The Legal System of Art Auction in China

Zhen Zheng

The Legal System of Art Auction in China

Springer

Zhen Zheng
School of Humanities
and Social Sciences
University of Science
and Technology Beijing
Beijing, China

ISBN 978-981-19-0127-0 ISBN 978-981-19-0128-7 (eBook)
https://doi.org/10.1007/978-981-19-0128-7

This Springer imprint is published by the registered company Springer Nature Singapore Pte Ltd.
The registered company address is: 152 Beach Road, #21-01/04 Gateway East, Singapore 189721, Singapore

Acknowledgements

This report was completed under the careful guidance and patient help of the co-tutor Prof. Wang Yi. I would like to express my sincere thanks. Mr. Wang Yi is knowledgeable, kind, rigorous in academic research and diligent in work. He is a gentleman and model of scientific research worth emulating. In addition, I would like to express my special thanks to Prof. Wang Wenjie and Prof. Wang Qianwei from Chengchi University of Taiwan and Prof. Chen Ziqiang from Taiwan University. During my study and exchange in Taiwan, these three teachers not only put forward many pertinent opinions on my thesis but also took good care of my life. The three teachers' unique views on problems and open-minded attitude toward academic life also inspire me to move forward on this road.

I would like to thank Dr. Li Zhongxian, Dr. Pan Yijia, Dr. Ning Yuan, Dr. Li Dingxi and other friends of the Law School for their support and help. I would like to thank Mr. Wang Yang from Tsinghua University, Mr. Nie Weifeng from Xi'an Jiaotong University and Mr. He Xuxu from East China University of Political Science and Law for their care and concern. Thanks to Judge Qiu Jiang and Judge Xian Hairong of Beijing No. 3 Intermediate People's Court for their support of the case; thanks to the Palace Museum, Taipei Palace Museum, China Auction Association, Artron Art Center and many other units of the art community for providing rich materials for this article; thanks to Dr. Anne Laure for providing foreign literature.

Finally, I would like to thank my parents and my wife Dr. Li Yulan for their selfless dedication and support. You have made me understand that where there is home and love is the starting point of courage and the return of heart. Thank you for your understanding and company!

Contents

Chapter 1
Introduction to Auction Legal System

1 China's Auction Legal System

1.1 The Auction Legal System is the Foundation of the Auction Legal System

China's auction legal system is based on China's auction laws and regulations. Since China affirmed auction transactions in the 1980s, numerous laws and regulations have been issued for auctions from the central government to local governments in China, and the effect of other relevant laws and regulations on auctions has objectively formed the system of auction laws and regulations.

The system of auction laws is what we call the auction law. The auction law can be understood in a narrow sense and a broad sense. In the narrow sense, the auction law only refers to the Auction Law, which is a single regulation. Auction law in the broad sense refers to the sum of all the laws and regulations related to auctions and adjusting legal relations and management relations based on the core laws and regulations of auctions. The auction law in a broad sense actually refers to the system of auction laws and regulations.

The system of auction laws and regulations exists objectively, but it is not easy to sort out this system, that is, how to make a scientific structure classification to show the logic, stereoscopic, hierarchical, complementary and so on between these laws and regulations. The number of auction-related laws in China and the breadth of their origins are obvious. These laws and regulations are enacted by both the NPC and government departments. There is both central and local legislation; There are legislation specifically designed for auction, and there are legislation related to auction because of its extensive relationship; There are both laws enacted in accordance with formal legislative procedures and interpretive legislation enacted by judicial organs to implement laws. There is both comprehensive legislation and single legislation made according to different auction targets. In addition, so on and so forth.

Z. Zheng, *The Legal System of Art Auction in China*,
https://doi.org/10.1007/978-981-19-0128-7_1

In the course of compiling the textbook for the national auctioneer qualification examination, the China Auction Industry Association obviously accepted the concept of the auction legal system. In the general theory of auction compiled by the China Auction Industry Association, the auction legal system is expressed in the structure of "auction regulations" and "relevant regulations". Although this statement is not perfect, the logic of which is not fully explained, this is undoubtedly a basic idea. "Practical Auction Manual: Laws and Rules", edited by Mr. Zheng Xinyao, etc., provides a relatively complete list of the current effective auction laws and regulations in China. Most of the classifications in it have the meaning of the auction legal system, which is not satisfactory, but it is a rare basic data for analyzing the auction legal system.

It is difficult to prove that Chinese legislatures or departments at all levels have systematically and systematically constructed a legal system for auctions. However, since this system has objectively existed, it is necessary to demonstrate the logic, stereoscopic, hierarchical and complementary nature of this system so that it truly becomes a system. Moreover, the demonstration of the auction legal system is not only a theoretical demonstration but also of far-reaching significance for our understanding of the auction legal system. The advantages and disadvantages of the auction legal system are inevitably accompanied by the advantages and disadvantages of the auction legal system, which are fully reflected in practice. This paper argues that China's auction law system can be classified as follows: auction core law, auction special law, compulsory auction law and auction-related law. Among them, the auction core law is or should be the basic point in the system, it is the scaffolding to build the auction law system, without this basic point and support, the so-called auction law system is just a simple collection of laws and regulations; Auction special laws and regulations play a supplementary role in this system, which makes the relevant contents of the auction core laws and regulations more specific and operable, and makes the auction core laws and regulations have regional characteristics. The compulsory auction law is the expression form of the core auction law in the judicial field, which opens a new and characteristic field for us in this system. Auction-related laws and regulations are or should be a natural extension of all the roads shown to us in this system, and its existence shows on the one hand that the auction legal system is intricate, on the other hand, it also shows that the auction legal system is open.

1.2 Auction Core Regulations

The auction core law plays an important role in the auction law system. It is the basic point and support of the auction law system and supports this huge system. Therefore, which regulations belong to auction core regulations? This paper first makes the following analysis. First, auction core regulations should come from central legislation. Since the mid-1980s, China has enacted much auction-related legislation, including central legislation and local legislation. It should be admitted that some local auction legislation should be superior to legislative reviews, such as the auction legislation of Shenzhen, Shanghai and other places. However, as a national system of laws and regulations, its core laws and regulations cannot and should not be selected from local laws and regulations. Second, the auction core laws and regulations should belong to the auction special laws and regulations. There are many auction-related laws and regulations in the legislation at the central level, including those specifically formulated for auctions and those only related to auctions, such as the civil Procedure Law and Contract Law. Regulations other than those specifically designed for auctions cannot perfect auctions. The legal basis of. Third, the core laws and regulations of auctions should have the function of establishing systems and laying foundations. In this sense, auction core regulations should belong to auction special regulations, but not all auction special regulations are auction core regulations.

In view of the above analysis, this paper holds that there are three core auction laws and regulations in China, namely, Auction Law, Auction Administration Measures and The Notice of The State Council on public Property Disposal and Public Auction. Here, this paper discusses the promulgation time sequence of these laws and regulations.

1.2.1 Circular of the State Council on Public Auction of Public Property Disposal (Hereinafter Referred to as the Circular)

The Circular is issued by The State Council to governments at all levels throughout the country. Although it does not have a typical legislative form, it has administrative regulations because of its content, effectiveness and practical impact.

The Notice consists of four articles with prefaces, the significance of which is as follows:

(1) The notice is the first national recognition of the auction industry in legal form. Auctions have experienced many twists and turns in the history of China. At the beginning of the founding of New China, although the state did not immediately ban the auction industry, it held a negative attitude toward the auction industry as a whole. This attitude led to the complete disappearance of auction houses across China from the mainland in the late 1950s. As auction houses reappeared in local markets after reform and opening-up, some local governments quickly passed legislation affirming the industry, but there is still no national legislation affirming the auction industry. Although the Civil Procedure Law (Trial) in 1982 became the basis of a few auction behaviors in the judicial practice of that special period, it was only an approval of judicial enforcement measures at best, rather than the approval of the auction industry. However, "notice" has taken a very bright affirmative attitude. Article 3 of the Notice stipulates that local governments should, according to their needs and possibilities, establish auction houses with appropriate scale and competent staff to undertake the auction business of public property disposal. To balance income and expenditure, the auction house of each city, in addition to undertaking public property disposal auctions under the guidance of the local government,

carries out the auction business of other items, and gives full play to the role of the public auction system in the development of the commodity economy.

(2) The notice sets the tone for disposing confiscated goods through auction. The notice defines confiscated goods as public property. Since the founding of the People's Republic of China, China has been dealing with confiscated goods and recovered stolen goods through state-owned commercial departments fixing prices, which has many drawbacks. To further strengthen the building of a clean government, manage state property and reduce financial losses, the circular stipulates: the state will gradually establish and improve the public auction system for the disposal of public property; Handling public property must be the state laws and regulations to allow the circulation of commodities, specifically refers to, in accordance with the law enforcement agencies confiscated goods do not return to recover stolen goods, postal, transportation and other departments for unowned goods, state organs, social organizations and state enterprises and institutions according to the relevant provisions of the articles needed in handling and other aspects need to sell off public property; Must first start from the confiscation of goods, the public auction law enforcement agencies confiscated goods in accordance with the law and ruling by law come into operation can be carried out after the auction, local governments must be entrust auction house appointed by way of public auction, shall not be passed to other channels for business acquisitions more The above directly became the source of Article 9 of the Auction Law.

(3) The notice lays down the basic framework for auction legal relations. Auctions are different from the general transaction method. How to identify the nature of the auctioneer, its position in the auction relationship and the source of income will directly affect the setting of rights and obligations. Therefore, article 3 of the Notice stipulates that the auction house is a service corporate enterprise, which shall be examined and approved by the department designated by the local government, registered by the industrial and commercial administrative department, and managed according to the special industry. The auction house acts as an intermediary between the consignor and the buyer, providing services to both the buyer and the seller and charging a certain percentage of the transaction fee. The income source of the auction house is limited to the auction fee and other legitimate income directly related to the auction. The auction house shall be responsible for its own profits and losses and shall not be subsidized by the state.

1.2.2 Auction Act

The Auction Law was promulgated in 1996 and came into force on January 1, 1997. On August 28, 2004, the 11th session of the standing Committee of the tenth National People's Congress decided to amend the Auction Law. This amendment involves two aspects: first, the third clause of Article 5 is deleted, that is, the content of "public security organs implement public security management on the auction industry according to the special industry" is deleted; Second, delete the fifth item of article 12, that is, delete the content of "special industry license issued by public security organs". The revised Auction Law consists of 6 chapters and 69 articles.

The Auction Law is the basic law of China's auction industry, the basis for the formulation of various regulations in the auction field, and the code of conduct that auction practitioners and all auction participants should abide by. To grasp the Auction Law on the whole, we should understand the following points. First, the auction activities regulated by the Auction Law of China have the nature of market operation. From the perspective of auction performance, auction activities are very extensive, but not all auction activities have the nature of market operation. For example, private individuals may dispose of idle daily necessities, enterprises or social organizations may allocate work tasks or production resources, and judicial organs may execute the property of persons subject to execution. However, since they do not have the nature of market operation, the Auction Law is not applicable. From another point of view, any enterprise, institution, organization, etc., such as the intention to carry out auction activities with the nature of market operation, should be regulated by the Auction Law. Second, the legal norms in China's Auction Law can be roughly divided into three categories: first, administrative norms, which aim to reflect the state's administrative or industrial management of the auction industry; second, substantive norms aim to determine the rights and obligations of auction parties or participants; and third, procedural norms aim to clarify the procedures that auction parties should follow in auction activities. Auction activities have a history of more than 2000 years. In such a long historical process, many rules have come into being. These rules have gone through vicissitudes and changes in different countries and different times, and the rules proved to be effective in practice are basically reflected in China's Auction Law. Therefore, the rule system in China's Auction Law is relatively complete. Third, the provisions in China's Auction Law are relatively strict on the whole. For example, strictly regulate the conditions for the establishment of auction enterprises; strictly regulate the negative influence of auctioneers and trustees on the bidding process; and strictly standardize auction procedures. Strict regulations are necessary to maintain and build a healthy auction market with Chinese characteristics. The development history of China's auction market is relatively short, and there are many disharmonious, dishonest and unhealthy factors in the market. Only strict regulations can establish a good market order. In addition, the auction legal order belongs to the domestic legal order, and within the effective coverage of the domestic legal order, it does not accept any modification from the so-called auction custom, auction custom practice.

1.2.3 Auction Administration Measures

The Measures for the Administration of Auction are formulated on the basis of the Auction Law and relevant laws, administrative regulations and rules on foreign investment. The Auction Administration Measures consist of 7 chapters and 61 articles.

The promulgation of auction administration measures is to meet the needs of the rapid development of China's auction industry, to regulate the order of the auction industry, to promote the healthy development of the auction industry, to fulfill the commitments of the Chinese government to the WTO and to promote the opening of the auction industry to the outside world. The Auction Administration Measures is an extension of the principles and rules established in the Auction Law in the auction industry. Compared with the Auction Law, the Measures for Auction Administration has the following three characteristics. First, the Measures for Auction Administration focuses on the administration and supervision of the auction industry. First, the Auction Administration Measures stipulate the establishment, alteration and termination of auction enterprises and foreign-invested auction enterprises in a large number of provisions and emphasize the administrative functions of the competent authorities of the auction industry in this respect. Second, in terms of auction activities, the Measures for Auction Administration highlights the management of auctioneers' qualifications and practice, highlights the operation and management of auction enterprises, and entrusts the competent authority of the auction industry and the auction industry association with the management and supervision functions in this regard. Finally, the legal liability set in the Auction Administration Measures is mainly aimed at the illegal business behaviors of auction enterprises and the illegal behaviors of auction industry managers. The comparison shows that the focus of the auction law is on the auction parties, while the focus of the auction administration measures is on the auction enterprises and administrative departments. Second, auction administration measures have added new content to the auction legal system to adapt to the development of the auction industry. Among the provisions of the Measures for the Administration of Auction, there are some new provisions, among which the most prominent provisions are in two aspects, namely, the market access of foreign-invested auction enterprises and the control of unfair competition in the auction market. The market access of foreign-invested auction enterprises belongs to the fulfillment of China's WTO commitments, and the comprehensive opening of the auction market to foreign capital will certainly have a certain degree of impact on domestic auction enterprises, but from the point of view of attracting foreign capital, absorbing foreign advanced management ideas and flourishing Chinese auction industry, it is of far-reaching significance. Controlling unfair competition in the auction market is an urgent matter in China's auction practice. With the increase in the number of Chinese auction enterprises, unscrupulous business behaviors emerge one after another. If not controlled, it will damage not only the relevant auction enterprises but also the whole auction industry. All in all, these provisions with new content reflect the new concept of national development of the auction industry. Third, auction management measures make the auction legal system more specific and operable. From the point of view of practice, many provisions of the Auction Law are relatively principled, and their application in practice may cause differences. Therefore, the Auction Administration Measures have refined and reasonably extended the provisions of the Auction Law from the perspective of auction industry management. The detailed contents mainly include scope of application, conditions for the establishment of auction enterprises, qualifications of enterprises auctioning confiscated goods, registration of auction enterprises, professional qualifications of auctioneers, prohibited auction items or property rights, auction announcement and display, liability for guarantee of defects, etc. Involving a logical extension of the content mainly includes: set up the auction enterprises branch, set up the auction enterprises and branch should follow the procedures and shall be submitted to the material, auction enterprises exit mechanism, auction enterprises with foreign investment, the relevant provisions of the auctioneer, auction enterprises are prohibited and commissioned bidding seats, suspend and terminate the auction, the supervision and management of the auctioning industry, etc.

1.3 Special Laws and Regulations for Auction

Special auction regulations refer to legal documents formulated specifically to regulate auction behavior and auction market order. Some of these legal documents are very formal, such as the Interim Provisions on the Auction Practice Qualification System; Some are not very formal, such as the Notice of the State Administration of Taxation on the collection of VALUE-ADDED tax and business tax on the auction income obtained by the auction house. However, formal or not, they serve to regulate behavior and market order. There are two main categories of special auction regulations in China: legal documents formulated by the relevant ministries and commissions according to the Auction Law and relevant laws and regulations, combined with their own relevant responsibilities; and China's local governments.

Legal documents are formulated to regulate auction behavior and maintain the order of the auction market in the region.

Relevant state ministries and commissions issued special auction regulations mainly include: The interim provisions on the auctioneer qualification system, the state administration of taxation on calligraphy and painting works, such as antique auction of notice of individual tax income, the state administration of taxation for the auction house auction revenues impose value added tax, business tax related issues notice ", "interim measures for the supervision and administration of the auction", the state economic and trade commission, the General Administration of Customs on Anti-smuggling confiscated vehicles designated work auction notice, the State Tobacco Monopoly Administration on strengthening the management of the tobacco auction notice ", "state-owned land use right of competitive bidding, auction and listing-for-sale sets", "the several provisions on the strengthening the supervision and administration of the auctioneer (provisional)", "mine exploration right to adopt measures for the management of bidding, auction and quotation (try out)", "cultural relics auction management interim provisions"," Trial measures for the Auction and Sale of Tax Deductible Property.

The auction special regulations issued by relevant ministries and commissions are obviously combined with their respective responsibilities. These laws and regulations can be roughly divided into two categories: one is the legal documents formulated by the relevant ministries and commissions of the state to implement supervision and management of the auction market according to the authorization of relevant laws including the Auction Law, such as the Interim Measures for Auction Supervision and Management and the Interim Provisions on the Auctioneer's Professional Qualification System; The other is the legal documents issued by the relevant ministries and commissions of the state to introduce the auction method into their areas in charge, such as the Interim Provisions on the Administration of The Auction of cultural relics and the Provisions on the Right to use State-owned land by bidding, Auction and Listing. These two kinds of auction special laws and regulations have different effects in practice.

There are numerous special auction regulations issued by local governments in China, mainly including: The Fujian province people's government on the auction of the small businesses owned by the whole people the interim provisions on the (1988) 4 property auction rules) of Fujian province (1997 revision), "the supervision and administration of Fujian province auction sets" (1998), the management method of bidding, auction of state-owned land access) in Fujian province (2001), the auction enterprises in Fujian province audit if permission and supervision and management Dry Provisions (2005); House Auction Measures of Shanghai Municipality (1988), Property Auction Provisions of Shanghai Municipality (1994); Interim Provisions on auction Market Management of Hebei Province (1993)"Shenzhen Special Economic Zone Property Auction Regulations" (1993), "Shenzhen Special Economic Zone Land Use Right Bidding and Auction Provisions" (1998)4 Shenzhen Special Economic Zone Property Auction Regulations implementation Rules (1999); "Beijing Urban Real Estate Auction Measures" (1994)4 Beijing Bidding Auction Listing Of state-owned Land use rights interim Provisions "(2005)4 Beijing Bidding Auction Listing of State-owned land use rights to determine the minimum price of trial measures" (2005); (Provisions of Sichuan Province on the Administration of Auction Market) (1994)4 Interim Provisions of Sichuan Province on the Administration of Auction Contract) (1998); (Measures of Hainan Province for the Administration of Auction of Confiscated Anti-Smuggling Materials (revised in 1997); Measures of Guangdong Province for the Administration of Public Bidding and Auction of State-owned Land Use Right in Urban Areas (1998); Measures for the Administration of Tianjin Public Property Auction (revised in 1998); Interim Measures for the Administration of Yunnan Province Auction Industry (2002); Measures for the Bidding, Auction and Listing of State-owned Land Use Right in Jiangsu Province) (2003); (Measures for the Administration of Hubei Province Bidding, Auction and Listing of State-owned Land Use Right) (2003); And (Measures for the Administration of Tianjin Public Property Auction and Listing and Listing of State-owned Land Use Right) (revised in 1998). (Measures of Ningxia Hui Autonomous Region for Bidding, Auction and Listing of State-owned Land Use Right) (2003); (Measures of Shandong Province for Bidding and Auctioning of State-owned Land Use Right) (2004 revised); Measures for Bidding, Auction and Listing transfer of State-owned Land Use Right of Liaoning Province M2004); Administrative Provisions on Auction Industry of Chongqing Municipality (2005); Administrative Measures on Auction

Industry of Qinghai Province (2005); Administrative Measures on Auction Industry of Guizhou Province (2005), etc.

According to the above incomplete listing, almost all local governments in China have enacted special auction regulations, and some places have more than one special auction regulation. Some of the local special laws and regulations on auctions that are currently in effect were formulated before the promulgation of the Auction Law, but most of them were formulated after the promulgation of the Auction Law. The local auction special laws and regulations all talk about basing on local characteristics in their purposes, but the contents involved are similar with minor differences. Among the local special laws and regulations for auctions, there are many comprehensive laws and regulations concerning the conduct of auction parties, but more of them are administrative laws and regulations for the auction of land use rights. The special local auction laws and regulations of all provinces, cities and autonomous regions in China have difficulty forming their own systems, and they can only play a supplementary and localized role in the national auction law system.

1.4 Compulsory Auction Regulations

Compulsory auction law, also known as judicial auction law, is a relatively independent system in China's auction law system. The relative independence of compulsory auction law stems from the fact that compulsory auctions do not belong to the adjustment scope of auction law in principle and the special relationship between compulsory auctions and auction law. Although in a practical sense, we can say that the compulsory auction law is the manifestation of the core auction law in the judicial field, the enactment of the compulsory auction law is based on a series of Procedural laws in China, including the Civil Procedure Law and the Maritime Litigation Special Procedure Law. The compulsory auction laws and regulations, in addition to their enactment basis, are derived from the norms formulated by China's judicial system to take compulsory measures, which can be roughly divided into two categories: first, from the judicial interpretation made by the Supreme People's Court to regulate the compulsory auction; second, it comes from the normative documents made by the local higher people's courts to regulate the compulsory auction.

The judicial interpretations made by the Supreme People's Court related to compulsory auction are as follows: The Supreme People's Court on some issues for <the People's Republic of China civil procedure law> the opinion of ", the Supreme People's Court on some issues of the people's court for execution work regulations (try out)", the Supreme People's Court on some issues of judicial compensation in civil administrative litigation explanation", "the Supreme People's Court for freezing and auction of state-owned shares of listed companies and the social legal person share, regulations on several issues of the Supreme People's Court on the judicial authentication management regulations", the Supreme People's Court about the provisions on some issues of enterprise bankruptcy cases, the Supreme's Court on the applicable if <maritime's special law of the People's Court>. Dry problem explanation ", "the Supreme People's Court of the people's court civil execution auction or sale of goods Provisions on property, provisions of the Supreme People's Court on the Execution of mortgaged Houses by the People's Court, etc.

Local each higher people's court for compulsory auction related regulatory documents are: "hunan province higher people's court on the people's court to auction or sell off assets evaluation must be conducted when the notice of state-owned assets) (1996) 4, hunan province higher people's court of the people's court can auction land use problems in execution of opinion" (2002); Notice of Beijing Higher People's Court on retransmission of "Measures for Implementing Auction Valuation of Confiscated Articles at Auction" issued by Beijing Price Office and Beijing Auction House (1998), and Several Provisions of Beijing Higher People's Court on Entrusting Evaluation, Auction and Selling in The Implementation (Trial) (2001); Several Provisions of The Higher People's Court of Zhejiang Province on The Appraisal, Auction and Sale in The Process of Execution (2001); (Administrative Measures of The People's Court of Jiangsu Province on The Entrustment of Judicial Expertise externally (trial)) (2002) 4 Provisions of the People's Court of Jiangsu Province on the Entrustment of Judicial Expertise externally (Trial) (2002); The anhui province higher people's court about assessment and auction work commissioned by the execution of the interim provisions on the (2002) 4, the anhui province higher people's court about the establishment of the provincial court case on evaluation expert advisory committee (notice) (2003), the higher people's court in anhui province on the execution of assessment review related matters notice (2003); (Implementation Rules of Shandong Provincial People's Court for The Administration of Externally Entrusted Judicial Expertise (2002);Evaluation, sale, the Shenzhen intermediate people's court in detailed rules "(2003)," the door frozen province higher people's court about evaluation, auction work commissioned by certain rules) (2005) 4, Guangdong higher people's court of the people's court review to determine the parties negotiated opinions on some issues of evaluation, auction agencies (try out) "(2006); "Measures for the Administration of Entrusted Forensic Expertise by Hubei Provincial People's Courts (For Trial Implementation)" (2003); "Shanghai Court Entrusted Auction Work Operation Rules (Trial)" (2004), "Shanghai Court Entrusted Auction Work Operation Rules (Trial) supplementary Rules" (2005), "Shanghai Court Entrusted Auction Work Supplementary Provisions" (2005); (Provisional Provisions of Sichuan Higher People's Court on Issues Related to Entrusting Appraisal, Auction and Selling in The Execution Procedure (2005); "Several Provisions of Jiangxi Provincial Higher People's Court on Entrusting Appraisal and Auction Work in Execution" (2005) X Implementation Measures of Jiangxi Provincial Higher People's Court on Property Auction in Civil Execution (trial) X2005); (Notice of Chongqing Higher People's Court on Issues related to the Auction Site of Operational State-owned Property Rights in Civil Execution (2QQ5); Provisions of Hainan Higher People's Court on The Administration of Entrusted Auction execution (2006/4 Operation Methods of Hainan Higher People's Court on Entrusted Auction Execution) (2006); (Operational Measures of Guizhou Higher People's Court on The Execution of Entrusted Auction) (2006), etc.

Both the compulsory auction laws from the Supreme People's Court and the compulsory auction laws from the local higher people's courts reflect the core of compulsory execution, and their judicial nature makes compulsory execution in a relatively independent position. However, the compulsory auction law cannot and should not be completely independent. Together with other categories of auction law, it regulates the way in which the auction is a unique transfer of rights. Thus, mandatory auction statutes and other categories of auction statutes may share some major principles and rules, and they may complement and be interpreted by each other unless the nature of the jurisdiction and transaction requires it.

1.5 Laws and Regulations Related to Auction

"Auction-related regulations" means all regulations relating to the manner in which this transfer right is auctioned. For example, the ability of auction parties needs to be defined by law, and the rules for defining the ability of auction parties are mainly stipulated in the General Principles of the Civil Law and other laws. Therefore, the General Principles of the Civil Law and other laws are auction-related regulations. Since the auction relationship needs to be in the form of a contract and the rules on the contract are mainly stipulated in the Contract Law and other laws, the Contract Law and other laws are related to the auction.

The scope of auction legislation is a difficult issue to define. On the one hand, due to the universality of auction parties, the diversity of auction behaviors and the infinite nature of auction targets, there are numerous laws and regulations that can affect the auction relationship. Therefore, auction-related laws and regulations should be an open concept that is difficult to define and does not need to be defined. However, as auctions belong to civil and commercial relations, laws and regulations that can affect auction relations are different from each other, and the requirements for a classified legal system are relative, so the relevant laws and regulations of auctions should have a certain scope.

In terms of the importance to the construction of auction legal system, the following laws and regulations are considered as auction-related regulations: General Principles of Civil Law (1986), Law on Sino-Foreign Joint Ventures (1990 amendment), Law on Anti-Unfair Competition (1993), Law on Protection of Consumer Rights and Interests (1993), Law on Urban Real Estate Administration (1994), Labor Law (1994), Contract Law (1999), Law on Tendering and Bidding (1999 Product Quality Law (amended in 2000), Law on Sino-foreign Contractual Joint Ventures (amended in 2000), Patent Law (amended in 2000), Customs Law (amended in 2000), Trademark Law (amended in 2001), Copyright Law (amended in 2001), Law on Foreign-funded Enterprises (amended in 2001), Law on Tax Collection and Administration (20)), The Law on the Protection of Cultural Relics (2002), the Company Law (2004), the Land Administration Law (2004), the Securities Law (2004), the Regulations on The Administration of Company Registration (2005), etc. In addition, the supporting regulations, implementation rules and judicial interpretations of the above laws should also be incorporated into the system.

The reason why the abovementioned laws and regulations are included in the relevant scope is that they are either significantly related to auction relations, to the ability and behavior of auction parties, to the management of auction enterprises, or to the order of the auction market. Without the norms of these laws and regulations, the legal system of auctions is incomplete.

2 Relations of Fundamental Rights and Obligations of Auction

The basic rights and obligations of auctions refer to the rights and obligations of auction parties and their rights and obligations to auction targets. Due to the legal norms of these rights and obligations, these basic rights and obligations are also the basic legal relations of auctions.

2.1 Parties to the Auction

The auction parties regulated by China's Auction Law include auctioneers, trustees, bidders and buyers.

2.1.1 Auctioneers

Auctioneers are also called auction enterprises, auction houses and so on. Auctioneers have broad and narrow definitions. The auctioneer in the broad sense refers to anyone who appears as the seller and presides over the auction activities; In the narrow sense, auctioneer only refers to an enterprise legal person entrusted by others to auction other people's property in their own name and obtain remuneration (commission). The Auction Law of China clearly regulates auctioneers in a narrow sense and makes strict provisions on the qualifications and conditions of auctioneers. Article 10 of China's Auction Law stipulates that an auctioneer refers to an enterprise legal person established in accordance with the Auction Law and the Company Law to engage in auction activities. This article can be understood as follows: First, it is clear that the auctioneer can only be an enterprise legal person, so in Chinese legal terms, "auctioneer" and "auction enterprise" are synonymous; Second, the auctioneer's corporate nature is either limited liability company or joint stock limited company. Third, it emphasizes that the establishment of auction enterprises should be in accordance with the conditions stipulated in the Auction Law and the Company Law, but in fact, the establishment of auction enterprises is regulated not only by the above two laws and regulations.

The auctioneer is the most important party in the legal relationship of the auction, and its position in the legal relationship has the nature of an intermediary. Specifically, it is the agent of the client, and within the scope of agency, the consequences of its behavior shall be borne by the client. However, at the same time, the position of the auctioneer is relatively independent. It acts in its own name and has relations with bidders and buyers in its own name. Auctioneers enjoy a wide range of rights according to law but also undertake corresponding obligations.

2.1.2 Trustor

The trustee is one of the parties in the legal relationship of auctions. Article 25 of China's Auction Law stipulates that a trustee refers to a citizen, legal person or other organization that entrusts an auctioneer to auction articles or property rights. In China's core auction laws and regulations, there are no special restrictions on the qualifications of the trustor, but it is not to say that the trustor does not have any qualifications. The qualifications of an entrusting party shall refer to relevant auction laws and regulations. When a citizen (natural person) acts as a client, he shall be required to be at least 18 years of age and have no cause of incapacity or limited capacity for civil conduct, or at least 16 years of age and have his income from labor as his main source of income and have no cause of incapacity or limited capacity for civil conduct. When a legal person (company) acts as a client, it is required to possess capacity for civil rights and civil conduct. When organizations act as clients, they are required to bear civil liability independently.

The trustee referred to in China's Auction Law has no nationality or domicile restriction. Article 67 of the Auction Law stipulates that this law applies to foreigners, foreign enterprises and organizations that entrust auctions or participate in bidding within the territory of the People's Republic of China. Of course, when the client is a foreigner, foreign enterprise or organization, the qualification conditions on which the civil capacity is based shall be determined in accordance with the rules of private international law.

2.1.3 Bidders and Buyers

The bidder and the buyer are the same party in the legal relationship of the auction. The party is referred to differently because he is at different stages of the auction process. When he is in the process of competing with others, we call him a "bidder"; We call him a "buyer" when he has completed the bidding and finally purchased the auction item. For an auction target, there can be more than one bidder but only one buyer, and the buyer must be one of the bidders. China's Auction Law stipulates that bidders refer to citizens, legal persons or other organizations participating in bidding for auction targets. A buyer is a bidder who buys an auction object at the highest bidding price. Like the trustee, the qualifications of the bidder and the buyer shall refer to the relevant auction laws and regulations.

However, in some cases, the law has special requirements on the qualifications and abilities of bidders and buyers. The special requirements of law on the qualifications and abilities of bidders and buyers are rooted in the particularity of auction targets. For example, Chinese laws and regulations often have special requirements on the transfer of auction objects such as land use rights, land contract rights, cultural relics and bulk tobacco and alcohol. Article 33 of China's Auction Law stipulates that if laws and administrative regulations have provisions on the buying and selling conditions of auction targets, bidders shall meet the prescribed conditions. In practice, special qualifications and abilities are mainly related to nationality, residence, business scope and government approval. The requirement of the economic capacity of the bidder and the buyer does not belong to the qualification and capacity issues discussed in the legal category.

Unless special qualifications and abilities are involved, the bidders and buyers referred to in China's Auction Law have no nationality or domicile restrictions. Article 67 of the Auction Law stipulates that this law applies to foreigners, foreign enterprises and organizations that entrust auctions or participate in bidding within the territory of the People's Republic of China. Of course, when the bidder and the buyer are foreigners, foreign enterprises and organizations, the qualification conditions on which their civil capacity is based shall be determined in accordance with the rules of private international law.

2.2 *Auction Targets*

Auction targets commonly known as "lots" and "auctions" generally refer to all kinds of property that can be transferred through auctions, including tangible property and intangible property. Article 6 of The Auction Law of The People's Republic of China stipulates that the auction target shall be articles or property rights owned or disposed of by the trustee according to law. Among them, "goods" should be understood as tangible property with substantial existence, and "property rights" should be understood as intangible property without substantial existence, which is drawn up by people subjectively. Auction targets are very important in the legal relationship of auctions; they are the object of rights and obligations of auction parties. Without this object, the rights and obligations of auction parties will lose the significance of existence because there is no target.

2.2.1 Legal Standards for Determining Auction Targets

Can an article or property right be auctioned? Does it have to be auctioned? In what kind of auction can it be auctioned? The first thing that determines the answers to these questions is what the law says. China's Auction Law has a special chapter to define auction objects, and other core auction laws, special auction laws, compulsory auction laws and auction-related laws and regulations all have provisions concerning auction objects. The legal system surrounding auction objects is relatively perfect.

According to the norms of China's auction legal system, auction targets can be divided into four categories according to the degree of legal constraints on auction targets: items allowed to be auctioned or property rights, items restricted to be auctioned or property rights, items legally auctioned or property rights, and items prohibited to be auctioned or property rights.

(1) Items or property rights that are allowed to be auctioned. Such articles or property rights refer to property that can circulate freely in the auction market without any legal restrictions. Most items or property rights fall into this category, such as household items, business products, works of art, etc.
(2) Articles or property rights that are restricted from auctions. Such articles or property rights refer to properties that can be auctioned only after being examined and approved, appraised or approved by the relevant authorities. Article 8 of China's Auction Law stipulates that articles or property rights that can only be transferred according to law or according to the provisions of The State Council shall go through the examination and approval procedures according to law before auction. Cultural relics entrusted for auctions shall, before being auctioned, be appraised and licensed according to law by the administrative department for cultural relics in the place where they are auctioned. In China's auction practice, there are many such items or property rights, such as cultural relics, land use rights, land contract rights, exploration rights and mining rights, telecommunications network code resources, and state-owned property rights of enterprises. A small analysis is not difficult to find in the auction market restricted goods or property rights relatively concentrated in state-owned assets.
(3) Articles or property rights auctioned by law. The term "such articles or property rights" refers to the property that can only be transferred by auction or which has priority to be transferred by auction. "Notice" stipulated in article 1: must first start from the confiscation of goods, the public auction law enforcement agencies confiscated goods in accordance with the law and ruling by law come into operation can be carried out after the auction, local governments must entrust auction house appointed by way of public auction, shall not be passed on to other business channels for acquisitions, more do not allow law enforcement agencies within the system for processing. Article 9 of the Auction Law stipulates that articles confiscated by state administrative organs according to law, articles used to pay taxes or fines and other articles, which should be auctioned by the auctioneer appointed by the people's government of the province, autonomous region or municipality directly under the Central Government where the property is located, shall be auctioned by the auctioneer. The provisions of the preceding paragraph shall apply to the auction of articles confiscated by the people's court according to law, articles used to pay for fines or fines, and recovered articles that cannot be returned. Article 9, Paragraph 2 of the Auction Administration Measures stipulates: Auction of items confiscated by state administrative organs according to law, items used

to offset taxes and fines, items confiscated by people's courts according to law, items used to offset fines and fines, items that cannot be returned and other special state-owned assets shall be undertaken by auction enterprises with corresponding auction qualifications. Specific qualifications shall be formulated by provincial commercial administrative departments jointly with other relevant departments in accordance with the principle of standardized management and selection of the best and shall be reported to the Ministry of Commerce for the record. To summarize the contents of the above provisions, the target of legal auctions mainly refers to confiscated goods, ownerless goods and some special state-owned assets.

(4) Articles or property rights prohibited from auctions. Such articles or property rights refer to properties that are not allowed to enter the auction market. Article 7 of China's Auction Law stipulates that articles or property rights prohibited by laws and administrative regulations shall not be used as auction targets. Article 29 of the Measures for the Administration of Auction stipulates that the auction of the following articles or property rights shall be prohibited: Disputes over ownership or disposal rights have not been confirmed by judicial or administrative organs; Goods under customs control that have not gone through customs formalities. According to the above provisions, articles or property rights that cannot be auctioned in this paper are divided into two categories. The first category refers to articles or property rights prohibited from sale by laws and administrative regulations, including but not limited to persons and their rights of body and person, land, forests, grasslands, mineral resources, weapons and ammunition, drugs, stolen goods, smuggled articles, obscene articles, related cultural relics, goods under customs supervision, state secrets, etc. Second, articles or property rights in which the ownership or disposal right is in dispute; Any article or property right, as long as its ownership or disposal right is in a realistic state of dispute, that is, has been submitted to judicial or administrative authorities for confirmation of the right but its rights have not been finalized, shall not be auctioned as a target.

2.2.2 Social Standards for Determining Auction Targets

The so-called social standard refers to some criteria that decide whether goods or property rights are suitable for auctions in addition to legal norms. Social standards are of little significance to the construction of the auction legal system, but they affect auction practice. In practice, some goods or property rights have a definite value, and the state does not prohibit their transfer, but they never appear at auction. What is the reason for this? This paper argues that whether goods or property rights can be used as auction targets is restricted not only by legal norms but also by a series of social factors. The difference is that legal norms determine whether goods or property rights can be auctioned, while social factors determine whether goods or property rights are suitable for auctions.

First, consider the social effects that make some goods or property rights unsuitable for auctions. Auctions are carried out openly in the market, and the public has a high degree of awareness and participation. Therefore, it is necessary to pay great attention to grasping the appropriate measures so as not to have a negative impact on social morality, ethics, right and wrong views, likes and wrongs views, etc. For example, the sale of sex products is not prohibited or restricted, but auction companies that organize the sale of sex products in a large way will have negative social effects.

Second, consider the economic effects that make some goods or property rights unsuitable for auctions.

An auction is a means of profit for both the trustee and the auctioneer, so it is impossible not to consider the economic effect. There are many differences between the auction and the general way of buying and selling. One of them is that the auction must go through certain procedures. The client and auctioneer spend more on procedures than the general way of buying and selling. Therefore, auctions are a relatively expensive way of buying and selling, and whether an article is suitable for auctions should consider the economic effect. For example, a consignor would not choose an auction because he had a half kilogram of candy to sell, and an auctioneer would not accept a commission to sell a half kilogram of candy. This example illustrates the fact that sporadic items are not suitable for auctions unless they are of special value. Therefore, the auction target not only has a qualitative limit but also has a quantitative limit. A kilo of candy is not suitable for auction, but a ton might be.

Finally, the nature of the item or property rights may make it unsuitable for auctions. Auctions have characteristics such as auctions needing to go through a process, auctions advocating openness, auctions emphasizing buyer competition and so on. Considering the criterion of "fit for auction", the characteristics of auctions cannot be ignored. If the properties of an article or property rights conflict with the characteristics of an auction, it may not be suitable for auctions. For example, the auditability of trade secrets is highly questionable. Trade secrets are "property rights" and can be bought and sold without question. However, are trade secrets suitable for auction? To answer this question, we need to compare the characteristics of the two. Among all the characteristics of trade secrets, confidentiality is one of the most significant characteristics. Trade secrets maintain their value because of confidentiality. The greatest characteristic of the auction method is that it is open, and all bidders have the right to know the content of auction targets before participating in bidding. The requirements of the two are in conflict with each other. Once the trade secret is disclosed to all bidders, it will lose its value, while if it is not disclosed to bidders, it cannot achieve the auction. Therefore, it can be concluded that trade secrets are not suitable for auctions.

In addition, some items or property rights whose sale price has been completely fixed or whose sale price can only float in a very small range are also not suitable for auctions because they conflict with the competitive characteristics of auctions. Auction competition is price competition. If the price of goods or property rights has been set, what are the bidders bidding for?

2.2.3 Basic Rights and Obligations of Auction Parties

Constituting legal auction relationships, in addition to auction parties, auction targets also need to have the rights and obligations between the auction parties and the parties to the auction targets. Auctions in legal relationships with the content of the rights and obligations of the parties, including the auctioneer accepting entrust auction-related articles or property rights, the rights and obligations of the trustor authorizing others to dispose of by auction his or her own articles or property rights, and the rights and obligations of the bidder or buyer by taking part in bidding for the rights and obligations of the relevant articles or property rights. Rights and obligations play an important role in maintaining and combining the legal relationship of auctions. People and things in society are isolated, and it is precisely because of rights and obligations that these isolated people and things are linked together, forming legal relations. Rights and obligations are interdependent. The auctioneer's rights and obligations correspond to those of the trustee, the bidder and the buyer, and the trustee's rights and obligations correspond to those of the bidder, the buyer and the auctioneer. In the legal relationship of auctions, rights and obligations are concrete and depend on the actual interests of the parties in social life.

The basic rights of an auctioneer are: to accept or reject the auction entrustment of others; Requiring the trustee to explain the source and defects of the auction target; To decide on the appraisal of an auction target; To decide the time and place of the auction; To announce the suspension or termination of an auction; Conduct auctions through auctioneers; Collect margin; To decide whether the auction is completed; Collect auction commissions or reasonable fees; Pursue others for breach of contract or infringement caused by their own losses, etc. The basic obligations of an auctioneer are: to take care of the items delivered by the trustee for auction; Keep secret the identity of the client and the buyer at their request; Issue auction announcements according to law; Display auction targets according to law; Do not participate in the auction activities organized by oneself as a bidder; Not to auction his own articles or property rights in the auction activities organized by himself; Explain the defects of the auction target to the bidder; Making auction records; Transfer of an auction target to the buyer if the auction is completed; If an auction is completed, the price paid to the trustee for an auction target; If the auction fails to conclude, the auction target shall be returned to the trustee; Properly keep account books, auction records and relevant materials; To assist the buyer in handling the law of changing certificates and transferring ownership of property punishments;

The basic rights of a trustee are as follows: sign an entrusted auction contract with the auctioneer in his own name or by entrusting others; Determining the retentive price of an auction target; Require the auctioneer to keep the reserve price confidential; Requiring auctioneers to keep their identities secret; Withdrawing an auction target before the auction begins; The decision whether to auction again if the auction does not clinch a deal; Take back the auction target if the auction fails to be completed; The price for collecting auction targets after the auction is completed; Pursue others for breach of contract or infringement caused by their own losses, etc. The basic obligations of the trustee are: to prove that he has the right to own or dispose of the auction target; Deliver an auction target to the auctioneer as agreed; Explain to the auctioneer the origin and defects of the auction target; Not participating in bidding for articles or property rights entrusted by oneself; To pay commissions or reasonable expenses; Deliver the auction target to the buyer upon completion of the auction as agreed; To assist the buyer in handling the procedures of changing certificates and transferring ownership; Accept law enforcement inspection and punishment of law enforcement departments.

The basic rights of bidders and buyers include: participating in bidding in their own name or entrusting others; Require the auctioneer to explain the source and defects of the auction target; Examining auction targets and consulting relevant auction materials; Requiring auctioneers to keep their identities secret; According to the quotation rules freely choose quotation and not quotation; Claim one's highest price; If the auction is completed, the auction target is obtained; Require the auctioneer and trustee to assist in handling the procedures of changing certificates and transferring ownership of property rights; Pursue others for breach of contract or infringement caused by their own losses, etc. The basic obligations of bidders and buyers are: to explain or prove their identity; To pay a deposit for participating in an auction; Abide by the auction rules and notes announced by the auctioneer at the auction; Once the offer is made, it cannot be withdrawn; Do not collude maliciously with others; Payment of auction target price and commission upon completion of auction; To accept an auction target without delay; Accept law enforcement inspection and punishment of law enforcement departments.

The rights and obligations of the parties mentioned above mainly involve the legal relationship of auctions and basically do not include the relationship of auction management. It is in this sense that these rights and obligations are fundamental. These basic rights and obligations are based on the system of auction laws and regulations, which shows us a relatively complete framework of auction legal relations. Regardless of whether any party or auction target has its proper place in this framework, it develops in accordance with its established direction.

2.2.4 The Emergence and Termination of the Auction Legal Relationship

The Emergence of the Legal Relationship of Auction

The emergence of legal relationships is the result of the action of events and actions in accordance with the law between the parties. The main reason for the legal relationship of auctions is the behavior of concluding a contract between auction parties. The contract that proves the legal relation of the auction mainly includes the contract of the entrustment auction and the contract of the auction transaction.

(1) Conclude an entrusted auction contract. An entrusted auction contract is an agreement whereby an auctioneer accepts the entrustment of others, performs

certain acts in his own name for the benefit of the trustee, and obtains remuneration from the trustee. The conclusion of an entrusted auction contract shall comply with the provisions of the Auction Law, the Contract Law and other laws and regulations.

Although the auction contract has great particularity, as far as the conclusion of entrusted auction contract is concerned, generally adopt the negotiation contract. When adopting the negotiation contracting mode, its contracting process can be roughly divided into three stages: prepare for a negotiation and sign a contract. An entrusted auction contract is a consensual contract. When one party makes an offer and the other party commits, the contract is established, that is, the time when the offeror receives the commitment is the time when the contract is established. Where the parties agree to conclude a contract in the form of a memorandum of contract, the contract is formed when it is signed or sealed by both parties. The place where the offeror receives the acceptance is the place where the contract is formed; Where the parties agree to conclude a contract by a memorandum of contract, the place of formation of the contract is the place where the parties sign or seal the contract. In practice, the conclusion of an entrustment auction contract is usually based on the standard terms provided by the auctioneer, which are restricted by the relevant standard terms in the Contract Law of China.

Generally, the establishment of auction contracts marks the emergence of legal auction relationships.

(2) Conclude an auction contract. The term "auction contract" refers to the agreement reached between the auctioneer and the buyer on the sale of auction targets according to the agreement or the established auction rules. The conclusion of an auction contract shall mainly comply with the provisions of the Auction Law and other laws and regulations.

For the auctioneer, the conclusion of the auction contract is the key to fulfilling the entrusted auction contract, and the auctioneer must pay full attention to his obligations in the entrusted auction contract. In this sense, the auction contract is the continuation of the entrusted auction contract, and the auctioneer's conclusion and performance of the auction contract is the performance of the entrusted auction contract. For the buyer, the conclusion of the auction contract has nothing to do with the entrusted auction contract. Regardless of what kind of commitment the auctioneer makes to the trustee, it cannot directly bind the buyer, who only regards the auctioneer as the opposite party. In this sense, the auction contract is independent of the entrusted auction contract.

The auction contract adopts a special contracting mode, which is called "quotation and hammer" in the auction legal system. Generally, the conclusion of a contract is the result of mutual agreement between the parties, and the formation process of mutual agreement is the bargaining between the parties. The Contract Law of China divides this process of mutual agreement into two stages: offer and acceptance. On the surface, "offer and hammer" is similar to "offer and acceptance" in the Contract Law, that is, "offer" corresponds to "offer" and "hammer" corresponds to "promise". However, a careful analysis shows that the so-called "offer and hammer" contracting mode in the Auction Law is different from the so-called "offer and promise" contracting mode in the Contract Law. First, the status of the offeror and promisee in the contract law is not fixed, and both the buyer and the seller can be in the position of the offeror or promisee. However, in the auction law, the position of the bidder and hammer is fixed, the bidder is fixed in the position of the bidder, and the auctioneer is fixed in the position of the hammer. Second, "offer and acceptance" in contract law is restricted by a series of rules, including counteroffer rules, alteration and withdrawal rules of offer and acceptance. However, the "quotation and hammer" in the Auction Law are made and completed face to face by the auctioneer and the bidder without going back on their words, so there are no problems such as counter quotation, change and withdrawal. Therefore, strictly speaking, auction contracts are a kind of special contract outside the norms of Contract Law. The process of concluding an auction contract is that the bidders bid in turn, and the highest bid is confirmed by the auctioneer dropping his gavel or by other publicly expressed means of purchase, and the auction is concluded.

Termination and Discontinuation of the Legal Relationship of Auctions

China's Auction Law does not make relevant provisions on termination and suspension, but termination and suspension are inevitable in practice, which is a pity. Fortunately, the Measures for the Administration of Auction promulgated subsequently have made provisions on the termination and suspension of auctions. The following is a discussion on the termination and suspension according to the relevant provisions of the Auction Administration Measures.

(1) Termination of legal relationships on auctions. The termination of auction legal relationships refers to the elimination of rights and obligations between auction parties due to certain circumstances. The termination of auction legal relationships can be divided into normal termination and abnormal termination. Normal termination refers to the termination of rights and obligations by the parties to an auction who have fulfilled all their obligations in accordance with the relevant auction contract or legal provisions. Normal termination may or may not be concluded. Regardless of whether the transaction is concluded, as long as the auction parties have fulfilled their obligations, it is normally terminated. Abnormal termination refers to the occurrence of some circumstances so that the auction parties cannot or are not allowed to continue to perform their obligations, resulting in the elimination of rights and obligations.

    The Measures for the Administration of Auction stipulates the circumstances for the termination of auction, which is intended to terminate the auction act or procedure, but theoretically, the termination of the auction act or procedure means the termination of the legal relationship of auction. Article 41 of the measures for the administration of auction stipulates that an auction shall be terminated under any of the following circumstances: (1) where the people's court, arbitration institution or relevant administrative organ determines that the trustee has no authority over the auction target and notifies the auction enterprise in writing; (2) the auction target is identified as stolen goods; (3) The auction activity cannot be carried out due to force majeure or accidents; (4) The auction target is damaged or lost before the auction; (5) The trustee notifies the auction enterprise in writing to terminate the auction before the auction meeting; (6) Other circumstances that should be terminated according to law occur. The termination of an auction shall be announced by the auction enterprise. If the trustee requests to continue the auction after the auction is terminated, he shall go through the auction procedures anew.

(2) Termination of legal relationship on auction. The termination of auction legal relationships refers to the occurrence of some special circumstances that make the auction behavior or procedure temporarily unable or not allowed to continue. The termination of auction legal relationships is obviously different from the termination of auction legal relationships. First, the suspension only suspends the auction act or procedure. After the suspension is eliminated, the auction act or procedure will continue. Termination means permanently ending the auction act or procedure, and the original auction act or procedure will not continue even after the termination is eliminated. Second, during the suspension, auction law. The relationship continues, the rights and obligations are still valid, but the execution is suspended; Termination means the end of the auction legal relationship, the rights and obligations between the auction parties thus eliminated. Third, the termination is not like the termination of the normal situation, causing the termination of the situation to be abnormal.

The Measures for the Administration of Auction stipulates the circumstances of the suspension of auction, which is intended to suspend the auction act or procedure, but theoretically, the suspension of auction act or procedure means the suspension of the legal relationship of auction. Article 40 of the measures for the administration of auction stipulates that an auction shall be suspended under any of the following circumstances: (1) where no bidder participates in the auction; (2) The third party disputes the ownership or disposal right of the auction target and provides effective certificates on the spot; (3) The trustee notifies the auction enterprise in writing to suspend the auction with justifiable reasons before the auction meeting; (4) Auction activities cannot be carried out temporarily due to accidents; (5) Other circumstances that should be suspended occur. The suspension of auctions should be announced by the auction enterprise. The auction is resumed after the reasons for suspending the auction disappear.

3 Several Basic Issues Related to the Legal System of Auctions

3.1 System of Auction Legal System

A legal system is a set of established customs, customs, or practices and the legal rules formed around them. The legal system itself is systematic and cannot be constructed by a single legal rule but requires a set of legal rules. The legal system varies, such as the marriage legal system, property legal system, and contract legal system. From the above discussion on the auction legal system, the auction legal system naturally belongs to one of the many legal systems in China.

China's auction legal system is a system that contains a series of legal rules involving the status and qualification of auctioneers, the status and qualification of clients, the status and qualification of bidders (buyers), auction targets, auction transactions, auction procedures, auction enterprise management, auction market management, etc. This paper argues that no other country has so many auction laws and regulations as China. However, the question is whether China's numerous auction laws and regulations are harmonious in the institutional system. Are there any conflicts between regulations, rules or contents? Can they be interpreted under common principles? Another way of thinking, under China's current system, does China need one unified auction legal system or two or more auction legal systems? These problems have long troubled the auction industry, resulting in confusion in some parts of the auction practice but also related to the perfection of the auction legal system.

A considerable number of auction insiders always adhere to the concept of a unified auction legal system. They think that the core of the legal system of China's auction laws and regulations is the "auction rate", "auction law" established by the principles and rules is auction laws and regulations in China, the basic according to appropriate the principles and rules in his auction rules cannot be established with the auction law principles and rules contradict, so the Chinese auction law system, waste system is unified. The concept of a unified auction legal system should be investigated and studied in two aspects: first, whether it is a fact; second, whether it is reasonable and feasible.

First, we examine and study the fact that the unified auction legal system is not the current auction legal system. First, a considerable number of auction laws and regulations in China are not formulated according to the Auction Law, including all auction-related laws and regulations, compulsory auction laws and a large number of auction-specific laws and regulations. Of course, there is a good reason why auction-related laws and regulations are not based on the Auction Act because many important auction-related laws and regulations are themselves coeval with the Auction Act, and their legislative objectives are different. Many important auction-related laws and regulations were enacted prior to the Auction Act. Therefore, the fact that auction-related laws and regulations are not formulated according to the Auction Law does not mean that China's auction legal system is not unified. However, the forced sale or auction special rules and regulations are different, the rules of auction is one of the core goals or legislation goal, these regulations are basically after "auction law", they will not be "auction law" as making basis, clearly from the outside in "auction law" as the core of legal system of the auction system. Second, there are different auction operation modes in China's auction practice. According to the auction law, the leading power of auction operation belongs to the auctioneer, and the rights and obligations of the auctioneer are the core of the legal relationship of the auction. However, according to mandatory auction law, the auction operation of the dominant power belongs to the court. According to a series of special auction laws and regulations, the leading power of auction operation belongs to relevant government departments, such as land administrative departments, tobacco monopoly administrative departments, land and resources administrative departments, marine administrative departments, cultural relics administrative departments, tax authorities and so on. Third, different auction operation modes follow completely different requirements, resulting in conflicts between certain rules and contents. Such as "the State Tobacco Monopoly Administration requirements: engaged in tobacco auction houses must be dubbed" tobacco ", the name of the qualification by the state tobacco monopoly bureau approval, tobacco auction business led by provincial bureau of monopoly management department, tobacco auction houses, appointed by the provincial tobacco monopoly bureau, the head of the newspaper, country monopoly department for the record, etc., for example, national land and resources required: Auction of state-owned land access auction notice issued by the land administrative departments of the government and decided to auction, the time and place of state-owned land access floor price, bidding decision implementation of collective decision-making, bidding auction of state-owned land access when less than three may be undertaken, the auction should be by the land administrative departments of the government and the buyer signed the collective decision-making, etc. These requirements are obviously in conflict with the contents stipulated in the Auction Law. Although the above three aspects are not comprehensive, they are enough to illustrate the following facts: China's auction legal system is not unified.

Second, it investigates and studies whether the unified auction legal system is reasonable and feasible. This is a question of necessity, and it is difficult to simply say yes or no. First, look at it from a negative perspective. The auction legal system, especially the current Auction legal system in China, should not be completely unified. Here, the so-called "not completely unified" is the retention of compulsory auctions and noncompulsory auctions in the two system systems. Compulsory auctions and noncompulsory auctions are very different in nature. The former is the people's court in the execution of civil and commercial judgments, and the debtor's property has been sealed up and distracted by the relevant units in accordance with the auction disposal. To realize the interests of creditors compulsory enforcement measures, it is mainly judicial behavior. The latter is that the trustee hands over the property he owns or has the right to dispose to the auctioneer for the purpose of realizing his own interests, which belongs to transaction behavior. The huge difference in nature makes it impossible for them to operate in the same mode and follow the same rules. For example, optional auctions are dominated by auctioneers, and compulsory auctions are dominated by courts. In the case of a noncompulsory auction, the trustee shall bear the liability of guarantee for defects, while the court shall not bear the liability of guarantee for defects in the case of a compulsory auction. The noncompulsory auction procedure is decided by the Auction Law, and the compulsory auction procedure is mainly decided by the Civil Procedure Law. In addition, when China's Auction Law was promulgated, it excluded compulsory auctions from its scope of application. From this point of view, although the same auction, but different nature, rigid pursuit of a unified auction legal system is not reasonable, is not feasible in practice. Second, from a positive point of view. It is not appropriate to construct a relatively independent auction legal system based on the particularity of an auction target. Taking the auction of tobacco monopoly commodities as an example, according to the Notice of the State Tobacco Monopoly Administration on Strengthening the Management of Tobacco Auction Houses, the auction activities of tobacco monopoly commodities are deviating step by step from the norms of the Auction Law and forming a relatively independent auction legal system, which is neither reasonable nor feasible. First, The Auction Law of China does not exclude the auction activities of tobacco monopoly products from its scope of application, and the establishment of a separate auction legal system violates the provisions of the upper law. Second, tobacco monopoly products, in addition to their own restrictive content, do not affect disposal in accordance with the Auction Law. In fact, there are many auction objects similar to tobacco monopoly products, such as state-owned land use rights, cultural relics, exploration rights and mining rights, telecommunications resources, etc., which obviously cannot be managed by the administrative system to which they belong, and exclusive auction houses should be set up for auctions. Third, in the Notice of The State Tobacco Monopoly Administration on Strengthening the Management of Tobacco Auction Houses, in addition to incorporating the tobacco auction houses into its own system management, the auction house is not only responsible for the management of tobacco auction houses. The substantive rules and procedural rules are basically not stipulated. In fact, the particularity of auction targets does not affect their operation in the unified legal system of auctions. For example, national laws and regulations, on the one hand, emphasize the supervision of cultural relic administration departments and, on the other hand, emphasize that it should be carried out in the legal system with the auction law as the core.

According to the above investigation and research, this paper believes that there are two relatively independent auction legal systems in China, namely, compulsory auction legal systems and noncompulsory auction legal systems. In these two legal systems, there are different objectives and grounds, different contents of the parties and their rights and obligations, different substantive rules and their understandings, and different procedural requirements and their interpretations. Is, of course, the system of two legal systems are not opposite, between them also have intersection, asked the court since the Supreme People's Court "shall entrust auction institution", "auction law" of some important physical rules, such as price aircrafts to rules, barred from bidding rules, etc., in compulsory auction also influence; However, the differences between them are still basic, and only by considering them as two institutional systems can we make a correct and reasonable explanation for these differences.

3.2 Industry Self-regulation Rules and Enterprise Auction Rules

3.2.1 Rules on Industry Self-regulation

Industry self-regulation refers to the industry internal norms formulated by the auction industry association. At present, there are two types of auction industry associations in China. One is the China Auction Industry Association, which was established in Beijing in June 1995. It is a national nonprofit industry organization voluntarily formed by national auction enterprises, public institutions and social groups and has the legal person status of social groups. The second is the local auction industry association. China's provinces and municipalities are directly under the central government, and autonomous regions have their own local auction industry association, founded at different times. Article 17 of the Auction Law of The People's Republic of China stipulates that auction industry associations have the right to supervise auction enterprises and auctioneers in accordance with the Auction Law and their articles of association. According to the articles of association of Auction Association, auction association can assist government departments to carry out industry management work, formulate industry regulations, meeting agreement, promote standardized management and standardized operation of enterprises. At present, the self-regulatory rules of the auction industry mainly come from the China Auction Industry Association, while the local associations of various industries have relatively weak functions in this respect.

The self-disciplinary rules formulated by the China Auction Industry Association mainly include the following: auction industry in China the general principles of the auction (public property and other text category) "(1998)," China's auction industry auction rules (cultural and art category) "(1998)," several provisions on strengthening the supervision and administration of the auctioneer (provisional) "(2002) 4, provisions on strengthening industry self-discipline) (2004) 4 auction data management standard (trial) X2 Administrative Measures for Auctioneer Qualification Examination (2005), Supplementary Provisions for Auctioneer Registration Administration (2006), etc.

Strictly speaking, both the China Auction Industry Association and all local auction industry associations are nongovernmental organizations, which determines the effectiveness level of the self-disciplinary rules of the industry. The state does not endow nongovernmental institutions with the power to formulate laws and regulations. Even according to the articles of the Association of China Auction Industry, it only has the power to formulate rules and conventions, which do not belong to the scope of national laws and regulations. In this sense, this paper does not regard the self-regulatory rules formulated by the auction industry association as auction regulations, nor can they be included in China's auction regulatory system. Industry self-regulation rules that do not belong to national regulations have no universal effect, but they are not a piece of paper with no normative significance. They also have legal binding forces, but the legal binding force does not come from the industry rules and the convention itself. The evaluation of the legal binding force of industry self-discipline rules mainly comes from three aspects. First, the explicit provisions of China's auction law. By analyzing the abovementioned rules formulated by the China Auction Industry Association, it can be found that a considerable number of rules directly express various auction laws and regulations in China. For example, "Auction enterprises shall not engage in auction activities in violation of the Provisions of the Auction Law"; "An auction enterprise shall not, in violation of the agreement or in violation of the requirements of the trustor, bidder or buyer, disclose, use or allow others to use the commercial secrets of the abovementioned parties in its possession"; "When the trustee auctions state-owned assets, he shall evaluate the auction target in accordance with the law before the auction, to determine the reserve price. "There are too many of these rules to list them all. Such rules are, of course, legally binding, and their violation is no different from a violation of national auction regulations. Second, the auction law or the authorization of the state administrative organs. Due to the authorization of the Auction Law, the Auction Industry Association has the following rights: organizing the auctioneer qualification examination uniformly, issuing the auctioneer qualification certificate, supervising auction enterprises and auctioneers, etc. In addition, the auction industry association can also exercise some industry management rights authorized by the government management department. Among the abovementioned rules formulated by the China Auction Industry Association, a large number of rules belong to this category, such as Measures for the Administration of Auctioneer Qualification Examination, Several Provisions on Strengthening supervision and Administration of Auctioneers (Trial), etc. Such rules shall have legal effects as long as they do not exceed the authorization of the law or the relevant administrative authority and are reasonable in themselves. Third, the commitment was made by auction enterprises and auctioneers. The auction industry association adopts the membership system. If the member units of the auction industry association reach a consensus on some rules or make a joint commitment on some behaviors, the rules thus formed shall be legally binding on each other as long as they are reasonable and do not violate national laws and regulations. Among the rules formulated by the China Auction Industry Association listed above, a certain number of rules belong to this category, such as "General Rules for Auction in China Auction Industry (Public Property and Other Property Categories)" and "General Rules for Auction in China Auction Industry (Culture and Art Categories)". However, it should be noted that the legal effect of such rules originates from the binding force of the contract.

It is of great significance to clarify the source of the legal effect of self-regulation. On the one hand, it makes all the people who may be regulated by the self-discipline rules understand that the self-discipline rules should be observed, and the violation of the self-discipline rules may also be punished by the law; On the other hand, it also makes all the people who may be regulated by the self-discipline rules understand that the self-discipline rules themselves are not laws and regulations, except the self-discipline rules that directly express the legal rules, the validity of the self-discipline rules is relative.

The effect of the trade self-regulation rules generated in accordance with the Auction Law or the authorization of the state administrative authority is relative. The reason is that although the Auction Law or the state administrative organ authorizes the auction industry association to perform certain duties, neither of them authorizes it to formulate regulations, nor may they be authorized to formulate regulations. In this context, the industry self-regulation rules should be tested from two aspects: first, whether the rights and obligations set by the industry self-regulation rules exceed the authorized authority; second, whether the rights and obligations set by the self-discipline rules of the industry abuse the authority granted. In this sense, the rights and obligations set by the self-disciplinary rules of the industry are not established; even if the violation of the self-disciplinary rules of the industry is punished, it is also possible to obtain judicial relief.

According to the auction enterprises and auctioneers who made a point of commitment to the industry self-regulation rules, its effectiveness is also relative. The rights and obligations set by such industry self-discipline rules are only binding in the sense of contract law, which can restrain the person who has made the promise, specifically the auction house.

The member units of a trade association and their working personnel, but not binding on others. In this sense, the industry self-discipline rules generated according to the promises made by auction enterprises and auctioneers cannot set up rights and obligations for society; for example, they cannot set rights and obligations for consignors, bidders and buyers. Because these people have not made promises, they are naturally not bound by such industry self-discipline rules.

3.2.2 Rules on Enterprise Auction

Enterprise auction rules refer to the rules of conduct formulated by auction enterprises to regulate auction transactions. At present, there are thousands of auction enterprises in China, and almost every auction enterprise has its own auction rules, so there are numerous auction rules in China.

Enterprise auction rules do not have any legal nature. In practice, some auction enterprises regard the auction rules unilaterally formulated by themselves as regulations and require national law enforcement departments to apply them forcibly, which is not feasible.

However, corporate auction rules can be binding. The binding force of enterprise auction rules is manifested in two aspects. First, as the service code of auction enterprises, it constrains the auction enterprises. The enterprise auction rules are formulated by the auction enterprises. The promises made by the auction enterprises in the auction rules have a binding force on the auction enterprises as long as they do not violate laws, regulations and public order, and the auction enterprises shall act in accordance with the rules. Second, as a contract term binding auction parties. Although the enterprise auction rules are unilaterally formulated by the auction enterprise, they do not affect the contract terms, such as the terms of the entrusted auction contract or the terms of the auction contract, binding the contract parties. In practice, the main purpose of almost all corporate auction rules is just this. However, the enterprise auction rules as contract terms binding auction parties need to meet some preconditions, these preconditions include: do not violate laws, regulations and public order; Known, understood and accepted by the trustor and the bidder (buyer);The content is fair and reasonable. Auction enterprises have no right to impose enterprise auction rules on other auction parties.

3.3 Legal Principles on Auction Activities

The legal principles of auction activities are related to the theoretical basis or principle of various rules of conduct in the legal system of auctions, which is a major problem that cannot be ignored. There are many legal principles related to auction activities in China's auction laws and regulations, which can be summed up as nothing more than the principles of openness, fairness, justice and honesty.

Openness is the legal principle of auction activity, and the open form of auction and incomparable public participation are the concentrated embodiment of the openness principle. Openness is the most commendable attribute of auction. The basic difference between auction and other buying and selling methods is that the degree of openness of the former is incomparable to the latter. The principle of openness runs through auction activities, which is the external requirement of the principle for auction activity and movement. It requires auction transactions to be carried out as transparently as possible. For example, auction targets should be publicly solicited; Auction targets and their contents shall be publicized; The holding of auction activities shall be announced; Bids and offers must be made in public; The transaction process shall be made public, etc. The principle of openness makes the auction "public sale", which is especially suitable for the transaction of state-owned assets. When a deal is made public, it is hard to fake and easy to monitor. From the logic connection of many principles of auction activities, the principle of openness is the premise, first there is openness, then there is fairness and justice; With openness, it is difficult to form unfairness and injustice, or even if it is formed, it is easy to expose. Therefore, openness provides a kind of guarantee for fairness and justice.

The principle of fairness and justice runs through auction activities, which is the inherent requirement of the principle for auction activities. The principle of fairness reflects the equal participation of auction activities. Unless otherwise stipulated by law, everyone can participate and has the right to participate. It requires the establishment of equal legal status between the auction parties and rejects the unfair phenomenon that the big oppress the small and the strong bully the weak due to the unequal social and economic status between the parties. It requires that competition in the auction process be fair competition, and no party is allowed to dominate the competition process by means of collusion, fraud and falsification. Justice principle pay more attention to the rationality of the rights and obligations in the auction, an auctioneer and a trustee, bidding, and the rights and obligations of the buyer in the auction activity is various, the rights and obligations may come from the auction law expressly provided otherwise, may also come from the agreed between the parties, but it does not matter where come from, to be fair principle of inspection; The principle of justice does not recognize that a party only has rights without obligations, nor does it recognize that the party enjoys more rights than its obligations; The system of rights and obligations under the principle of justice should be balanced.

The principle of honesty and credit runs through auction activities, which is the requirement of the principle for the inner quality of the auction parties. Legal relationships are essentially relationships between people, so the legal system to maintain the healthy operation of legal relationships can not only be limited to the external form of the requirements but also ignore the internal quality of people. As far as the auction legal system is concerned, the auction regulations attempt to comprehensively regulate the auction parties and put all the words and deeds of the auction parties under the halo of the auction legal system. However, words and deeds are controlled not only by external forms but also by people's inner qualities. It has been proven that without the norms of intrinsic quality, the legal system is quite fragile, and in some cases, its social efficacy is almost nil. For example, article 30 of the Auction Law stipulates that the trustee shall not participate in the bidding or entrust others to bid on his behalf. The social efficacy of this prohibition depends to a large extent on the honesty of the client; otherwise, the social efficacy of this prohibition would be greatly compromised. In the auction law, similar provisions are numerous. Strictly speaking, no auction law can be thoroughly enforced on the basis of lack of good faith, and the principle of good faith is everywhere. Honesty is first and foremost a moral principle, and in the business world, honesty is the highest moral principle. The incorporation of such moral principles into legal norms as a general principle reflects the evolution of society on the one hand and people's expectation for a more perfect legal system on the other.

Openness, fairness, justice and honesty are the legal principles established for auction activities in China's Auction Law, which have various functions. First, they are the basis and principle for auction parties to understand the rules of auction behavior. It is obvious that the legislator establishes the system of auction parties' rights and obligations according to these principles. This requires that every auction party understand the rules of auction behavior from the height of principle. It should be realized that principles are highly abstract rules. Although rules are different and may have different understandings due to different interests in practice, all rules must be unified in principles and can be contained and explained by principles. Second, they are the basis and principle for law enforcement departments to implement the rules of auction behavior. It is well known that there are gaps in the established system of regulation, as is the auction system. This is because as a legislator, there will inevitably be blind spots in understanding, and there will be no false rules.

Alternatively, it is impossible to assume the situation, which leads to the distance between the established legal system and social practice, resulting in a specific behavior without corresponding rule guidance. There is no lack of such situations in auction practice. For example, the behavior rules of online auctions, whether a bidder can achieve the auction, and the liability for defects when an auction enterprise accepts a mandate to carry out a forced auction, etc. In this regard, the law enforcement department can only solve the problems in practice by expanding the interpretation of the existing rules, but the expansion of interpretation should not be arbitrary; the law enforcement department should have the basis of principle.

3.4 The Connotation and Extension of Auction in the System

Article 3 of The Auction Law of the People's Republic of China defines "auction" as follows: Auction is a trading method in which specific articles or property rights are transferred to the highest bidder in the form of open bidding. This is by far the shortest definition of an auction seen in this article. In other authoritative dictionaries, the definition of auctions is not simple.

Ci Hai defines "auction" as: also known as bidding; A way of buying and selling in business; A seller sells an item to the highest bidder (bidder) by bidding for it; Auction is generally by the seller of spot or sample display auction site, auction by number bidding; Bids are on the increase and decline in two: the former is by the auctioneer to shout a lowest price first, and then let the bidders to tariffs, until there is no one to go above, the auctioneer then with a hammer or a clap on the table, according to clinch a deal, which is by the auctioneer to shout a highest price first, if no one to buy, then gradually falling in price, until there is answer buyers, an auctioneer is a thump, trades; Auction has voluntary and compulsory two kinds, the former is the owner of goods voluntarily arily entrust house bection half of the banking, the latter is the owner of goods due to compulsory other reasons.

The Dictionary of Law defines "auction" as: also called auction; A method of buying and selling based on competitive bids; Divided into voluntary and compulsory two kinds, the former is the seller and the auction house to conclude a commissioned auction contract, the latter is the goods owner due to bankruptcy or other reasons by forced auction, such as the court entrusted auction house to auction the debtor's property; Its way for the auction house to accept the consignment, post a notice or advertisement, explaining the variety of goods, storage location, auction date and location, let people go to see the goods, then by the auction house presided over the public auction, the goods will be sold to the highest bidder buyer, on the spot transaction; In an auction, the auctioneer announces the starting point of bidding, and the buyers compete to price. When no one continues to increase the price, the auctioneer beats a small wooden hammer to clinch a deal. However, there are also auctioneers who shout out the highest price first. When there is no buyer, the auctioneers reduce the price one after another. When there is a buyer, the auction is called a "Dutch auction". The auction house is paid either by the seller or by both buyers and sellers.

The Oxford Law Dictionary defines "auction" as a way of selling or renting; In this way, people at the scene compete to buy or lease by offering a higher price; It usually takes place in public; An authorized auctioneer who, following the Posting of an advertisement, signals his acceptance of the final offer or bid by striking a hammer, may reclaim the property for sale before the hammer is dropped; It can be determined that the auction can be carried out under the reserve price, and the seller can freely reserve his bid; Bids can be withdrawn before the hammer falls.

This paper holds that it is not unreasonable for the abovementioned authoritative dictionaries to take pains to define "auctions", especially in the legal system, which is not "a way of buying and selling". First, auctions are fraught with complex behavior. On three sides of most of the parties involved in the auction process, participants each have their own behavior to attain the goal of participation, including the client, auction and bidding (the buyer) of behavior, which is the basic behavior in auction activity. The behavioral purpose of transferring the rights of an auction target as the core determines that the participants engaged in activities generally have a civil nature. Second, the auction is full of the stage and period of the process. In the case of a successful auction, the auction is usually an auctioneer or client offer (its aim is to sign a contract on trust auction). After signing the contract on trust auction, the auction of organizing and planning, auction notice, check the said auction target and live auction several stages until the buyer has certain rights and delivery of an auction target clearly. In the legal system, the stage and period of auction is clear, and orderly, auction is the implementation of a legal procedure. Finally, auctions can also be understood as a measure of enforcement. China's Civil Procedure Law stipulates auctions in the chapter on enforcement measures. Auction refers to the court enforcing the property of the person subjected to execution at the request of creditors or in accordance with legal provisions. Therefore, the auction in the compulsory auction law is no longer a civil activity or a way of sale, and its behavior and process have obvious judicial nature.

In summary, in the auction legal system, the meaning of auction, its connotation and extension is difficult to use "a way of buying and selling" to summarize. Of course, there is nothing wrong with saying auction is a way of buying and selling, but the problem is that this definition loses its institutional meaning. The auction legal system does not intend to regulate a way of buying and selling, nor can it regulate a way of buying and selling. What it wants to regulate are activities (behaviors), procedures and compulsory measures. In fact, China's auction laws and regulations do not establish a normative system according to "auction" as defined in the Auction Law but are much broader and deeper than that.

4 Past and Future of Auction Legal System

4.1 The Development Trajectory of China's Auction Industry

China's auction industry took shape after the middle of the nineteenth century. In 1874, the largest auction house in Britain opened a subsidiary company in Shanghai, where China's commodity economy was developing rapidly. Subsequently, a number of foreign firms have been listed in China to carry out auction businesses. The auction industry is not indigenous to China but has evolved with the entry of foreign capital. In its early days, the industry was largely in foreign hands, and the Chinese treated this foreign novelty as a sideshow. Soon, the Chinese civilization absorbed this new thing with its extensive and profound nature, and the auction industry took root in China.

At the beginning of the formation of China's auction industry, there were few auction houses because they were all controlled by foreign businessmen, so most of them were called "certain foreign firms". Examples include Shanghai Lu Yi Si Mo auction company, Rui and foreign firm, Rosentai foreign firm, three law foreign firm and Beijing lu Lin foreign firm. These foreign firms operate a wider range, in addition to auction businesses but also operate, such as import and export and retail Qing businesses. When the category of an auction target is relatively simple, mainly diplomat he did not want to take away the clothes, furniture, decoration, customs confiscated goods, sea transport of water damage, as well as Banks, insurance companies, mortgage items, occasionally the auction of the Qing dynasty royal calligraphy and painting and antique dignitaries, but far from form art auction climate. There were also limited bids, mainly from other auctioneers and a few secondhand dealers. In short, although there was a sensation in the early days of the auction industry, the style was not high. The country's economic situation cannot provide a larger market for auctions, domestic troubles and foreign wars. People's livelihood is not guaranteed. How to talk about economic development and how to talk about auctions are more important.

Around the republic of China, auction houses founded by The Chinese appeared in Beijing, Shanghai, Guangzhou and other places. The auction entities that broke free of foreign control quickly joined forces with homegrown pawnbrokers and consigners, often addressing the lack of auction bids by selling off the most desirable items in pawn or by consigning hard-to-sell items. Auction houses are therefore also called "pawn auction houses" or "consignment auction houses". Although the combination of auctions with pawns and consignments has more disadvantages, it is sufficient to show that auctions have been widely accepted by Chinese people. The auction industry had its ups and downs for a while. For example, during the victory of the War of Resistance against Japan, the auction industry prospered when society was full of dancing and dancing. By the time the Kuomintang government was about to fall, the economy was about to collapse, and the auction industry was rapidly shrinking.

After the founding of new China, ten thousand industries recovered, but the auction industry was restricted. There are only two reasons. First, the leading economic theory of new China is the planned economy, and all other economic elements will be transformed to integrate into the planned economy system. However, the auction industry is based on the typical market economy. The development of the auction industry means the development of a market economy, which is contrary to the country's leading economic theory. Second, in China's practice, the auction industry has long been associated with the pawnshop industry, and pawnshop is considered a tool for exploiting working people, coupled with the infiltration of underworld and evil forces into the auction industry in old China, resulting in many illegal acts in the auction industry and a poor social image. All this has become a reason for the government to restrict and gradually eliminate the auction business. Take Shanghai as an example. In the early days of the founding of New China, there were 25 auction houses in Shanghai. After the industry was rectified, 11 auction houses remained in 1955. By 1958, with the disappearance of auction houses, the auction industry had ceased to exist.

In the 1980s, an extremely large and profound change in the economic system hit the original economic structure. When the foundation of planned economy theory began to loosen, people began to re-evaluate the function of auctions. The reform of the economic system aims at establishing the whole market system, and auctions, as a special market means, play a special and irreplaceable role in promoting the reasonable flow and allocation of factors of production. The driving force of economic operation comes from fair competition, and auction is exactly the trading way that can best reflect the openness, fairness, justice and competitiveness of the market. The theory of the market economy has given green light to a revival of the auction industry.

In 1986, some firms in Guangzhou began to run the auction business to ask the market for directions. In January 1987, Guangzhou Auction House was officially established, which marked the beginning of the Renaissance of the Chinese auction industry. In April 1988, Shanghai Wuzi Auction House was formally established in Shanghai, the birthplace of China's auction industry. In May, the Beijing auction market opened. In June, Tianjin auction house listing and so on. 1988 was a year of comprehensive revival of China's auction industry, and professional auction houses were established successively in major and medium-sized cities across the country. In August 1992, the Notice of The General Office of the State Council on the Implementation of Public Auction for the Disposal of Public Property was published, formally recognizing the auction industry in legal form. In June 1995, the China Auction Industry Association was established, which marked the auction industry's cohesion, and self-protection, self-restraint, and self-development ability were significantly enhanced. In July 1996, the state promulgated the Auction Law, which not only indicates the maturity of the auction legal system but also indicates that the legalization of the auction industry has reached a new level. Approximately 1997, according to the provisions of Article 10 of the Auction Law, auction enterprises throughout the country began to be transformed into corporations, such as auction enterprises owned by the whole people and collectively owned auction enterprises into auction limited liability companies or ^^ selling limited liability companies. Since 2001, under the auspices of the China Auction Industry Association, the auction industry has carried out an annual qualification assessment of auction enterprises, which has played a very important role in promoting enterprises to strengthen management, improve the overall quality and enhance the overall level of the whole industry. Since 2004, to fulfill the commitments made when China entered WTO, China's auction market has been opened to foreign investment, and the auction industry has ushered in new opportunities and challenges. By the end of 2004, China's auction industry had a total of more than 2,000 auction enterprises, more than 1,000 of them with a-level qualifications. There were nearly 50,000 auction employees, of whom more than 23,000 had received training and obtained professional certificates. More than 5,000 auctioneers; the annual auction turnover is more than 200 billion yuan.

As seen from the above development trajectory of China's auction industry, China's auction industry has neither a long history nor a small scale. However, thanks to the support of the market system and the regulation of auction laws and regulations, it has been full of vitality and rapid development since the 1980s, so it has become a school of its own among many industries in China and has brilliant development prospects. However, with the rapid development of the auction industry, there are also some problems that need to be solved. These problems mainly include (1) unreasonable business structures, and specialized markets have not yet formed. At present, China's auction enterprises are small in scale and large in number, with the same business scope. Most of them mainly rely on judicial entrustment and the auction of confiscated goods, and the competition among them is becoming increasingly fierce. However, in agricultural and sideline product transactions, motor vehicle transactions, property rights and equity transfer and other fields, auction enterprises account for a very small share of the transactions that need to be developed. (2) The management level of auction enterprises is low, the overall quality of employees is not high, and professional technical personnel and high-quality management personnel are lacking. (3) The overall development of the auction industry is unbalanced, and the gap is gradually widening. These differences exist not only between enterprises but also between China's eastern and western regions. To solve the above problems, on the one hand, joint efforts of the industry are needed; on the other hand, the industry also depends on the perfection of the auction legal system.

4.2 Auction Custom System and Auction Law System

Historically, China's auction industry has long been guided by auction habits. The system of auction customs refers to the system of rules that auction traders follow by common conventions without the enactment of national legislative procedures. The auction practices include: the auction shall be conducted in public; The auction subject shall be sold to the bidder with the highest bid; The price competition in the auction spreads out among the buyers; When the buyer's quotation does not reach the bottom price, the transaction will not be concluded; The auction parties should be subject to some restrictions in the auction process; An auction may be conducted in the form of price increase or price reduction. Bidders should follow certain rules and so on. The custom auction entered Into China along with auction transactions. As some of the rules are very suitable for the characteristics of auctions and almost inseparable from auctions, they are not forced by national legislation, but they do not affect their popularity in the industry. Over time, auction habits were generally considered to have legal force, and auction parties should follow them.

In China, auction customs have a long history of dominating the legal relations of auctions. From the late Qing Dynasty to the early Republic of China, China's legal system underwent great changes. The Chinese legal system formed since the Tang Dynasty was greatly impacted and faced disintegration, while the modern legal system was far from being established, and there was no basis for formulating auction laws and regulations. Auctions in this period were completely subject to auction habits. During the Period of the Republic of China, although China's modern legal system had been established, there was no opportunity and motivation to legislate for auction because the auction industry was not well developed and the civil war had no time to take into account. Auctions in this period were mainly restricted by auction habits. From the founding of The People's Republic of China to the 1980s, the auction industry was restricted and then banned, and there was no social need to enact laws and regulations for auctions. The sporadic auction that remained during this period was subject to the inertia effect of long-standing effective auction habits. Therefore, the historical role of auction customs in the development of China's auction industry cannot be underestimated. In fact, from the beginning of the formation of the auction industry to the 1980s, the core of China's so-called auction legal system was a system based on an auction custom system.

The system of auction customs is quite different from the current system of auction law. First, China's auction habit system is derived from foreign (mainly British) auction habits. Although these foreign auction habits have changed somewhat through the long-term adaptation of Chinese culture, their basic spirit and principles have not been changed. The system of auction habits reflects a high degree of autonomy of intention, and the rights and obligations of auction parties are basically agreed upon between them. There are few prohibitive rules in the system, and some established rules can also be changed according to the consent of the parties. The system of auction customs assures that what the parties freely agree is reasonable. However, the current auction legal system is formulated by Chinese authorities according to the long-term practice of auctions in China and the national conditions of China, with Chinese characteristics. The guiding principle of the auction legal system is the organic combination of autonomy and state intervention. On the one hand, the system allows the parties to set their rights and obligations freely; on the other hand, the system sets an insurmountable forbidden area for the parties' freedom. In the face of auction parties, the initiative and strength of the auction law system is incomparable to that of the auction habit system. The auction regulatory system is convinced that the parties' agreements are reasonable only if they conform to openness, fairness, justice and good faith. Second, although there is a system of auction habits that have been used for a long time in China's auction practice, it is far from perfect. There are few auction habits that can be known to people, and they only focus on a few behaviors of auction parties and some auction procedures. For the maintenance of the order of the auction market, the management of the auction industry (including auction enterprises, auctioneers and auction practitioners), as well as most of the auction procedures and the behavior of the parties, are outside the norms of auction customs. However, today's auction law system is a relatively perfect system: from the big aspect, it includes the auction entity rule system, the auction procedure rule system, the compulsory auction rule system and the auction industry management rule system; From a small point of view, it almost involves the words and deeds of auction parties and related subjects, and strives to be specific and meticulous in content, and strives to be clear and detailed in specification. Third, auction habits are never unified, which includes not only the establishment of rules but also the understanding of rules. The disunity of rules establishment refers to whether a practice is a habit or not, there are different understandings in the industry and outside the industry, such as auctioneer bidding agent, some people think it belongs to the auction habit, some people deny it belongs to the auction habit. Do not have a unified understanding of the rules is to point to one way of doing this is to belong to the auction habit, but for the custom content contained in have different understanding, such as "statement does not guarantee", admittedly, it belongs to the auction habit, but for the habit should be absolutely understanding or relatively understanding, what are the limits to exemption conditions, etc., can say, unable to agree. The disunity of auction customs greatly affects their function as a law. However, today's auction legal system is unified. Centralized and unified legislative organs ensure the unified formulation of regulations, centralized and unified law enforcement agencies ensure the unified operation of rules, and common legal principles ensure that there can be unified understanding. Of course, in the face of such a unified auction legal system, there will be disharmonious voices in practice, but it is impossible to affect a truth; that is, the auction legal system essentially requires unification. Fourth, the rationality of auction habits lacks a solid social foundation. The auction habit is formed in the industry, in this process, although it cannot be said that there is no participation of the public, but its participation is limited, coupled with the strong interpretation of the so-called auction habit by the auction industry, all kinds of factors may tilt the rights and obligations of the auction habit to the auction enterprise. Compared with auction habits, auction laws and regulations have a much more solid social foundation. China's auction laws and regulations come from legislative, administrative, judicial and other institutions, which are detached from the auction parties and represent the interests of all the people. Their broad representativeness provides a solid social foundation for the rationality of auction laws and regulations.

This paper does not intend to erase the auction custom and its system, and there is a certain relationship between the auction custom system and the auction law system. China's auction legal system is not created out of thin air. At the beginning of the establishment of the auction legal system, enough nutrients were absorbed from the auction custom system, so it was not difficult to find that some of today's auction rules and past custom rules had roughly the same outline. However, it is necessary to clarify that the system of auction customs does not belong to the present system of auction laws and regulations. In terms of the history of the auction legal system, the auction custom system and the auction legal system represent two different times. Before the 1980s, China's auction was regulated by the auction custom system, thus forming the auction legal system at that time. After the 1980s, China's auction was regulated by the system of auction laws and regulations, thus forming the current auction legal system. There is an inheritance relationship, but it cannot be compared with the actual effect. It should be seen that when the auction legal system absorbs the auction habit, it seldom accepts all the bills. Most of it has been reformed and deepened according to China's national conditions, making it into two different versions. It is not feasible to interpret auction laws and regulations by auction habits or even to break them by auction habits.

This book focuses on the current auction legal system.

4.3 Prospect of Auction Legal System

China's auction legal system is unique in the world, and its specialization, comprehensive content and strict specification are rare among the auction legal systems of many countries. However, China's auction legal system is also flawed and needs to be improved. In the middle of April 2003, some newspapers and periodicals published or reprinted the report about exposing the dark curtain of the auction industry, making people shocking. Of course, there are some things wrong with the report, but the questions raised are not groundless, they are used to warn others and have positive significance. The report summarizes three points of view, two of which are: lagging phenomenon of auction law should be changed; The quality of auction practitioners needs to be improved. This is basically consistent with the view of auction industry insiders, including the China Auction Industry Association.

Looking forward to the perfection of the auction legal system, we need to have a clear understanding of the defects of the current auction legal system. This paper agrees with the above report on the reasons for some bad phenomena but thinks that it is not all, and the evaluation is not comprehensive. In the following, this paper will be divided into various issues to explore the improvement of the auction legal system.

4.3.1 The Lag of Auction Laws and Regulations

Auction laws and regulations lag behind the problem, but not seriously, there is a deviation in the understanding of the industry. First, from the formal investigation. China's auction legal system was formed in 2. After this, the late 1980s were constantly updated and enriched to improve. At present, the key laws and regulations in this system have the background of the new century. For example, the Auction Law was revised in 2004; The Auction Administration Measures was formulated in 2004; Most of the special laws and regulations related to auction were formulated after

2001. The provisions of the Supreme People's Court on compulsory auctions were formulated after 2001. Local auction laws and regulations have been revised since 2001. These regulations have not been implemented for a long time, and how can they be criticized as lagging? Not formally, at least. Second, examine from content. There are indeed many problems reflected in China's auction practice, but most of these problems are based on rights and incorrect auction laws. Take the problems mentioned in the above report as an example. It is reported that some auction houses pursue monetary interests, acquire in the black box operation of buyers and sellers or participate in the black box operation themselves to embezzle bank funds or seize state-owned assets. For this kind of behavior, is there no normative basis in Chinese auction laws and regulations or the normative basis is not clear? The report says that some auction houses sell their own goods to make huge profits. For this kind of behavior, is there no clear prohibition in Chinese auction law? The report said some auction houses hid defects and sold fake items, hurting consumers' interests. For this kind of behavior, is there no right and wrong basis or sanctions in Chinese auction laws and regulations? In fact, the problems reflected in the report can be found in China's auction law system. Why do people inside and outside the industry think auction regulations lag behind?

This paper argues that the serious lag of auction law is caused by the lack of unified interpretation and understanding. In the practice of auctions, the majority of disputes arise not from the rule of no action but from the different interpretations and understandings of the same rule, especially the different interpretations and understandings of the rules in the Auction Law. For example, article 22 of the Auction Law stipulates that "auctioneers and their staff shall not participate in the auction activities organized by themselves as bidders, and shall not entrust others to bid for them. "This article has produced two problems in practice: the first problem is whether the personnel hired by auction enterprises to organize auction activities belong to the scope of "staff" in the provisions; The second question is whether it is prohibited by the rules for auctioneers to accept the entrustments of bidders to participate in their own auction activities. There is no unified understanding of the disputes surrounding these two issues. For example, article 3 of the Auction Law stipulates: "Auction refers to the sale method of transferring specific articles or property rights to the highest bidder in the form of open bidding. "In practice, the problem of "whether only one bidder can participate in the auction" arises.

Different interpretations and understandings of auction law are caused by different reasons. First, some regulations in auction law are too principled, leaving the source of ambiguity in practice. Second, parties with conflicting interests arbitrarily interpret the rules in auction regulations for their own interests, while authorities or departments rarely come forward to clarify them.

To solve the above problems, this paper holds that first, it is necessary to formulate implementation rules or judicial interpretations for the application of the Auction Law as soon as possible. At present, most of the ambiguities in auction practice originate from or are rooted in the Auction Law. In practice, the provisions of the auction law involve articles 2, 3, 5, 7, 8, 9, 11, 14, 17, 21, 22, 28, 34, 52, 57, 59, 60, 61, 62 and so on, which need to be further clarified. Second, the law enforcement and publicity of auction laws and regulations should be strengthened, and people's understanding of the content of auction laws and regulations should be unified. For a country with a tradition of written law, the written expression of laws and regulations always has boundaries. Even if the implementation rules of the Auction Law are formulated, it is impossible to directly answer all the questions in practice, which requires understanding and publicity in law enforcement. This paper argues that the false perception of auction laws and regulations lagging behind is mainly caused by insufficient publicity of law enforcement. Some market behaviors that have long been considered illegal by law enforcement authorities are still considered ambiguous gray areas in the industry, and some clearly defined regulations are still controversial in the industry. Therefore, it is necessary to strengthen the law enforcement and publicity requirements, people's courts at all levels, industrial and commercial administrative departments, the competent departments of the auction industry and other relevant cases should be unveiled to the world, in order to unify people's understanding of the auction laws and regulations and their contents.

4.3.2 Coordination Between Auction Laws and Regulations

There is a huge legal system around auctions in China, which includes auction core law, auction special law, compulsory auction law and auction-related law. Longitudinally, it includes central auction regulations and local auction regulations. In this large system, the coordination between laws and regulations is a major problem that directly affects the evaluation of the perfection of the auction legal system.

As far as horizontal coordination is concerned, the coordination between regulations should first solve the coordination between the first three types of regulations and auction-related regulations. Auction-related laws and regulations are basic laws and supporting laws in various fields. Therefore, the principle of consistency between the first three types of laws and auction-related laws and regulations should be maintained unless special requirements of auctions are involved. Second, there should be coordination between the auction core law and compulsory auction law. The compulsory auction law has the nature of judicial enforcement, and its contents are inevitably different from those of the core auction law due to the differences in purpose and methods. However, since they both belong to the category of auction, they should be consistent in the principle of auction. Third, the auction core regulations and auction special regulations should be coordinated. The auction special law is derived from the auction core law, and there is no auction special law without the auction core law; therefore, the two should be consistent in principle and in the main content. Finally, regulations should be harmonised within themselves. Each type of regulation is composed of several regulations, and the differences between these regulations are intricate. Some have only small differences, such as between the auction core regulations, and some have great differences, such as between the auction related regulations. Therefore, coordination within various regulations can only be principled.

In terms of vertical coordination, local auction laws and regulations should be based on central auction laws and regulations, and they should be highly consistent.

To evaluate the coordination of auction laws and regulations in China, two points should be made clear. First, a healthy regulatory system does not require the content of different laws and regulations to be completely consistent. In fact, a regulation, no matter what level it is, is not a simple repetition of other regulations; therefore, the content differences between regulations are inevitable, but the differences are different degrees. Such differences in content can also be seen, for example, between central and local auction regulations, which are most easily reconciled. Second, a healthy regulatory system requires that differences in content between regulations should not lead to substantive conflicts with each other. Substantive conflicts cannot be tolerated because substantive conflicts will lead to functional cancellations between laws and regulations, the complementary relationship no longer exists, and then confusion in practice. Substantive conflicts arise from differences in principles and principles and may also arise from differences in main provisions. For example, if there is a conflict in principle between the contract regulated by the Auction Act and the Contract Law, there will be a material conflict.

It can be said that there are both joys and sorrows in analyzing the coordination between Chinese auction laws and regulations. Coordination in the following areas is basically nonexistent. First, the coordination between the central auction law and local auction law. Historically, China's local auction laws and regulations occurred earlier than the central auction laws and regulations. As early as the early 1990s, when central auction laws and regulations had not yet taken shape, local auction laws and regulations now had a relatively complete pattern. In fact, China's central auction laws and regulations are the result of local auction laws and regulations. However, after the formation of the central auction law, the unification of local auction law played a very good role. China's local auction laws and regulations were all corrected and reconstructed in approximately 2000 based on central auction laws and regulations. At present, China's local auction laws and regulations are highly unified with the central auction laws and regulations, and there is basically no conflict between the two in practice. Second, there is coordination between three kinds of laws and regulations (auction core law, auction special law and compulsory auction law) and auction-related laws and regulations. At present, the three types of laws and regulations maintain good coordination with auction-related laws and regulations, and the principles, principles and main provisions of auction-related laws and regulations are fully reflected in the three types of laws and regulations. For example, the principles of auctions established by the three types of laws are rooted in the principles of civil legislation established by laws such as the general principles of civil law. The provisions of the three types of laws and regulations on contracts follow the principles of contracts established in the Contract Law. The provisions on auction enterprises in the three kinds of laws and regulations are in line with the Company Law and other laws. The contents related to the auction of cultural relics in the three laws and regulations reflect the provisions of the Cultural Relics Protection Law. In addition, the internal coordination of various regulations does not exist too large a problem.

There are also inconsistencies between Chinese auction laws. First, there is disharmony between auction core regulations and auction special regulations. The main performance is as follows: (1) From the formulation of the basis to dissociate from the auction Law. Apart from the special local auction laws and regulations, there are few auction laws and regulations issued by ministries and commissions in China that take the Auction Law as the basis for enactment. For example, the Notice of the State Tobacco Monopoly Administration on Strengthening the Administration of Tobacco Auction, The Provisions on The Transfer of State-owned Land Use Right through Bidding, Auction and Listing, The Administrative Measures for Bidding, Auction and Listing of Mining Rights (Trial), and the Trial Measures for Auctioning and Selling Off Property against Tax, etc. The auction law is not explicitly taken as the basis of enactment or as one of the bases of enactment, thus foreshadowing the disharmony between regulations. (2) Adopt different basic structure of auction. In the core laws and regulations of auction, the basic structure of auction is as follows: the transaction is carried out between the three parties (auctioneer, trustee, bidder/buyer), and the three parties have their own independent interests in the transaction; In some special auction regulations, the auctioneer and the trustee are one, or the interests of the auctioneer and the trustee are completely consistent. The basic architecture of change fundamentally overturns the principle of the auction, and agents change the auction trading way for buyers and sellers of way to trade directly, thus playing down the auction to sell core rules to choose the unification of the auctioning industry management system, including the commerce administrative departments for auctioning industry supervision and management, the administrative department for industry and commerce to market supervision and management of the auctioning industry. Other competent administrative departments shall guide and supervise the auction of specific auction targets only within the scope of their competence when the auction targets are involved. However, some special auction laws and regulations have chosen segmented auction industry management systems to establish industry management according to the category of auction targets. For example, the tobacco auction belongs to the national tobacco administrative department for industry management, and the land use right auction belongs to the land and resources administrative department for industry management. Different management systems of the auction industry produce great conflicts in practice. Second, there is disharmony between the core auction law and the mandatory auction law. The main performance is as follows: (1) the scope of their effectiveness is not clear. China has established two systems according to the core auction laws and the compulsory auction laws, and these two systems have been substantially connected through the court entrusting auction enterprises to implement the compulsory auction, but there is no clear provision on the consequences of the connection, which easily leads to practical conflicts. For example, should an auction enterprise entrusted by the court act in accordance with the Auction Law or the provisions of the Supreme People's Court? After the court entrusts an auction enterprise, should the trustee also follow the relevant provisions of the Auction Law? (2) The lack of perfect regulations after the linkage of the system, especially the regulation of compulsory auctions. There is a difference between compulsory auction systems and noncompulsory auction systems. A compulsory auction system and a noncompulsory auction system need to be connected in practice, which has been proven in the previous discussion and will be further proven in the following discussion. Since there are differences between systems and there is a need for convergence, they need to have their own perfect provisions; otherwise, it is difficult to coordinate the application of laws after convergence. At present, in the scope regulated by compulsory auction law, incomplete content is difficult to make up by noncompulsory auction law. For example, the liability for defects in compulsory auctions has not been stipulated in compulsory auction law, and the liability for defects in noncompulsory auction law is difficult to apply, which leaves an unsolvable problem for auction practice.

In summary, this paper argues that one of the important tasks is to coordinate auction laws and regulations to further improve China's auction legal system. There are many kinds of auction laws and regulations in China, but the function of these laws and regulations is greatly reduced due to the uncoordinated situation. Without solving this problem, China's auction legal system can hardly make substantial progress.

4.3.3 The Implementation of Auction Laws and Regulations

A sound legal system should not only ensure that there are laws to follow but also, more importantly, ensure that there are laws to abide by and laws to be corrected. China has a complete regulatory system for auctions, but by comparison,

Enforcement of auction laws is weak. This is mainly manifested in two aspects: weak law-abiding consciousness and weak law enforcement.

(1) Improving law-abiding consciousness is an urgent task for better implementation of auction laws and regulations. The improvement of law-abiding consciousness mainly involves the publicity of auction laws and the training around auction laws, among which the publicity of auction laws and regulations is conducive to improving the law-abiding consciousness of the whole people, while the training around auction laws and regulations is conducive to improving the law-abiding consciousness of auction practitioners.

    As far as the publicity of auction laws and regulations is concerned, the publicity of auction laws and regulations at all levels in China is not enough at present. First, the popularization of auction laws and regulations lacks publicity. Although the scale of the auction industry is small, the participation of all walks of life and the public is very high, which requires that the publicity of auction laws and regulations be national. However, since the promulgation and implementation of the Auction Law, China has not effectively and extensively publicized the auction laws and regulations, let alone systematically publicized them, which directly leads to the following phenomenon: some people only know that auction exists but do not know that there are laws and regulations on auction; Some people just know the auction law in general but do not know how the auction law sets rights and obligations; Some people do not know the relationship between the rules of auction regulations and the agreed rules of auction enterprises, and they always regard the agreed rules of auction enterprises as the rules of auction regulations. Some people think that as long as they want and others do not object, auction rules and regulations are optional and so on. Second, theoretical research on auction laws is insufficient. The auction law is highly professional, and every provision and rule has its profound origin, background and principle, connotation and extension, applicable conditions and scope, etc. To understand the auction law and improve the awareness of obeying the auction law, theoretical research is not easy. However, in China, people from all walks of life pay little attention to auction law research. The legal profession has few experts in auction law. Research in the auction industry focuses on management skills and ignores auction laws and regulations. Auction seminars are less about legal issues. The above situation directly leads to the following phenomena: some people do not understand the correct meaning of the auction law and its rules; Some people interpret the auction law and its rules arbitrarily to suit their own interests; Some put the rules applied in foreign auctions above Those in China; Some people create conflicts between China's various auction laws and regulations. Therefore, on the one hand, China should improve the popularization of auction law publicity; on the other hand, it should strengthen the theoretical research on auction law.

As far as training on auction laws and regulations is concerned, training on auction laws and regulations related to improving law-abiding awareness in China is mainly carried out by auction industry associations. The training of auction industry associations can be divided into three levels: the training of practitioners, the training of auctioneers and the training of persons in charge of auction enterprises. The national.

Auction industry associations and local auction industry associations always hold several training sessions at various levels every year. The content of the training includes the general knowledge of the auction, the auction practice, auction enterprises planning, operation and management, an auctioneer qualities and skills, all kinds of the implementation of the auction target auction (including the public property auction, art auction, auction real estate auction, the bankrupt enterprise, enterprise property rights auction, intangible assets, equity, motor vehicle auction, auction, online auction, etc.), Auction regulations, etc. It is a scientific approach to train people at all levels in the auction industry to improve the level of compliance with auction laws and regulations by improving their law-abiding consciousness and has achieved certain effects in the past decade. However, there are some downsides, including the increasingly commercial nature of training. There is a disharmony between the number of training participants and the improvement of the quality of the participants after training. There are defects in the standardization and unification of training materials, which affect the quality of training. The content of training fails to keep up with the development of China's legal construction. Most of the above-mentioned irregularities in China's auction market come from the low quality of the auctioneers, which is related to the form and content of training. This paper emphasizes the training of auction laws and regulations. The training should be pragmatic, focusing on a comprehensive understanding of auction laws and regulations, a correct understanding of auction rules, the establishment of links between rules and practice, clear responsibility for violations, etc.

(2) Strengthening law enforcement is a top priority for better enforcement of auction laws. Strengthening law enforcement involves both judicial and administrative law enforcement.

First, the issue of strengthening law enforcement in the judicial field. Judicature is the last means of relief set up in a society ruled by law. It should be timely, accurate and effective in the implementation of the law. Since the implementation of China's Auction Law, there have been many legal disputes within the scope of its adjustment, including: disputes caused by auctioneers' participation in their own auction activities; Disputes caused by bidding on behalf of auctioneers; Disputes caused by auctioneers auctioning their own articles or property rights; Disputes arising from the trustee's participation in the bidding of his own commissioned auction targets; Disputes arising from the auction of fakes; Disputes arising from the auction of defective auction targets; Disputes caused by the auctioneer and trustee abusing their right of nonguarantee; Disputes caused by malicious collusion between bidders or bidders and auctioneers; Disputes caused by the buyer's refusal to pay the price after the auction is completed; Disputes arising from the refusal of the trustee to hand over the auction target after the auction is completed; Only one bidder participates in the disputes caused by bidding; Disputes arising from failure to exercise the pre-emption right; Disputes arising from the failure of the auctioneer to properly perform the obligation of keeping auction targets during the auction; Disputes arising from illegal auction procedures; Disputes caused by the auctioneer's refusal to accept the punishment by the administrative authority. Some of the above disputes have already had judicial practice, and some have not. To achieve the goal of judicial promotion of the implementation of the Auction Law, it is suggested to consider the following two points: First, judicial interpretation of the application of the Auction Law. As mentioned above, the content of China's Auction Law is relatively principled, and some provisions have different understandings in practice. The content of China's Auction Law is not perfect, and some practical problems have no legal basis. Judicial interpretation, no matter what form is adopted, has much to be done in the application of auction law. At present, the judicial interpretation of auctions focuses on the field of compulsory auctions, and there is almost no judicial interpretation of the application of auction laws. Second, attention should be given to the coordination between various auction laws and regulations. As mentioned above, China's various auction laws and regulations are not fully coordinated, which will affect the implementation effect of auction laws and regulations. The people's court can regulate the applicable scope and validity of different types of auction laws and regulations by means of trial, judgment and mediation, which is particularly beneficial to the improvement of China's auction legal system.

Second, the issue of strengthening administrative law enforcement is discussed. The scope of administrative law enforcement related to auctions is very wide. Here, we focus on market law enforcement related to auctions by government law enforcement departments. In China, there are a number of government administrative departments involved in the law enforcement of auction and sale markets, including industrial and commercial administrative departments, cultural relics administrative departments, price control departments, tax administration departments, public security departments, etc. The market law enforcement power of these government administrative departments has its own legal basis and is beyond doubt. To strengthen administrative law enforcement, the following issues are worth paying attention to: First, the institutionalization of law enforcement. Each government administrative department with market law enforcement power should, on the basis of the Auction Law, formulate corresponding government regulations according to the characteristics of the auction market and institutionalize law enforcement around the auction market. In addition to the corresponding rules and regulations, the law enforcement system should also include the construction of law enforcement teams, channels to grasp market information, and means to punish illegal acts. For example, the State Administration for Industry and Commerce, through the promulgation of the Interim Measures for Auction Supervision and Administration, aims to legalize auction market law enforcement. Although there are controversies in practice, the auction activity record system and the auction site supervision system, if reasonably implemented, will be conducive to strengthening administrative law enforcement. Second, the coordination of law enforcement. Multidepartmental law enforcement for auction market norms has a favorable aspect; it can strengthen the investigation and punishment of illegal market behavior. However, there are also downsides, such as over enforcement or gaps in enforcement. The negative aspects of multiagency law enforcement can only be avoided through coordination and integrated law enforcement. Auction market of law enforcement shall establish a joint law enforcement and law enforcement system, because of all the illegal behaviors, including violation of cultural relic management regulations, violation of price regulations, disobey action of public security management regulations, the first is violation of market order, so in this system, the administrative authority for industry and commerce is normal law enforcement, Other law enforcement agencies are professional law enforcement agencies and should be duty-bound in regard to their scope of law enforcement. In the process of law enforcement, administrative departments for industry and commerce shall either lead law enforcement jointly or notify each other of law enforcement independently to ensure full coverage of law enforcement and no overlapping penalties. Third, the problem of standardized punishment. Looking at China's auction laws and regulations, there are many and multifarious administrative punishments for illegal acts. They include fine, confiscation of illegal income, warning, revocation of business license, administrative sanction, banning illegal enterprises, order to correct, delay auction, cancellation of establishment license, revocation of license, suspension of practice, revocation of practice qualification, not being allowed to preside over auction activities, administrative personal compensation, notice of criticism, etc. It is not difficult to find some problems by analyzing the above administrative punishment methods: (1) some punishment methods are very nonstandard, such as "postponed auction", "shall not host auction activities", unclear meaning, unclear boundaries, as administrative punishment methods are very inappropriate. (2) Some punishment methods are illegal, such as "administrative personal compensation". Generally, if the auction price is lower than the reserve price due to the auctioneer's own reasons, the auctioneer shall compensate the trustee for the loss caused to the trustee because the auctioneer is not a party to the auction legal relationship, and the trustee has no right to hold the auctioneer responsible for the loss. Of course, the auctioneer can ask the auctioneer to assume responsibility afterwards, but this is the internal responsibility of the auction enterprise, and it is illegal to change it into administrative responsibility. (3) The above punishment methods are stipulated in different laws and regulations, and the corresponding behaviors vary greatly; that is, for the same behavior, some laws and regulations give excessive punishment. Some regulations are too lenient. In the same legal system, for the same act, the punishment of terse and terse is taboo. Therefore, how to standardize punishment is also an urgent problem to be solved to strengthen China's administrative law enforcement.

Chapter 2
Art Works that Are Subject to Adjustment Under the Auction Law

The art market in China and around the world has been booming in recent years. According to the TEFAF Global Art Market Report 2017, the global art market reached $45 billion in sales in 2016, comprising both the dealer market and the auction market. When dealer sales are included, the US remains the world's largest art market, with 29.5% of the market, followed by the UK at 24%; China was third with 18%. The auction market remains the main sales channel in Asia, where China (including Hong Kong and Taiwan) dominates, accounting for nearly 90% of the market. In the Internet era, many offline transactions have moved online, and art transactions are no exception. Online auctions, art e-commerce, online galleries, art finance and other modes are developing rapidly.[1]

However, the existing laws and regulations governing the creation, circulation and collection of works of art are not matched with China's leading position in the world. Art industry in our country, there is no separate legislation related to this clause referring to each department, mainly for civil and commercial law (including contract law, auction law, property law, tort law and intellectual property law, etc.), economic law, including tax law, the protection of cultural relics and anti-unfair competition law, etc.) as well as criminal law, including the crime of infringement of intellectual property rights, hindering cultural relic management, etc. It is difficult to understand the connotation of auction law because of the scattered legislative model and interdisciplinary background requirements, and it also leads to a relatively scattered situation in academic research on auction law.

Artwork has an important position in auction law, but the boundary of artwork is not so clear. For example, a work of art is a work created by an artist. If an artist designates a commodity he or she buys from a store as a work of art and then exhibits it everywhere, is that commodity a work of art? What is the difference between art and goods? What rights do works of art carry? What protection should be afforded? Another example is performance art or performance art. Does the artist's performance itself constitute a work of art? Does the work of art have to be in physical form? How

[1] Zhao (2016).

Z. Zheng, *The Legal System of Art Auction in China*,
https://doi.org/10.1007/978-981-19-0128-7_2

to make a definition to artwork from law? In addition, if one digs up some old cultural relics from the courtyard of one's ancestral home, are these relics works of art? Once traded, can it be sold or auctioned directly on the market?

This section aims to respond to the above questions by sorting out scholars' views, legal cases and data materials. The structure includes the following three parts: first, art and artists, as well as the relationship between artists and artworks; second, the essence of the artwork, as well as the various legal rights carried by the artwork; third, the difference between artwork and other similar concepts, including cultural relics, works of art or fine art, cultural property and the definition from the perspective of tax law.

1 Artists and Works of Art

1.1 The Meaning of Art

The meaning of art is very broad; from philosophy, literature, sociology, ethics, art and law, the understanding of art is different. Although it is difficult to express in one sentence, everyone has been exposed to art, and it is easy to find a few things or events related to art around him. Everyone can also express their views on these things or events based on their own inner feelings. In short, art is about craft, that is, the creator expresses himself to the outside world with some skill or with some medium. Art is subjective because everyone can participate in the creation, have different ways of expression and effect, and convey different feelings of joy, disgust and anger to the same object. Art is also objective because some art is universally popular, while others are not accepted by most people. Art is also interlinked, transcending the limitations of race, language, culture and region. It can spread globally and be accepted by people outside the region. The function of art is to cultivate the character and moral character of social people imperceptibly, deeply and universally.[2]

Beauty and art are two different things. Beauty is a philosophical concept that includes natural beauty and artistic beauty. Art is closely related to beauty, but art is not beauty. Tolstoy criticized "beauty is the essence of art" in "art theory". Art must possess the form of beauty, but beauty cannot be regarded as the whole characteristic of art.[3] Both the beauty of nature and the beauty of art exist in people's perception or imagination; the difference is that the former exists in the transient general representation or idea of the mind, while the latter exists in the artist's intuition. The artist recorded this intuition and explained it.[4]

Art in a broad sense is a reflection on beauty and the social and human significance of the artist's time. Art should reflect the social life and the object in the social life,

[2] Zong (2011).

[3] Ma (1981).

[4] Bernard (2010).

so art is a kind of cognitive activity. Since ancient times, the perception of art has changed with the development of people's consciousness.[5]

In the narrow sense, art refers to other art categories besides literature, mainly including the following categories. First, practical art refers to the combination of practical and aesthetic performance of space art, including architecture, gardens, arts and crafts and design. Second, plastic art refers to the use of certain material through the creation of a static visual image to reflect social life and the expression of artists' thoughts and emotions of art, including painting, sculpture, photography, calligraphy and so on. Practical art and plastic art belong to space art, with visual sense being directly felt, so they are also known as art or visual art. Third, expression art is a general term for art that directly expresses people's emotions and indirectly reflects social life through certain material media (sound and human body), including music and dance. Fourth, comprehensive art is a general term for drama, traditional Chinese opera, film, television and other arts. It combines the characteristics of time art and space art, visual art and auditory art, reproduction art and performance art, plastic art and performance art and has strong artistic appeal.[6]

On the origin of art, Peng Jixiang summed up a variety of theories, including imitation theory, game theory, performance theory, witchcraft theory, labor theory and multideterminism. According to pluralistic determinism, the development of society is not unitary but pluralistic. It is difficult to distinguish production labor, religious witchcraft and artistic activities in the primitive society, which together constitute the practice of human beings in the primitive society. The origin of art should be a long process. According to this theory, the emergence of art has experienced a long historical development process from practical to aesthetic, with witchcraft as the medium and labor as the premise, which is also permeated with the need for human imitation, the impulse of expression and the instinct of play.[7]

1.2 The Definition of Artist

Artists are the producers and creators of works of art. An artist is a creator who specializes in the production of art. Artists should have artistic talent and artistic ability, master special artistic skills and techniques, have rich emotions and profound artistic accomplishment, and be able to meet people's special spiritual needs through their own creative work.[8]

Theoretically, anyone can be an artist, but there should be certain criteria for being an artist in a strict sense. An artist is first and foremost a craftsman or a craftsman. A sculptor is good at making shapes out of clay or stone, and a painter is good at combining paint and canvas to make a scene. An artist usually has two elements: a

---

[5] Yan (2004).

[6] Peng (2013a).

[7] Peng (2013b).

[8] Peng (2013c).

keen mind that can capture extraordinary emotions from the prosaic of everyday life, and a skillful skill that can bring such extraordinary emotions to life.[9]

What it means to be an artist is ultimately ambiguous because there are no qualifications and certificates in the industry, unlike lawyers, accountants or architects with professional qualifications. Sometimes judging whether a person is an artist depends on the artistic image and aesthetic value reflected by the works he or she creates. First, what the artist shows through his creation must be true art. The views and ideas expressed by artists through their works usually create a sense of beauty and resonance in the audience. Some so-called performance art violates the rules of artistic creation, even social order and good customs, so in the eyes of most people, these actors are not artists.[10]

Second, art should draw a clear line with life. Everyday objects (or commodities) are different from art. We cannot refer to everyday objects or their simple stitching as works of art, otherwise we would not need artists, because anyone can simply refer to the objects around them as works of art.[11] Therefore, it is necessary to clarify the boundaries of the artwork itself, which is an important basis to identify artists.

In other words, a work of art is the embodiment of an artist's inspiration. A work of art without inspiration is also a work of art, but it lacks some vitality. Inspired works of art, people will have a strong resonance.[12] The birth of a work of art is the process in which the artist truly presents his inspiration and reflects it on a specific material. A work of art is a tangible thing created by an artist, and people can observe, appreciate and feel its beauty. Works of art carry the functions of recording, decoration, education and aesthetics.[13] Art is a way for artists to communicate and communicate with society. It is also a medium for artists to give feedback or convey feedback to society by absorbing their social experience, emotion and experience and processing it in their minds. For the same thing or event, different artists may have different understandings or views, relying on their own familiar skills and tools, to present a wide range of artworks.

2 Artworks from Different Perspectives

2.1 The Meaning of a Work of Art

China's "Art management Measures" with the word "art" replacing the previous "fine art" will be limited to the scope of cultural works of art, not including cultural relics of art. According to Article 2 of the rules, works of art are paintings, calligraphy

[9] Wang (2005a).

[10] Cao (2005).

[11] Feng (2009).

[12] Wang (2005b).

[13] Dong (2016).

and seal cutting, sculptures and carvings, art photography, decorative arts, arts and crafts, and limited copies of the above works. The essence of a work of art consists of three levels. First, a work of art belongs to a whole, that is, to all the works of the author. There are striking similarities between many of the works of an artist. Second, artists and their works are not isolated but belong to contemporaneous and contemporaneous art schools or art families. Third, the artistic sect or family is also included in a larger whole, that is, its time or society. To understand a work of art, an artist, a group of artists, one must relate it to the spirit and customs of its time.

Taine concludes: "The object of a work of art is to express some principal or projecting feature, that is, some important idea, more clearly and completely than the actual thing; To do this, the artwork must be a totality of many interconnected parts. "Artwork has three dimensions: the first is its original dimension. Tracing back to its origin, artwork is the inner expression of the artist. Artists use certain skills and specific materials to express their mind's view of the world. The original attribute is concerned with the inner ideological, artistic and social nature of the artwork.[14]

Anthony O'dwyer believes that art consists of two elements, namely, the original expression of ideas and tangible carriers. Unlike literature or music, the materiality (carrier) and intangibility (thought) of a work of art are fused and cannot be separated. The public internalizes these works in different ways, with art lovers "seeing" and literature or music lovers "reading" or "listening". Only the original can make people feel the original expression of the artist's ideas, and a copy or fake cannot convey the idea.[15]

The second is its economic dimension. Goods are not works of art, but works of art may be goods. When an artist creates a work of art, it may be for economic or other purposes. Regardless of the purpose, once the artwork enters the circulation field, that is, there are buyers and sellers, and the circulation is carried out in society, then the economic attributes of the artwork will appear. Most works of art do not have a fair value, but there are some works of art that are often traded on the auction market and generate an economic value that can be reflected in the auction price.

The third is its legal dimension. Works of art should have material materials as the carrier, and these material materials themselves are the objects in the property law, existing owners, protected by law. After the creation of a work of art, in addition to ownership, there are other rights such as copyright. The legal attribute is concerned with the civil and commercial subjects, the rights they enjoy and the obligations they undertake.

Artwork also has an important characteristic, namely, authenticity. When viewing, the audience will of course assume that the artwork is the work of the artist himself. The beauty, perception and value of a work of art is greatly diminished by the knowledge that it was created by someone else as art. Authenticity should be determined by the market, not the courts. Courts are not equipped to provide meaningful statements of truth. A statement that is valid in the market or art world must be supported by

---

[14] Hippolyte Adolphe Taine, Philosophie de l'art, Translated by Fu Lei, Beijing: Life, Reading, New Knowledge Sanlian Bookstore, 2016.

[15] Anthony (2017).

experts who are well known and recognized in the relevant field of expertise. A claim of authenticity would not solve the plaintiff's problem since the market ultimately decides whether his holdings can be sold. If a work of art is not included in a foundation's verified catalog, it becomes a matter of the art world voluntarily relinquishing its authority and handing it over to a single entity.[16]

Although there is no unified legislation, in judicial practice, there have been a number of cases involving nonfidelity auction houses,

Awards on ownership of cultural relics and copyright infringement of works of art. For works of art appraisal, the court's attitude at home and abroad is similar, the judge not to art authenticity, because it belongs to the surveyor, scientists or art history expert, the duty of a judge to judge, the works of art appraisal of each process, involving lawsuit parties whether there is fault, whether or not to be liable for the damage caused by the ramifications, etc. In one case, the perpetrator infringed upon the civil rights and interests of others due to his fault and should bear tort liability. If the collection holder signs the Engagement Letter of Collection Appraisal and Letter of Commitment with the program under clear rules, based on the autonomy of the meaning of the contract, it shall be deemed that the party agrees with the appraisal opinions of the experts invited by the program and bears the risk of being destroyed if the collection is fake. The program crew and appraisers are not at fault when they destroy the collection after identifying it as fake and shall not bear tort liability.

2.2 *Works of Art from the Perspective of Law*

The legal meaning of artwork includes three levels. First, works of art are what property law calls, and the subject of rights has property rights to works of art. This property right can be either ownership or usufructuary right such as pledge. A person who buys a painting by bidding at an auction house becomes the owner of the painting and has the right to possess, use, profit from or dispose of it. If a debtor transfers a painting he owns as collateral to the creditor, a pledge is created on the painting, and the creditor becomes the pledgee. Since a work of art is a kind of thing, it should be jointly owned by several parties.

The division of common works of art also needs to refer to the division rules of common property in civil law. Common ownership, it is to point to some property by two or more right subjects jointly enjoying ownership, can be divided into by share common and common. According to article 103 of The Property Law of China, if the co-owner does not agree that the co-owned realty or chattel is co-owned by shares or jointly owned by shares, or the agreement is not clear, the co-owner shall be regarded as co-owned by shares unless the co-owner has family relations.

The common legal characteristics of works of art are mainly reflected in the following aspects. First, the common subject is plural, which can be either a natural person or legal person. Second, the common object is the work of art. During the

[16] John (2012).

existence of the co-ownership relationship, the ownership of the common property cannot be divided into various parts shared by each co-owner but jointly enjoyed by each co-owner, and the rights of each co-owner extend to the whole of the common property. Third, the co-owner of the artwork can be jointly owned or co-owned by shares. However, the co-owners are not completely independent in exercising their own rights. In many cases, the will of all co-owners should be reflected and restricted by the interests of other co-owners. In accordance with the law, where a co-owner agrees that the jointly owned realty or chattel shall not be divided to maintain the co-ownership relationship, the agreement shall be followed. However, if the co-owners have a major reason for the division, they may request the division. If there is no agreement or the agreement is not clear, the co-owners by shares may request division at any time, and the co-owners may request division when the co-owned foundation is lost or there is a major reason for division. Where damage is caused to any other co-owner due to the division, compensation shall be made. A work of art may be co-owned by shares, and in the case that the co-owners have not agreed on the partitioning of the common property, the co-owners by shares may request partitioning at any time.

Second, the author of a work of art (that is, the artist) enjoys copyright. Copyright and ownership belong to absolute rights, and both have absoluteness, exclusivity and other characteristics, but there are still many differences between them. First, the object is different. The object of copyright has immateriality, while the object of ownership is substantial. Taking an oil painting as an example, the oil painting itself is a tangible object and the object of ownership, while the author's idea or concept carried by the oil painting is the object of copyright. Second, different ways of use. The use of ownership includes tangible uses such as possession, use, profit and disposal, while the use of copyright includes special uses such as reproduction, distribution, performance and information network transmission. Third, the temporality is different. The duration of copyright is limited, and the law clearly stipulates the duration of copyright protection. Ownership has sustainability, which means that the existence of ownership cannot predetermine its duration of existence, and the agreed duration of ownership is invalid.[17] Fourth, exclusivity is different. The monopoly of copyright is relative and limited, and its monopoly is often restricted by power, such as reasonable application and compulsory license systems. Ownership is the most complete property right, the owner has the right to exclude anyone's interference in its possession, and there can only be one ownership on the same thing, but can not coexist two or more than two ownership. Ownership is restricted by law only when its exercise is detrimental to the legitimate interests of others or endangers the public interest. Professor Herbert Lazerow claimed in his book "Mastering the Auction Law" that "the transfer of art is the transfer of copyright", which is clearly wrong. Ownership and copyright are independent of each other. The transfer of copyright usually requires written evidence, while the authorization of copyright can be oral.[18]

---

[17] Wu (2014).

[18] Odenkirk and Sarah (2015).

Artists' copyright includes spiritual rights and economic rights. Spiritual right, also known as the personal right of works, is the nonproperty right that the author enjoys for his works, which is inseparable from his person. It is the exclusive right that the author enjoys for his works, which is related to his personality and identity. It is the exclusive right that the author enjoys for the spirit and personality reflected in his works. The main characteristics of personal rights of works include the following contents.

First, this right is inseparable from the author's specific identity and is linked to the author's reputation, personality, identity and moral character. The author's works can be regarded as an extension of his personality. Second, the right does not have direct property content. Third, the right can exist independently of the existence of the property right to a work. Even if the property right of the work is transferred, the author still enjoys the personal right of the work. Fourth, the right is not transferable and can only be enjoyed and exercised by the author. Fifth, the right is unlimited in terms of duration of protection. Sixth, this right shall not be deprived or declared invalid by force.

In China, the personal rights of works mainly include the right of publication (the author has the right to decide whether to publish his unpublished works to the public), the right of authorship (the author has the right to ask others to recognize his creation qualifications, Decision whether signed and to sign the right), the right to modify and the right to recover the author (or authorizing others to change their rights and change the author by his own ideas and reclaim their rights has published works), the right of integrity, (protecting the rights of work is not subject to distortion, tampering with).[19]

Auction is a special form of buying and selling. The auction of painting and calligraphy is an act of selling works of art. In one case, the defendant challenged the plaintiff by analyzing it, and there is no conclusive evidence to prove that the work of the plaintiff inscribed on the plaintiff himself sign, put it into auction sale, and gained an advantage. In violation of the "copyright law", the provisions of article 46 item 7 belonged to the sell fake signature art copyright infringement behavior of others. Therefore, the original claim that the two defendants sold fake their signature works of art, infringement of their copyright, has factual and legal basis, won the court support.

In another case, the plaintiff failed to prove that the calligraphic works auctioned by the auction company were copyrighted works with fake signatures. The dispute in this case stems from the auction company accepting the commission of an outsider to the case and auctioning calligraphy works signed as the plaintiff. According to Article 61 of the Auction Law, if an auctioneer and a trustee declare before an auction that they cannot guarantee the authenticity or quality of an auction target, they shall not bear the liability of guaranteeing defects. According to this, if the auction company has made a statement before the auction that it will not bear the liability for guarantee of defects, it is not at fault and should not bear the responsibility.

[19] Feng (2010a).

Economic rights, also known as property rights of works, refer to the right of authors or other copyright owners to exploit their works by themselves or by authorizing others in various ways according to law, as well as the right to obtain economic benefits from such use. With the development of science and technology, the content of property rights of works is continuously expanded. Obtaining income is the main purpose of exercising the property rights of works, and the rights of earnings are one of the core contents of the property rights of works. Copyright owners may obtain remuneration by licensing others to exercise their copyright or by transferring all or part of their copyright. In addition, the property rights of works related to artists and artistic creation mainly include the right of reproduction, the right of distribution, the right of projection, the right of exhibition, the right of information network transmission, the right of deduction (including the right of adaptation, translation, filming and compilation), the right of renting, the right of performance, the right of broadcasting and so on.[20]

Take two examples. In a case about the right of distribution, the oil painting Drunken Concubine adopts the method of combining the virtual and the real and combines the techniques of Traditional Chinese painting, printmaking and oil painting to describe the drunken concubine's expression. It has certain originality in expression and can be protected by copyright law as fine art work. The plaintiff, an artwork development co., Ltd. is authorized by the copyright owner to obtain the exclusive right of use and the right to file a lawsuit in its own name and has the qualification of the main body of the plaintiff. The defendant, without the permission of the plaintiff, provided the public with embroidery products that were substantially similar to the painting for sale, which constituted an infringement of the plaintiff's right of distribution of fine art works. Another case involves exhibition rights. One of the final destinations of a work of art is to be collected by museums and other public institutions and is not used for exhibitions from time to time. Therefore, the object of exhibition rights includes and is limited to works of art. Obtaining the ownership of an artwork does not mean that the owner has the right to exercise the copyright of the artwork, but the right to exhibit is an exception. After a person obtains the ownership of the original artwork, this person has the right to exercise the exhibition right of the original artwork. The Kiefer controversy shows the conflict between exhibition rights and ownership. According to Article 18 of the Copyright Law, the original owner has the legal right to exhibit kiefer's work, so it is legal to exhibit Kiefer's work. In addition, the issue also involves the rights of the author's name in the exhibition title. According to the General Principles of the Civil Law, citizens enjoy the right to use and change their names in accordance with regulations, and others are prohibited from interfering, stealing or counterfeiting their names. If Kiefer does not agree with cafA's use of his name, the exhibition has no right to use the artist's name without authorization.

In addition, there is a right, in our country does not provide for but is very important, that is, the right of renewal. This right means that when a work is resold, the author of the work is entitled to a percentage of the difference if the buyer resells

[20] Feng (2010b).

it to others for more than the amount paid at the time of purchase. We can grasp the connotation of this right from the following aspects. First, the right of renewal is the author's right to share a certain amount of profits when the original work is sold again, with economic interests as the main content. Second, the right of renewal reflects the relationship of rights and obligations between art dealers and creators in the art market based on the economic conflicts of interest between the original works in the market circulation. Third, the right of renewal ADAPTS should be set to meet the needs of the development of the art market. Fourth, the right of renewal guarantees the author's inalienable expectation of the original work.[21]

Liu Chunlin discussed the legislative conception of the right of renewal, including two parts. First, the subject and object of the right of renewal. The subject of the right of renewal is the author and his successor. The owner and legal holder of the original art work (except the author) cannot enjoy the right of renewal. The right of succession can be inherited; that is, if the author dies, his successor can enjoy the right of succession, which is also an extension of the protection of the author's interests. However, the subject scope of the right of renewal should not include the legatee of the original work of art to reduce the unnecessary obstacles caused by the right of renewal to the circulation of the work of art. If the author transfers the original work of art (including sales or gifts) to the museum and other public institutions, then it is considered that the author has given up the right to profit from the original work and gives up the right to pursue renewal. The object of the right of renewal shall be limited to the origins of the artistic work. The works of art here mainly refer to the works of art in China's copyright law. Music works, drama works, folk art works, dance works, acrobatic art works, photographic works, graphics and model works are also commonly known as works of art in the broad sense, but as the object of the renewal of the right of art cannot be so extensive. Only works of art, some photographic works and model works can be the objects of the right of renewal. If the scope of objects is not properly expanded, the circulation of copyright will be hindered, and the prosperity of the cultural market will be restrained.

Second, the content and exercise of the right of renewal. On the one hand, the copyright law should clarify the applicable conditions of the right of renewal. The exercise of this right is only applicable to "public resale" with the participation of intermediaries such as auction houses, galleries or art dealers, aiming to facilitate the author to accurately understand the trend of his works of art, to timely landlord and exercise the right. Only when the public resale price exceeds a certain percentage of the previous sale price can the author or his heirs claim a certain percentage of the resale proceed. The amount to be withdrawn shall be calculated from the difference before and after the resale of the work. On the other hand, copyright law should clarify the way of exercising the right to renew works. The advantage of authorizing intermediary agencies or entrusted agents is that it can reduce the cost and expense of the author and his heir to exercise the right of renewal, and at the same time, it can

[21] Ding and Zou (2005).

ensure the operability of the claim and exercise of the right of the copyright owner and turn the legal right into the real right.[22]

2.3 The Status of Works of Art in Auction Law

Liu Guolin believes that the subject of auction law includes a series of subjects, such as artists and art dealers, collectors and critics, in the field of art circulation, and the object of auction law refers to specific works of art and cultural property.[23] Song Zhen pointed out that the object of auction law should be a specific part of artistic works and a specific part of cultural heritage. Artistic work refers to the original expression in the field of art, but not all original artistic expressions can become the object of auction law protection. For example, works of art with an illegal purpose (obscenity, violation of national sovereignty or damage to the public interest, etc.) are excluded. Cultural heritage includes material cultural heritage and intangible cultural heritage, but cultural relics that only have historical value or scientific value but lack artistic value are not protected objects of auction law. It can be concluded that auction law is a special legal department that protects artistic works and specific parts of cultural heritage and is the sum of social norms with universal binding force that regulate the interests of specific artistic works and specific cultural heritage as well as their rights and obligations.[24]

Experts in their works, the content structure of the auction law is not the same. For example, Paul Kearns divided his book "the legal meaning of works of art", which is regarded as the first monograph in the UK, to discuss auction law as a whole, into seven parts: indecency law, copyright law, libel law, public funding of art, law relating to charitable trusts, customary provisions, and law relating to the removal of national treasures.[25]

Auction law not only involves the contents of private law but also includes the contents of public law. The former refers to the legal relations, rights and obligations and responsibilities arising from artwork between equal subjects, such as the sale contract signed due to artwork transfer, the infringement lawsuit caused by damage to artwork, and the copyright disputes arising from the use of artwork. The latter refers to art censorship, art management, art funding and other systems involving public interests. Auction law is different from communication law and entertainment law. Communication law mainly studies the legal issues related to news communication activities and mass media, including the protection and restriction of freedom of speech, the control of power over mass media and the relevant rights of the communicator. Communication law focuses on the rights of the media as a communicator, while auction law focuses on the rights of the artwork creator or copyright owner.

---

22 Liu (2013).

23 Liu (1989).

24 Song (2014a).

25 Anne (2000).

The works involved in the communication law are not limited to the field of art, and the overall structure of the auction law is built on the art. Entertainment law, on the other hand, is a broad concept covering many legal fields. From the industry sector, entertainment law involves film, television, drama, music and other entertainment industries. The object of entertainment law protection includes not only works but also creativity and influence, while the object of auction law protection is the creative expression of works of art.[26]

The auction act is also different from the cultural industry Act. The cultural industry is a vague concept with unclear boundaries. Some scholars have proposed that, according to theory, the cultural industry can be divided into three levels: the product layer, service layer and cross layer. Method of culture industry, it is to point to in order to realize the national cultural industry development strategy, to promote and safeguard social orderly and healthy development of cultural industry, for the purpose of adjusting engaged in cultural products in the process of production and business operation and providing cultural services the floorboard of the legal norms of the various social relations, social and economy, dispersion, policy, etc. Characteristics.[27]

In summary, for the narrow sense of auction law, artwork is the foundation of the entire legal system. The auction law is to study and solve the legal problems involved in the creation, excavation, production, sale, circulation, exhibition and collection of works of art. These problems cannot be solved by a single line of laws and regulations but must be adjusted by a variety of laws and regulations.[28]

3 The Difference Between Artwork and Similar Concepts

3.1 Works of Art and Cultural Relics

There is a cross relationship between cultural relics and works of art: some cultural relics are works of art, some are not; and vice versa.

According to the Regulations on Auction of Cultural Relics and Artworks issued by the Ministry of Commerce on July 1, 2010, the auction targets are limited to the collection of cultural relics, which shall comply with the state provisions on the scope of cultural relics auction targets and conform to the qualification of the enterprise for cultural relics auction. When soliciting auction targets from abroad, an auctioneer shall abide by the relevant provisions of the state on the administration of the entry and exit of cultural relics. From the use of the term "cultural relics of art" and its applicable auction target analysis, cultural relics should be a kind of art. The term can also be seen in the reply to the Establishment and Registration of the All-China Chamber

[26] Song (2014b).

[27] Tao (2016).

[28] Duboff (1994a).

of Commerce for Folk Cultural Relics and Artworks issued by the Ministry of Civil Affairs on December 14, 2011. There are two terms parallel to the artifacts: One is cultural artifacts, See the ministry released on October 12, 1993 "abroad culture art and exhibition management rules" and the central propaganda department, the Ministry of Commerce, the ministry of culture, the state administration of radio, film and television, press and publication (gapp) released on December 30, 2011 "about the implementation of the State Council decided to strengthen the management of the trading of cultural property and art opinion", However, neither of the two documents defines the extension of cultural works of art. The other is jewelry works of art. See the Notice on Regulating the Evaluation and Management of Jewelry works of Art issued by the Ministry of Finance on July 18, 2007. According to the circular system, jewelry works refer to raw materials and semifinished products of jewelry, jade and precious metals, as well as accessories, craft decorations and art collections made of jewelry, jade and precious metals. Thus, it can be seen that the two terms are settled on works of art, and the prefix is used to modify works of art, indicating a wide range of works of art.

Relics under state protection include: (1) sites of ancient culture, ancient tombs, ancient buildings, cave temples, stone carvings and frescoes of historical, artistic or scientific value; (2) Important historical sites, objects and representative buildings in modern times that are related to major historical events, revolutionary movements or famous figures and that are of great significance for commemoration, education or historical data; (3) precious works of art and arts and crafts from different periods in history; (4) important documents and materials of various historical periods as well as manuscripts and books of historical, artistic or scientific value; (5) representative objects that reflect the social systems, social production and social life of different ethnic groups in different historical periods. In addition, cultural relics can be divided into two categories: immovable cultural relics, including ancient cultural sites, ancient tombs, ancient buildings, grotto temples, stone carvings, murals, modern and important historical sites and representative buildings. The other is movable cultural relics, including important objects, works of art, documents, manuscripts, books, representative objects, etc.

Fu Ying pointed out that as a legal concept, "cultural relics" in the Law of the Protection of Cultural Relics bear important values such as "history", "science" and "art", which are widely recognized. It must be tangible, controllable and definite in scope, and the concept of "cultural relics" itself also has two important characteristics of legal stipulation and clarity. Therefore, vague and broad terms such as "cultural route" and "cultural landscape" should not be included in the category of "cultural relics".[29]

Li Yuxue believes that cultural relics in the sense of special law are different from cultural relics in the sense of civil basic law, and the former is narrower than the latter. Cultural relics in the sense of civil basic law are objects in the sense of private law, but cultural relics themselves have some characteristics. Cultural relics in the sense of special law were initially defined as two traditional categories: important

[29] Fu (2014).

relics and relics left over from ancient times. With the development of the theory and practice of international cultural heritage legal protection, the importance of cultural relics has become more prominent and gone beyond its traditional meaning.[30]

Cultural relics are protected by private law as a kind of "object", but they are different from ordinary objects and have special legal status. The infringement of cultural relics should not only be based on the adjustment of private law but also conform to the goal of "cultural relic protection". Therefore, the regulation of cultural relic ownership has a special arrangement, which is manifested in the object of cultural relic ownership, which is the limitation and particularity of the object of ownership. In terms of the subject of ownership of cultural relics, it is the main structure dominated by the state, the advantage of the state in obtaining the way and the "permanence" of the state ownership.

3.2 *Works of Art, Works of Art and Works of Fine Art*

A work of art is different from a work of art, which refers to the intellectual creation of art and its related fields that is original and can be reproduced in a tangible form. Art types mainly include viewing classes (such as art or photography, performance class (such as music, dance, drama or vocal works), audio-visual classes (such as a movie or in the work of the analogous method of film creation) and correlation work (e.g., and several other kinds of works of creation, transmission and related interpretation of the text or oral works) and so on four classes.[31] The works of art mentioned in this article only refer to ornamental works of art.

According to the Copyright Law amended by the Standing Committee of the National People's Congress on February 26, 2010, works protected by the law fall into three categories, namely, literary, artistic and scientific works. Article 3 of the law points out that works include works of literature, art, natural sciences, social sciences and engineering technology created in the following forms: (1) written works; (2) oral works; (3) works of music, drama, quyi, dance and acrobatic art; (4) works of fine art and architecture; (5) photographic works; (6) cinematographic works and works created by a method similar to that used in cinematographic production; (7) graphic works and model works such as engineering design drawings, product design drawings, maps and schematic diagrams; Computer software; (9) Other works provided for by laws and administrative regulations. Article 2 of the Regulations on the Implementation of the Copyright Law amended by The State Council on January 30, 2013, defines the works referred to in the Copyright Law as intellectual achievements that are original and can be reproduced in a tangible form in the fields of literature, art and science. Article 4 illustrates all kinds of works by enumeration.

In summary, works of art coexist with literary works and scientific works. Works of fine art use a narrow sense of interpretation; as a work of art, only refers to plastic art

[30] Li (2007).

[31] Song (2008).

works, not including photographic works. The copyright law and its implementation regulations do not define the status and meaning of works of art.

Released in 2009, according to the Ministry of Culture and the General Administration of Customs import and export management interim provisions, "the fine art of article 1, fine art refers to art creators to line, color or other ways the modeling of the aesthetic significance of creative works of art, including painting, calligraphy, sculpture, photography, installation works, and artistic creator approval and signature, Copies within 200 pieces. Industrial mass-produced industrial arts and craft products and cultural relics are not included. The definition of fine art in the above-mentioned documents is greater than that of fine art in copyright law. The former not only includes fine art in the narrow sense (painting, calligraphy, sculpture, etc. but also includes photographic works, installation art and industrial and craft works. Neither works of art nor works of art contain cultural relics.

In other words, fine art, works of art and works of art are all legal terms, which are defined differently in different laws and regulations. It is clear that the Ministry of Culture has replaced the original fine art with the term "artwork". In one case, the use of modeling, color, fabric, process elements such as clothes, independent of its art form, structure and external form, such as color, showed strong artistic quality and originality, showed practicability and artistic quality, and Chinese and Western culture blended modern aesthetic feelings and belonged to the copyright protection of practical works of fine art in China.

3.3 *Classification in Tax Rules*

Another way to define works of art is through customs duties on imports and exports. According to category 21 (Chapter 97) of the Customs Import and Export Tariff, the following categories are regarded as works of art, collections and antiquities: (1) the oil painting, powder painting, and other hand painting, but with the manual drawing and manual tracing act the role of the product or item 49.06 (namely, hand-painted architecture, engineering, industrial, commercial, terrain or similar purpose design drawings of the manuscript, the manuscript, written in sensitive paper photo copy or use carbon paper as soon as possible the above items copies) except the drawings; Collages and similar decorative boards; (2) the original woodblock painting, printed painting and lithographic painting; (3) sculptural pieces made of various materials; (4) used or unused stamp, stamp duty ticket and postage stamp, first day cover, the postal stationery paper (with stamp) and similar products, but item 49.07 (namely, after admitting or country will recognize its value circulation or new issue and without the use of stamps, stamp duty ticket and similar documents, bearing the stamp or stamp duty ticket paper, notes, blank check, Stocks, bonds and similar certificates of title); (5) collections and collections of zoological, botanical, mineralogical, anatomical, historical, archaeological, paleontological, ethnographic or numismological significance; (6) Antiques more than 100 years old.

"Wooded, printed, lithographic original" as referred to in the above categories means a black and white or color original directly printed from a single or multiple plate entirely handmade by the artist, regardless of the method or material used by the artist, but excluding the use of machines or photographic plates. The above categories do not apply to mass-produced copies and traditional handicrafts of a commercial nature, even if they are designed or created by artists.[32]

In the United States, the tax law on art is relatively narrow, and only pure art is exempt from import duty. These works of art include the following categories: original paintings and sketches, collages and decorative panels, original rubbing, engravings and prints, sculpture and statues, stamps, collections, and antiques. In addition, there are two other conditions for duty-free entry: one is that the work must be made by an artist rather than a craftsman; the other is that the work cannot be a practical object, nor can it be made for commercial use. Thus, the technical definition of a work of art in terms of tariffs is motivated by political or economic considerations, not aesthetic considerations. The key to defining a work of art is the context in which the word is used.[33]

3.4 *Works of Art and Cultural Property*

According to Mariman, cultural property refers to the objects that reflect human spiritual civilization, mainly referring to archaeological, anthropological and historical relics, artworks and buildings, but the category can be extended to almost anything created or changed by human beings.[34]

Article 1 of the 1954 UNESCO Convention on the Protection of Cultural Property in the Event of Armed Conflict (also known as the Hague Convention) defines cultural property as follows: Cultural property, irrespective of its origin or ownership, shall include (a) movable or immovable property of great significance to the cultural heritage of peoples, such as architectural, artistic or historical monuments, whether religious or secular; Archaeological sites; A complete building of historical or artistic value; Art; Manuscripts, books and other objects of artistic, historical or archaeological value; Scientific collections and important collections of books or archives or copies of any of the above. (b) Buildings whose primary purpose is to preserve or exhibit the movable cultural property referred to in paragraph (a), such as museums, large libraries and archives, and depositories prepared to cover the movable cultural property referred to in paragraph (a) in the event of armed conflict. (c) A central station for the storage of a large number of cultural properties referred to in subparagraphs (a) and (b) is referred to as a "Memorial Central Station".

According to article 1 of the 1970 UNESCO Convention on the Means for the Prohibition and Prevention of the Illicit Import, Export and Transfer of Ownership

---

[32] Editorial Board of Customs Tariff (2012).

[33] Duboff (1994b).

[34] Mariman (1990).

of Cultural Property, for the purposes of this Convention, the term "cultural property" means that each state, on religious or secular grounds, property specifically designated as of archaeological, prehistorical, historical, literary, artistic or scientific interest and belonging to (a) rare collections and specimens of fauna, flora, minerals and anatomy, and objects of paleontological significance. (b) Property relating to history, including scientific, technological, military and social history, the lives of national leaders, thinkers, scientists and artists, and important national events. (c) Archaeological excavations (both normal and secret) or archaeological findings. (d) Dismembered parts of an artistic or historical monument or archaeological site. (e) Objects from a hundred years ago, such as inscriptions, coins and seals. (f) Artifacts of ethnological significance. (g) property of artistic value, such as (1) drawings, drawings and drawings entirely by hand, irrespective of their frame and irrespective of the materials used (excluding industrial plans and hand-decorated industrial products); (2) original sculptural art and sculpture made of any material; (3) printmaking, the original copy of lithograph; and (4) original works of art assembled or assembled from any material. (h) Rare manuscripts and ancient editions, ancient books, documents and publications of special significance (historical, artistic, scientific, literary, etc.), whether in single copies or in complete sets. (I) Stamps, stamp duty stamps and similar tickets, whether in sheets or in sets (j) files, including audio, photographic and cinematographic files. (k) Furniture items and ancient Musical Instruments from 100 years ago.

Both of the abovementioned conventions refer to works of art as cultural property, so it can be considered that works of art and cultural property are subordinate. At the same time, we also need to discuss another concept related to cultural property, namely, "cultural heritage". The concept of cultural heritage was formalized in the 1972 Convention for the Protection of World Cultural and Natural Heritage. According to article 1 of the Convention, the following shall be classified as "cultural heritage": (1) Monuments: buildings, monuments and paintings of outstanding universal value from the point of view of history, art or science, elements or structures of archaeological character, inscriptions, caves and landscapes; (2) Architectural complex: a single or connected architectural complex of outstanding universal value in terms of architectural style, uniform distribution or combination with the environment and scenery from the perspective of history, art or science; and (3) Sites: human works or nature-man joint works of outstanding universal value from the historical, aesthetic, ethnographic or anthropological point of view, and areas containing archaeological sites.[35]

Although the concepts of cultural property and cultural heritage are relatively similar and often appear alternately in the relevant documents of UNESCO, there are still subtle differences between them: cultural heritage highlights nationality and identity inheritance and has wider connotations than cultural property; cultural property refers to tangible heritage and is closer to economic value. In addition, cultural heritage places more emphasis on the overall sites or remains between regions, and

[35] Guo (2011).

cultural property can also refer to the heritage that exists alone. Both cultural property and cultural heritage are interpreted in the context of international law. "There is no nation without culture, no country without heritage, and no heritage without a country. "Cultural property expresses and embodies the unique cultural identity of a nation or a country. In addition to the transmission of spiritual wealth, there are also some unsatisfactory aspects. It can trigger the identification of ethnic identities or become a prime target of armed conflict because of its cultural symbols. Therefore, at the level of international law, cultural property or cultural heritage contains not only cultural elements but also social and political elements.

4 Summary

What does not match the booming art market in China is that the art legal norms and systems governing the creation, trading and circulation, collection and donation and cross-border trade of artworks have not been systematically constructed, whether at the level of public law or private law. As an important branch of auction law, art auctions have been proposed by scholars and professionals, but they have little effect and have not been widely responded to by jurists and legislators. The reasons may be related to the strong professionalism of the art category; the proportion of the economic scale of the art market is still low and has little connection with the daily life of ordinary people. The establishment of the legal framework of art auctions is primarily to solve the legal definition of art. Different from its original dimension and economic dimension, works of art under the legal dimension emphasize more on the rights and obligations borne by works of art and the difference between them and adjacent concepts. First, works of art are called objects under property law, and the subject of rights enjoys property rights to works of art. This property right, including ownership and right of pledge and other usufructuary right. Second, the author of a work of art (that is, the artist) enjoys copyright. The copyright and ownership of works of art are independent of each other, and they are quite different in object, way of use and timeliness. Finally, artists should also enjoy the right of renewal in the follow-up transaction of artworks, which has great positive significance for protecting artists' rights and encouraging artistic creation.

References

Zhao shubo, Research on The Problem of Art Transaction Based on Internet. Beijing: Law Press, 2016: 17–29

Zong baihua, Yi Jing. Beijing: The Commercial Press, 2011: 239

Bernard Bosanquet, A History of Aesthetic, Translated by Zhang Jin, Beijing: China Renmin University Press, 2010: 3–4

Ma Qi, What art is. Journal of Zhengzhou University, 1981(3): 85–86

Yan QuanFa. The concept of art evolves. New Aesthetics, 2004(3): 38–47

Peng Jixiang. An introduction to the Science of Art: an intensive edition. Beijing: Peking University Press, 2013, 41, 73
Peng Jixiang. An introduction to the Science of Art: an intensive edition. Beijing: Peking University Press, 2013b, 2–16
Peng Jixiang. An introduction to the Science of Art: an intensive edition. Beijing: Peking University Press, 2013c, 202
Wang DeFeng, Philosophy of art. Shanghai: Fudan University Press, 2005a, 162–165
Cao Guisheng. Artists and nonartists, works of art and nonworks of art. Fine Arts, 2005(8): 68–70
Feng Minsheng. On art and artists in the aesthetic of daily life. Journal of Shaanxi Normal University, 2009(2): 79–80
Wang DeFeng, Philosophy of art. Shanghai: Fudan University Press, 2005b, 148–149
Dong tao. An exploration of the concept and function of artwork. Northwest Fine Arts, 2016(2): 94–97
Anthony O'Dwyer, The Nature of the Artists' Resale Right (Droit de Suite) from Antiquity to Modernity, Intellectual Property Quarterly, 2017(1): 95–122
John R Cahill, Keeping It Real: A Brief Primer on the Law of Art Authenticity, Columbia Journal of Law& Arts, 2012 (3):357–368
Wu HanDong, Intellectual Property Law: fourth edition. Beijing: Peking University Press, 2014
Odenkirk, and Sarah. Review of Herbert Lazerow, Mastering Art Law.International Journal of Cultural Property2015 (4): 541–544
Feng Xiaoqing. Copyright law. Beijing: Law Press, 2010a: 77–91
Feng Xiaoqing. Copyright law. Beijing: Law Press, 2010b. 94–97
Ding Liying, Zou Guoxiong. The theoretical basis and system construction of the right of follow-up. Legal Science, 2005(3): 33–40
Liu Chunlin. Legislative conception of the right of renewal. Hebei Law Science, 2013, 31(04): 49–51
Liu GuoLin, The conception of establishing art law system in China. Fine Arts, 1989(5): 58–61
Song Zhen. Art Law Restatement: Framework and Cases. Beijing: Intellectual Property Publishing House, 2014. 4–6
Anne Barron, The Legal Concept of Art, European Intellectual Property Review, 2000 (2): 100–101
Song Zhen. Art Law Restatement: Framework and Cases. Beijing: Intellectual Property Publishing House, 2014. 12–14
Tao XinPing. Introduction to cultural Industry Law. Beijing: China Renmin University Press, 2016: 4–5
Duboff, L. D., Art Law in a Autshell, Translated by Zhou Lin, Beijing: Intellectual Property Publishing House, 1994: 1
Fu Ying, Revisiting the Concept of Cultural Relics: From A Legislative Perspective, China Cultural Heritage Scientific Research, 2014(1): 35–38
Li YuXue, Private Law Concerning Cultural Relics: In View of Their Protection, Modern Law Science, 2007(6), 136–146
Song Zhen, Fundamentals of art law. Beijing: Culture and Art Publishing House, 2008. 7, 17-32
Editorial Board of Customs tariff. 2012 PRC Customs Import and Export tariff and declaration Guide. Beijing: China Business Press, 2012: 749–750
Duboff, L. D., Art Law in a Autshell, Translated by Zhou Lin, Beijing: Intellectual Property Publishing House, 1994: 2–4
J.H. Mariman. The public interest of cultural property. Global Law Review, 1990(4): 70–74
Guo YuJun, Research on cultural Heritage Protection from the perspective of International law and Comparative Law. Wuhan: Wuhan University Press, 2011: 2, 21

Chapter 3
Legal Relations of Artwork Auction

The Auction Law of the People's Republic of China was adopted at the 20th Session of the Standing Committee of the eighth National People's Congress in mainland China on July 5, 1996 to regulate auction behaviors, maintain auction order and protect the legitimate rights and interests of all parties involved in auction activities. The law came into force on January 1, 1997.[1] In addition, the law was revised twice in 2004 and 2015.

From the perspective of private law, the newly revised Auction Law of the People's Republic of China involves a series of important issues, such as auction targets, auction parties, auction procedures and legal liability. Because the provisions of this law are not very specific, there are disputes both in practice and theory, among which the legal relationship of arbitrary auctions is one of them. From the perspective of commercial disputes, it is a prominent issue whether the auctioneer is the seller and thus has to fulfill the relevant obligations of the seller. The Auction Law of the People's Republic of China and relevant laws and regulations do not provide an answer to this problem, and the explanatory documents compiled by the Civil Law Office of the Mainland Legal Commission of China hold that there is no legal relationship of direct agency between the trustee and the buyer.[2] From the perspective of judicial decisions in mainland China, the opinions of the Supreme People's Court in mainland China and the judgments of most local courts tend to support that the auctioneer is the seller, but a few judges in mainland China support that the trustee is the seller through judgments or articles, and even put forward other

---

[1] Article 1 of the Auction Law of the People's Republic of China (hereinafter referred to as the Auction Law).

[2] Civil law office, commission of legislative affairs, National People's Congress, auction law book, Beijing: China commercial press, 1997, 130.

Z. Zheng, *The Legal System of Art Auction in China*,
https://doi.org/10.1007/978-981-19-0128-7_3

explanations.[3,4,5,6] From the perspective of academic disputes in mainland China, some scholars advocate that one of the auctioneers or appointors should be identified as the seller, while others point out that the problem of who the seller should be constructed under the indirect agency.[7,8]

Although the Auction Law of the People's Republic of China does not directly stipulate who the seller is, Article 23 provides a very important clue. Article 23 of the Auction Law of the People's Republic of China stipulates that "an auctioneer shall not auction his or her own articles or property rights in the auction activities organized by himself or herself." On the other hand, the auctioneer can only auction other people's goods or property rights in the auction activities organized by himself, so the auctioneer can sell other people's goods or property rights as the seller. Can also

[3] Chief editor, civil law office of the Supreme People's Court, understanding and application of judicial interpretation of sales contract of the Supreme People's Court, Beijing: people's court press, 2012, 490.

[4] A more representative case is "Chen Yuanjun and Shandong hande auction co., LTD., and other auction contract dispute case" (2013 calendar business beginning word no. 2538), the auctioneer Shandong hande auction co., LTD., to provide the auction map finally attached "auction business rules" clearly said that "the parties to the sales contract are the principal and bidder". In this case, although the court judgment did not directly deny that the auctioneer showed the agency intention to act in the name of the principal, on the basis that the format rules fulfill the obligation to prompt and explain.

[5] Part of the courts claim that through Article 402 of the Contract Law of the Contract Law of the People's Republic of China (the Contract Law), that if the contract between the trustee and the third person within the authorization of the principal, it directly proves that the principal and the third person, except that the contract only binds the seller of the third person at any auction. However, the subject matter of these cases is mostly land or real estate, or the principal is the subject that is easily known by the third person, so the third person (buyer) can know the identity of the principal through its registration situation. Therefore, the third party (buyer) knows both the client and can presume the agency relationship between the client and the auctioneer, so it is no dispute to comply with Article 402 of the Contract Law. However, in real life, there are still the principal is the general civil subject or auction target will not register, the most typical example is art (not cultural relics) auction, in the auctioneer without the case of clearly disclosed the principal, the court judgment usually does not cite article 402 of the contract law as the sales contract effect to the basis of the principal. For details, see civil Judgment No. 682, New 23, Intermediate People's Court of Xinjiang Changji Hui Autonomous Prefecture (2017); Civil Judgment No. 1253, Ji 01 of Changchun Intermediate People's Court (2017); Civil Judgment No. 1071 of Haining People's Court (2015); Civil Judgment No. 30154 of Nanguan District People's Court (2016), etc.

[6] Wang Shen, Gao Wanquan, Ding Xiaoyan, Wu Tiesheng versus Shanghai Dekang Auction Company, Zhang Qi auction Dispute theory Seminar Review, Law, 2001 (7), 75; Ma Changjun, Xu Ziliang, Di Qing, The Assumption and exemption of the Auctioneer's Warranty liability for auction defects, People's Justice (Case), 2008 (22), 96.

[7] Guo Mingrui, Wang Yi, New Theory of Contract Law, pp. 55, August 1997. Liu Ningyuan, Principle and Practice of auction Law, p. 123, November 1998; Qiao Xinsheng, On the Legal Nature of Auction, Hebei Law Science, No. 4, p. 8–11, August 1989; Zhang Qiuhang, Liu Hui, My Opinion on the Meaning of basic Principles of auction Law, Application of Law, No. 2, p. 22, March 1996; Li Hailong, On the Improvement of China's Art Auction Legal System, Journal of Zhejiang University of Technology (Social Science Edition), No. 2, p. 230, June 2012; Chen Su, commission contracts, brokerage contracts, intermediation contracts, pp. 110, September 1999.

[8] Wu Teng, Contractual Relations and Agency Effect in Auction, Jurist, 2015(003). 110.

serve as a real seller (others) agent to sell the articles or property rights, and the key to the buyer to the seller or just agent, as professor Huang Maorong puts it, "depending on whether the auctioneer suggests that agents will, if the auctioneer shows that agent will (ACTS in the name of the appointed people), then the appointment of talent is the seller;The auctioneer is the seller if he fails to indicate his intention to act in his own name."[9] So the question of who the seller is at any auction becomes a question of who the auctioneer acts on behalf of. How to define who auctioneers act in the name of and how to integrate the basis of such a definition into the existing legal system in mainland China are rarely studied in academic circles in mainland China.[10] Therefore, this chapter will combine the comparative method to discuss this problem, which can provide a reference for theoretical and practical circles in mainland China.

1 Comparative Study on Legal Relations of Art Auctions

1.1 A Legal Relationship in the Name of the Appointee Representing the Purport of Agency

According to the agency system in mainland China, the legal relationship to indicate agency intention in any auction is based on Article 162 of the General Principles of the Civil Law of the People's Republic of China. From the perspective of the European civil law system, some scholars believe that "agency is extremely Offenkundigkeit-sprinzip, which is also known as an offensively appointed agent."[11] Professor wang zejian called Offenkundigkeitsprinzip an "open principle".[12] However, in Common law, as will be explained later, the form of agency which has the same effect as in the continental law system (the agency made public by me and the agency made public

[9] MaoRong, (2002).

[10] Specifically, on the one hand, the auctioneer, in accordance with the General Provisions of the Civil Law of the People's Republic of China (hereinafter referred to as the General Provisions of the Civil Law) of the auctioneer, shall be effective under the name of the agent. "Or if the vendee prior to the proviso of Article 402 of the Contract Law"… knows the agency relationship between the principal at the time of the contract, the contract directly binds the principal and the third party, "under the venant of Article 40 of the Auction Act. However, paragraph 1 of Article 61 of the Auction Law shows that when the auctioneer causes damages to the buyer, or the client violates the obligation of informing the defect, the buyer can only seek compensation to the auctioneer. However, there is no legal relationship between the auctioneer and the buyer, but it shall be liable to the buyer. What is the reason for this regulation?

On the other hand, when the auctioneer acts in his own name, when the trustee violates the obligation to inform the auctioneer, thus violates paragraph 1 of Article 61 of the Auction Law, and then causes losses to the buyer, in accordance with the liability of paragraph 1 of the Auction Law, the auctioneer shall directly recover from the trustee, or violates Article 58 of the Auction Law.

[11] Changqing (1997).

[12] Zejian (2009a).

but not specified by me) does not require that it be in the name of the principal. Therefore, when analyzing the legal relationship between auctioneers acting in the name of proxy in any auction in mainland China, it is biased to examine the principle of publicity in Continental Law, the public agency in Common law and the public but not specific agency in private law.

1.1.1 "Agency Disclosure Principle" in European Continental Law

Article 164 of the Civil Law of Germany, Article 32 and Article 38 of the Debt Law of Switzerland, Article 1984 of the Civil Law of France, Article 10 of the Nordic Contract Law and Article 103 of the Civil Law of Taiwan of China all have provisions similar to Article 162 of the General Principles of the Civil Law of the People's Republic of China, which all embody the principle of open agency. It is a feature of the agency law of European continental law countries to distinguish direct agency from indirect agency whether the agent decides the parties of the legal act in his own name or in his own name.[13]

Under the principle of open agency, the trustee and the auctioneer sign a contract of appointment (contratdemandat). This kind of contractual relationship can be applied to a wide range of single or multiple transactions, as well as long-term or short-term transactions. Direct agency does not require written agreement. However, if the parties have entered into a written agreement prior to the analysis of the authenticity of the subject matter by the relevant expert (within the auction house or by a third party expert), it will be beneficial for the parties to determine the manner and scope of performance, define their expectations and the risks involved, and predict the consequences of default.[14] In addition, the letter of appointment signed in person can serve as a reliable basis for parties and third parties to evaluate the contents of the agreement, which can help improve transaction security.[15]

It is worth mentioning that some scholars hold that the auctioneers owe an obliging debt rather than an obliging debt.[16] This is reflected in any auction that the auctioneer should perform the matters appointed by the trustee diligently and faithfully in accordance with the requirements of the contract, rather than achieve the specific results of the trustee, such as the sale of the entrusted property is one of the most typical specific results. Although some auction contracts have the lowest price purchase clause, regardless of the auction result, the auctioneer must pay the appointed lowest price, but this is only a special agreement between the parties and does not affect the nature of the auction contract. In an arbitrary auction, the instrument debt performed by the auctioneer is mainly reflected in the reserve price system, that is, the sale

[13] Ziqiang (2018).

[14] Alexander Jolles & Isabelle Roesle, Design of the Expert Contract in Swiss Law, 2 Artand law p. 35–36 (2013).

[15] Id. at 37.

[16] Joëlle Becker, Auction of Works of Art in Swiss Private Law: Representation, Contractual Relations and Liability, 21 Art Law, p. 167 (2011).

contract with suspensive condition signed between the auctioneer and the buyer. The contract of sale becomes effective when the price proposed by the buyer exceeds the reserve price fixed by the trustee or agreed upon between the trustee and the auctioneer.[17] It can be seen that the auctioneer does not guarantee that the appointed property will be sold, but it needs to guarantee that the price of the sale will be higher than the appointee's requirement.

The principle of proxy publicity requires the auctioneer to act in the name of the auctioneer; in other words, acting in the name of the auctioneer is an element of the principle of proxy publicity. If only from the narrow sense of "explicit name" principle, it is easy to enter into the dilemma of whether to express the name of the appointee.[18] In regard to the auction practice, "The name of the principal must be filled in the column of the parties when signing the contract, otherwise, the contract will be difficult to bind the principal."[19] In addition, there is the "confidentiality obligation" of the auctioneer in any auction, that is, "if the trustee or buyer requests to keep their identity secret, the auctioneer shall keep it secret for them".[20] Thus, it can be seen that the determination of the open principle under arbitrary auction is slightly different from that of the general agent. However, special rules similar to those for general agents may apply.

(1) **Subsequent disclosure**

Germany generally said that the key to the legal act in the name of myself (proxy) is not whether to reveal my (proxy) name, but that the effect of the agent shows its intention does not belong to their own[21]; The agent is not required to specify the name of myself (the appointor) when acting for the bank, or to later identify myself (the appointor).[22] Therefore, some scholars believe that direct agency relationship can be effectively concluded through appointment contract even if the name of the appointee is not disclosed.[23]

(2) **It can be inferred from the situation**

Article 164 (1) of The German Civil Code stipulates that "the expression of intention made by the agent in the name of the principal within the scope of his agency authority shall be directly effective for and against the principal. There is no difference between a definite expression of intention in the name of the principal and one that, in the circumstances, can be concluded to be made in the name of the principal." Article 32 (2) of the Swiss Debt Law has a similar provision: "The agent enters into the

[17] See Footnote 16.

[18] Chen Su, General Provisions of the Civil Law (Book below), p. 1148, May 2017.

[19] Geng Lin and Cui Jianyuan, How to treat indirect agents in the future General Provisions of the Civil Law, Journal of Social Science, Jilin University, Issue 3, p. 23, May 2016.

[20] Section 21 of the Auction Act.

[21] Muller-Freienfels, Die Vertretungbe im Rechtsges chäft, 1955, S.17; Larenz/Wolf, Allgemeiner Teildesdeutschen Bürgerlichen Rechts, 8. Aufl., 1997, S.877.

[22] Staudinger & Eberhard Schilken (2014) Vor bemer kungen zu§ §164ff., Rn. 35.

[23] Von Tuhr, Andreas and Hans Pete, GENERAL PART of the SWISS CODE of OBLIGATIONS vol. 1, 3de 387(1979).

contract without indicating that he is the principal, and only enters into the contract when the third party can infer the existence of the agency relationship based on specific circumstances... Where the principal directly acquires the rights or assumes the obligations." Some judgments also hold that when an agent expresses his intention in his own name but does not disclose his own name, such a situation can only have agency effect on him if the agent has the intention to represent him and the intention is known or available to the counterpart (third party).[24]

(3) **Acting as the agent of the person who is due**

Some scholars believe that if the buyer does not care who the client is, then the buyer can also bind the unnamed client through the contract.[25] This term is derived from the theory of Geschaftfurden (Denesangeht) in the European civil law system. It is also reflected in the statutory laws of some continental European countries. For example, article 32 (2) of Swiss Debt Law stipulates that "the agent does not indicate that he is the principal when concluding the contract... When the third party does not care about the counterparty, the principal directly acquires the rights or obligations". Some Korean scholars also discuss the principle of openness.[26]

It is still controversial whether the theory of "agent for the right person" can be applied to arbitrary auctions. Starting from the fact that the principle of agency disclosure does not protect the transaction itself, some scholars believe that it is mandatory to disclose the principal as a direct agent, and the disclosure time can only be made after the auctioneer drops the hammer. If the nature of the auction is a well-known collector single collector auctions (a single collector auction sale dedicated to the well-known collector), you may be in the catalog the auctioneer who is publicly released at the appointed person.[27]

When acting in the name of the auctioneer, whether the auctioneer needs to disclose the name of the auctioneer requires the judgment of the true intentions of the parties. First, if the buyer agrees with the true intentions expressed or implied by the auctioneer, then the person referred to by the auctioneer is the party to the contract. If the auctioneer does not indicate the name of the appointor when acting as an agent but the appointor is later identified, the purchaser's consent may be deemed to be that the auctioneer is acting in the name of the appointor. In contrast, even if the auctioneer indicates the name of the trustee but states that he or she will acquire the rights and obligations of the contract with the buyer, if the buyer agrees, it will not constitute an auctioneer acting in the trustee's name; Second, even if the auctioneer does not disclose the name of the trustee, if the buyer, depending on the circumstances, can infer the agency relationship, or does not care who the trustee is, it may

[24] Supreme Court Judgment No. 672 of Year 82, Supreme Court Rule No. 1774 of Year 101, and Supreme Court Rule Judgment No. 2069 of Year 103.

[25] Von Tuhr, Andreas and Hans Pete, GENERAL PART of the SWISS CODE of OBLIGATIONS vol. 1, 3de 389(1979).

[26] Zejian (2009b).

[27] Joëlle Becker, Auction of Works of Art in Swiss Private Law: Representation, Contractual Relations and Liability, 21 Art Law, p. 288 (2011).

constitute an auctioneer acting in the trustee's name; Finally, if any unstated disinterest is borne by the auctioneer, it shall be regarded as the auctioneer's own act.[28] Thus, rather than saying that the auctioneer is acting in the name of the trustee needs to reveal the trustee's name in the principle of disclosure of agency, the auctioneer needs to show that the final agency effect is own to his or her own.

1.1.2 Similar Agency Form in Common Law

According to article 101 of the third edition of the Agency Act of 2006 in the United States, agency is a faithful relationship between the principal and agent. Such a faithful relationship requires the agent to act in the principal's interest under the principal's supervision and is not limited to a contract. This definition is also found in the Bowstead & Reynolds Agency, the authoritative textbook on agency law in the UK.[29]

There are some differences in the definition of agency between the common law system and the continental law system. The key to the establishment of the agency relationship in Anglo-American law is not that the agent acts in his own name, but whether he acts for another or on behalf of another for (oron) account of; for the benefit of; In the interest of). In the European civil law system, "in my name" is not the same as "for the benefit of others". In the common law system, agency is not in my name but only for the benefit of others.[30] Compared with the principle of "open agency" in European law, the forms of agency that can achieve similar effects in common law are "open agency" in English law, "open agency" and "open but not specific agency" in American law.

(1) **"Public agency of oneself" in English Law**

In the case of an arbitrary auction, the auctioneer may or may not disclose the name of the appointee during the negotiation between the auctioneer and the buyer. The buyer may or may not know the name of the appointee. Whether disclosed or not by the auctioneer and known or not by the buyer, as long as the buyer knows at the time of transaction that he is not dealing only with the auctioneer, it can constitute the agent publicly represented by himself in English agency law, which is similar to the "agent for the proper person" in the above European law.[31] The effect of "my public agency" is basically the same as that of "direct agency" in European law, that is, the trustee has a direct relationship with the buyer, and the auctioneer is not a contract party.

Depending on the circumstances of the auction, if the auctioneer intends to exempt himself from contractual liability, he must disclose the agency relationship at the

---

[28] Moser, Die Offenkundig keitder Stellvertretung, 2010, S. 68–71.

[29] Reynolds Farncis M.B., Bowstead and Reynolds on agency, London: Sweet & Maxwell, 1–001, 1–002(2006).

[30] Chen Ziqiang, the determination of the Modernization of the—Contract Act V, p. 83, November 2018.

[31] Peel (2015).

time of signing the contract with the buyer.[32] If he fails to disclose his appointor, the auctioneer as agent will always be liable. For example, in Benton v. Campbell, Parker & Co Ltd, judge Salter J once made it clear that the auctioneer was not a party to the sale contract, which was binding only on the trustee and the parties.

Where the agency relationship has been disclosed but the name of the appointee has not been disclosed, this is controversial from an auction point of view, although a contractual relationship should be established between myself and the buyer as stated above. Although in most cases the disclosure of the appointee has nothing to do with the sale, in the case of art auctions, some scholars have pointed out that it may be important. Because the seller is part of the source of the artwork, if the commissioned person is a well-known collector, museum or other institution, the disclosure of the commissioned person not only contributes to the value of the artwork but also provides additional security for the authenticity of the artwork. Therefore, it is difficult to determine whether an auctioneer is a party to a contract of sale when acting in the interest of a public but anonymous client.[33]

Although the principles of European contract law (The Principles of European Contract Law) under paragraph 3 of article 203 of the regulation, if the agent in which is not disclosed to a third party appointed under the condition of people who sign a contract, agent will be subject to contract. However, British precedents have introduced some exceptions. In Pike, Sons & Co v. Ongley and Thornton, the English court of appeal held that an agent is not personally liable for entering into a contract on behalf of an anonymous appointee unless a particular custom of transaction grants a third party the right to treat the agent as the appointee.[34]

In Teheran-Europecoltd v. S.T. Belton (Tractor) Ltd The presiding judge, Sir Diplock, held that in ordinary commercial appointment contracts, in the absence of instructions to the contrary from the appointor, agents can assume that third parties are willing to enter into contracts with them, whoever the appointor may be.[35] However, Sir Francis Reynolds think Diplock explanation is not established, because there may be some "interferes with the third party and agent trade" (to the interference that the third party deal sonly with the agent). Francis Reynolds therefore argues that in the case of an anonymous appointee, under the rule of preponderance of evidence (prima facie), the agent should be held liable with the anonymous appointee unless the agent expressly states that he is not under contractual obligation.[36]

(2) In American law, "disclosed agent" and "Disclosed but not specified agent"

Article 1.04 of the Restatement of the Third Edition of the Agency Law of the United States in 2006 divides the agency form into three types according to whether the third party knows the person's name. First, the agency of the disclosure of the person's name: "when the agent deals with the third party, the third party knows that the

[32] Harvey and Meisel (2006).

[33] Reynolds (2006).

[34] Pike, Sons & Co v. Ongley and Thornton (1887) 18QBD708, 710.

[35] Teheran-Europe Co. Ltd. v. ST Belton (Tractors) Ltd. [1968]2QB545, at 555.

[36] See Footnote 33.

agent is acting for the person and knows the person's name"; 2. An agent whose name is not specified: "When an agent deals with a third party, the third party knows that the agent is acting for the principal's sake, but does not know the principal's name"; Third, I did not disclose the agent: "when the agent transacts with a third party, the third party does not know that the agent acts for me".[37] The restatement of American agency law not only focuses on whether the person is made public but also emphasizes whether the person's name and the third party know that the agent is acting for the person. These factors are critical to determine the legal effect of agency. The so-called disclosure of the name (disclosed principal) requires not only the disclosure of one's own existence but also the disclosure of one's own name, which is slightly different from British scholars who believe that whether one's name is disclosed or not, as long as one's existence is disclosed, is the disclosure of one's own name.

According to the agency law of the United States, the contract of sale and purchase in an auction is bound by the trustee and the buyer. It is indisputable that the auctioneer is not a seller in a buying and selling relationship but a simple broker facilitating the sale.[38] On the one hand, the auctioneer can arrange a contract as an agent rather than as a party to the contract by revealing the appointee.[39] On the other hand, if the auctioneer auctions the appointed property without disclosing that he is acting on behalf of the appointed person, the auctioneer himself is deemed to be the seller and liable to the buyer.[40]

In addition, if an agent acts for an unidentified appointee, the type of agent may change. An unidentified appointee is: "A third party observes that the agent is acting in the interests of the appointee but does not know who the appointee is".[41] Confidentiality of proxy status is very common in auctions, and since third parties do not have detailed information about the principal and its creditworthiness, it is reasonable to include an agent as a party.[42] In this case, all three parties are bound by a contract.[43] In the case of art auctions, for example, who commissioned the work forms part of the provenance and therefore part of the appraisal opinion. At the same time, it guarantees authenticity and quality. Therefore, who the appointee is important information about the buyer's intention to enter into the sale contract.

In cases where an auctioneer discloses that he is acting in the interest of an uncertain appointee, us courts usually hold the auctioneer to ultimate liability.[44]

---

[37] Restatement (Third) of Agency, para.1.04.

[38] Cristallina S.A.V Christie, Manson & Woods Intern., Inc., 502 N.Y.S.2d165; Krahmer v. Christie's Inc., 903A.2d773; New Texas Auto Auction Services, L.P. v. Gomez De Hernandez, 249S. W.3d400(Tex.2008); Doty v. Wilder(1854), 15Ill.407.

[39] Restatement (Third) of Agency, para.6.01.

[40] Restatement (Third) of Agency, para.1.04(2); 7Am. Jur. 2dAuctions and Auctioneers, para. 73.

[41] Restatement (Third) of Agency, para.1.04(2)(b).

[42] Restatement (Third) of Agency, para.6.02.

[43] See Footnote 42.

[44] Richard Bottorff v. Joe Ault et al., 374F. 2d832, 835(7thCir.1967); Richard A. Lord, Willistonon Contracts, University of Toronto Law Journal 4, §35:41(1990).

Thus, "a corollary to the understanding that the agent is a party to the contract exists unless the agent provides complete and easily identifiable information about the identity of his or her principal." If the auctioneer does not wish to be a party to the contract of sale, he or she must provide the purchaser with information about his or her appointment before the contract of sale is concluded.[45] Although the contract expressly provides for an agent to act on behalf of an unspecified appointee, the court may hold the agent liable based on policy considerations rather than on the general principles of the contract.[46]

Nevertheless, there are relevant laws in the United States that "the agent can clearly indicate in the contract that he does not enjoy any rights and bear any responsibilities, and all rights and responsibilities belong to the appointee".[47] The major auction houses take advantage of this rule to exclude themselves from contracts of sale and purchase, only between buyers and unspecified appointees. Typically, these auction houses state in their standard terms that the deed of sale will be directly between the appointee and the buyer. Therefore, the parties agree that the auctioneer is not bound by a buyer–seller relationship.[48] These terms clearly and unambiguously state that the auctioneer is not only acting on behalf of the unidentified appointee but also that the sale contract is entered directly between the buyer and the unspecified appointee. In this way, the buyer and the trustee have "the same rights, responsibilities, and defenses as if they had actually entered into a contract."[49] In addition, these terms expressly exclude the auctioneer's obligation to act on behalf of sales contracts not entered into by a specific appointee. The reason is that the court may give priority to the agreement of both parties. If the contract expression cannot clearly exclude the liability of the auctioneer, then the court will include the auctioneer as a party to the contract according to the provisions of Article 6.02 of the Restatement of the Third edition of the U.S. Agency Law.

From the perspective of precedents, some American precedents place more emphasis on protecting the anonymity of the appointee. Jenack Estate Appraisers and Auctioneers in William J., Inc. In Albert Rabizadeh, the New York Court of Appeals held that the anonymity of the appointee was justified under The State's Fraud law, which required that sales memos must contain "the name of the dealer," The appeals court found that Jenack, as auctioneer, met that requirement.[50,51] In view of the fact that the buyer does not know who is signing the contract with him,

---

[45] Restatement (First) of Agency, para.321.

[46] Richard A. Lord, Willistonon Contracts, University of Toronto Law Journal 4§35:41.

[47] See Footnote 47.

[48] The rule for determining that the principal is apparent but uncertain is: "If the agent provides sufficient information so that a reasonable person can understand from the surrounding circumstances that the agent represents the principal, even if the principal is not named, the party to the contract is the principal and not the agent".

[49] See Footnote 42.

[50] William Jenack Estate Appraisers and Auctioneers, Inc. v Albert Rabizadeh, 99A.D. 3d270, 952 N.Y.S.2d197, 2012 N.Y. App. Div. LEXIS6146(N.Y. App. Div.2d Dep't 2012); 22 N.Y. 3d470, 982 N.Y.S.2d813, 2013 N.Y. LEXIS3447, 2013 N.Y. Slip. Op.8373 (December 17, 2013).

[51] New York General Obligations Law. 5–701a6.

in order to secure the transaction, in practice the auctioneer will provide additional service of disclosing the trustee, but this requires the buyer to pay additional fees.

In summary, I can observe the characteristics of auctioneers acting in the name of trustees in the European and Anglo-American law systems from two dimensions of general and special. In general, the auctioneer ACTS in the name of the appointed person, the final effects are appointed people set up business relationship with the buyer, the difference is that agent public principle emphasizes the auctioneer continental law system needs to show that the final effect is inferior to itself, and the auctioneer need in Anglo-American law system, and the results show that the appointed person exist or that appointed person interest. The auctioneer without exposing appointed person information under special circumstances, given proxy public principle is strict requirements, generally difficult to in the appointment of a legal relationship between people and the buyer, but in the disclosure, the parties know and later to be the agent of the special system, such as appointed person also have established business relationship with the buyer may; The Anglo-American concept of agency is characterized by the relationship of loyalty, which is sufficient to cover all agents based on their actual agency or apparent agency. Therefore, even if the auctioneer does not disclose the information of the trustee, this situation can be evaluated by the Anglo-American agency system.[52]

Agency disclosure principle (European)	My open agent (UK)	My open Agent (US)	I am open however, no specific agent (USA)
The demonstration method is less effective than the auctioneer	Whether or not the person's name is disclosed, the third party knows that it is not only dealing with a middleman	When an auctioneer deals with a buyer, the buyer knows that the agent is acting for himself and knows his name	When an agent deals with a third party, the third party knows that the agent is acting for himself, but does not know his name

1.2 *The Legal Relationship in the Name of the Auctioneer Without Indicating His Intention to Act as Agent*

As previously stated, the legal effect of acting on my behalf under my authority shall be vested in me. If an appointee acts in his own name, what are the legal effects? According to Article 541 of Taiwan civil law, the appointed person should be a party himself, which is theoretically called an "indirect agent" (Mittelbar Vertretung; Indirekter Vertretung). Indirect agency is not the form of agency in European agency law.[53] There are few general provisions on indirect agency in European written code

[52] Chen Ziqiang, the determination of the Modernization of the—Contract Act V, p. 90, November 2018.

[53] Zejian (2009c).

countries, but the existence of indirect agency is inferred from the appointment. In addition, the contract type of dealing with others' affairs by indirect agency is also widely seen in the contract of commission, contract and transportation. The civil law of mainland China also follows this tradition. There is no explicit provision on indirect agency in the chapter of Agency in The General Principles of the Civil Law of the People's Republic of China, and the provisions on handling affairs by indirect agency are scattered in various contracts in the special provisions of the Contract Law of the People's Republic of China.[54]

However, in the common law system, the form of a similar agency effect is the agent without disclosure. Schmitthoff once believed that the basic concept of agent without disclosure is that the agent enters into a contract in his own name.[55] However, most scholars of Anglo-American law hold that the key to the establishment of private agency lies in whether the third party knows the existence of the private agency. I do not open agency refers to the contract when the third party does not know my existence, the third party has no intention to deal with myself, but is willing to deal with the agent of the individual situation, the Third edition of the Restatement of the United States agency law also do so understanding.[56,57]

1.2.1 Legal Relations and "Indirect Agency" Without Indicating the Intention of Agency

In the direct agency relationship, the legal effect of the contract concluded by the agent within the scope of agency authorization belongs to him directly, and the economic benefits or non-benefits are borne and borne by him of course. In indirect agency, although it is the middleman who actually contracts with the third party, the economic benefits and disadvantages are not borne and burdened by the middleman. In other words, a middleman makes a deal that is legally his own and may be economically his own for a time but ultimately belongs to him. Indirect agency and direct agency are no different from each other in terms of economic benefits and disadvantages.

The difference between indirect agency and direct agency lies in the fact that the middleman enters into a contract with the third party in his own name.[58] If a third party cannot be expected to know that the contractual relationship does not take place in the actual contracting party, the intermediary is a party to the contract, and if the intermediary is authorized to act in his own interest, it constitutes an indirect agency. In other words, when a third person neither knows nor can obtain the meaning of agency, it does not constitute direct agency because it cannot be explained that the

---

54 Geng Lin and Cui Jianyuan, How to treat indirect agents in the future General Provisions of the Civil Law, Journal of Social Science, Jilin University, Issue 3, p. 20, May 2016.

55 Schmitthoff (1969).

56 Reynolds Farncis M.B., Bowstead and Reynolds on agency. London: Sweet & Maxwell, 1–037.

57 Restatement (Third) of Agency, para.1.04(2b).

58 Busch (2005a).

intention of agency is manifested.[59] Even if the agent is granted the power of agency, he does not want to bear contractual obligations and acquire contractual rights, but he does not reveal his intention to act in the name of others. According to the provisions of Article 164 (2) of the German Civil Law, it does not constitute the lack of intention of the agent to act in his own name.

In any auction, although the auctioneer is selling the commissioned property in his own name, this does not mean that the rights of the commissioned property have been transferred. The nature of contract a trading-trust contract, in accordance with paragraph 1 of article 425 of the Swiss debt law regulation, the auctioneer has the right and obligation for the benefit of the appointed person to sign the contract.[60,61] In any auction of indirect agent, based on the Swiss debt law agency contract should be prescribed in paragraph 2 of article 396 of the be permissions as prescribed in paragraph 2 of article 425 of the general terms and the trustee-trader applicable rules of the where clause, even if the appointed person is not clearly authorized agent sell property, an auctioneer may also be determined by the nature of the appointment matters.[62,63] In this case, the auctioneer becomes the trustee for the sale. The auctioneer obtains the rights and obligations assigned by the trustee under the appointment agreement with the trustee, which means that the trustee is excluded from the sale contract.[64] Indirect agents are attractive to inexperienced appointees in transactions because they can access the auction market properly with the help of professionals. Since the appointee is not a party to the contract of sale, he can also ensure that his identity information will not be disclosed, which is not available in direct agency.

From the perspective of the auction rules formulated by the major auction houses in the world, they adopt provisions very similar to indirect agency in Swiss law.[65] In these auction rules, the appointee is invariably excluded from the contract of sale. In fact, if the purpose is to protect the information of the appointee from disclosure, then the indirect agency system is undoubtedly the best choice. From the point of view of privacy, auction houses place the highest priority on not disclosing information

---

59 Busch (2005b).

60 Joëlle Becker, Auction of Works of Art in Swiss Private Law: Representation, Contractual Relations and Liability, 21 Art Law, p. 143 (2011).

61 Yongsheng (2016a).

62 Yongsheng (2016b).

63 Yongsheng (2016c).

64 Joëlle Becker, Auction of Works of Art in Swiss Private Law: Representation, Contractual Relations and Liability, 21 Art Law, p. 155 (2011).

65 Joëlle Becker, Auction of Works of Art in Swiss Private Law: Representation, Contractual Relations and Liability, 21 Art Law, p. 107 (2011).

about their clients (usually their clients), even more so than avoiding disputes caused by the auction.[66]

1.2.2 The Legal Relationship Without Indicating the Intention of Agency and "The Agency that I Do not Disclose"

In the case of any auction, there is very little scope for the principle of personal secrecy to work. In American law, for example, it is generally believed that an auctioneer can make himself personally liable to the buyer in an auction through an explicit agreement, but the performance of the contract is still done by the appointee. The auctioneer may be liable to the buyer for fraud, fraudulent misrepresentation, negligent misrepresentation or personal assurance of the quality of the goods, but in the absence of such an agreement, the auctioneer is virtually free of any personal liability. The auctioneer may disclose who the trustee is unless the purchaser pays an additional fee when the auctioneer acts on behalf of the trustee.[67]

In addition, in accordance with the scholars Schmithoff point of view, and British and American agent theory is based on and my agency (doctrine of identity of principal and agent) identity theory as the foundation, therefore, The common law concept into a single agency (unitary concept of agency), based on the concept of single agent, agent to develop himself closed law (doctrine of the undisclosed principal).[68] The sale of the property by the auctioneer with full disclosure of the trustee's name will therefore be deemed to be the trustee's own act and the auctioneer shall not be liable to the purchaser for defects or breach of warranty.[69] For the auctioneer to fully disclose the appointee, it is not even necessary for the auctioneer to disclose the appointee by name. It is enough to point the appointee to the potential purchaser. In addition, if the buyer actually knows who the appointee is, the auctioneer is not required to make specific disclosures. At the same time, if the auctioneer declares that the goods are for sale as auctioneers of certain persons, the buyer is deemed to be aware of such notice, even if the buyer has not noticed or is unable to understand the contents of such notice.[70]

---

[66] Joëlle Becker, Auction of Works of Art in Swiss Private Law: Representation, Contractual Relations and Liability, 21 Art Law, p. 131 (2011).

[67] 7 Am Jur 2d Auctions and Auctioneers §71.P100.

[68] Clive M. Schmithoff, Agency in International Trade, A Study in Comparative Law, in Clive M. Schmitthoff's Selected Essays on International Trade Law 320–321 (1998).

[69] Joëlle Becker, Auction of Works of Art in Swiss Private Law: Representation, Contractual Relations and Liability, 21 Art Law, 104 (2010).

[70] See Footnote 69.

2 Reflection on the Legal Relationship of Arbitrary Auctions

2.1 Reflection on the Determination of Legal Relationships of Arbitrary Auctions

Regarding the classification of the legal relationship of whether the auctioneer discloses the agent's will in an arbitrary auction, we can draw the following conclusions based on the European civil law system and the common law system.

2.1.1 The Legal Relationship of the Auctioneer Disclosing the Agent's Will

(1) **Agency relationship**

In terms of the legal relationship of the auctioneer disclosing the will of agency, the European law system follows the "principle of publicity of agency". The auctioneer sells commodities in the name of the trustee, and its legal effect belongs to the trustee. In the common law system, the same legal effect can be achieved by the public agency of oneself based on the faithful relationship and the public agency of oneself but not specified. The provision that the legal effect belongs to the appointee is the general agency situation in mainland China and applies to any auction. In this case, the auctioneer shall, within the authority of the auctioneer, make public the name of the auctioneer, the intention of the auctioneer and the name of the agent. The so-called closed principal refers to the fact that when an agent transacts with a third party, the third party knows that the agent is acting for the person and that the person's name is known. Except that the requirement is not to use the name of the person, the disclosure of the person in United States law is similar to the direct agency in mainland China.

It is worth noting that Article 164 (1) of the German Civil Code and Article 32 of the Swiss Debt Act recognize the system of "extra phernalia in my name based on specific facts", while the Swiss Debt Act also recognizes the "agency of the appropriate person" (Geschaft fur den, Den es angeht). As Busch argues, in art auctions, even if the third party (buyer) does not know who he (the trustee) is but can reasonably infer that the auctioneer auctions in the name of others, it should be considered a direct agent.[71,72] Ruoss also believes that if the buyer does not care about the identity of the appointee, he can bind the anonymous appointee by contract.[73]

[71] Dieter Schwab, Zheng Chong translation, Introduction to the Civil Law, Beijing: Law Press, p. 234, 200.

[72] Danny Busch, Indirect Representation in European Contract Law, The Hague: Kluwer Law International 95.

[73] Reto Thomas Ruoss, Fake Auction Art Auctions—The Remedies of Swiss Civil Law to Fight Against False Bidding, in 14 Swiss writing Son Commercial And Business Law (1984). 71.

The assumption of specific facts in my name and the agency of such person can be regarded as a relaxation of the principle of open agency, even if the auctioneer does not disclose the agency order, it can still establish a legal relationship between the buyer and the trustee.

Generally, the European civil law system has strict requirements on auctioneers acting in the name of the trustee, but more situations can be brought into the scope of the principle through the easing of the principle of agency disclosure. In contrast, the Anglo-American public agency and the public but not specified agency require the auctioneer to act in the name of the trustee. On the other hand, the arbitrary auction in mainland China inherits the principle of open agency of the European continental law system from the type of agency and adopts relatively strict identification standards. However, in terms of the two kinds of easing system of the principle of public agency in the name of the person and the agency of the person, mainland China has not established the relevant theory of extrapolating in the name of the person based on concrete facts.[74] On the other hand, "agency of the proper person" is considered to be only applicable to cash transactions in daily life, which is only the reiteration of the transaction concept and has great limitations for the application of arbitrary auction. However, this does not mean that there is no room for easing the principle of agency disclosure in Mainland China. Some scholars believe that Article 402 of the Contract Law of the People's Republic of China in Mainland China is a kind of easing of the principle of agency disclosure, and arbitrary auctions can also be applied in the absence of special provisions.[75]

(2) **Intermediary relationship**

There is a view that when an auctioneer acts in his own name, the auctioneer, buyer and trustee are interlocutors. There are two reasons for this. First, the actual contracting party of the buyer is the trustee, and the auctioneer only plays the role of facilitating the successful conclusion of the contract, so there is an intermediary relationship between the auctioneer, the buyer and the trustee. Second, the auctioneer can charge a reasonable fee to the trustee.[76] This view in any auction of commercial practice also received certain support, such as in Christie's, a "special customer service group" (Special Client Service Group). Its main purpose was to explore the potential buyer, provide its interest in much information and technical support, and facilitate private transactions between potential buyers and consignors. At the same time, the court recognized that the transaction was only between the appointee and a specific buyer, so it was appropriate to understand it as a "sale" rather than an "auction."[77] In addition, according to article 51 of the Auction Law, the highest bid of the buyer is confirmed by the auctioneer dropping the hammer or other ways of publicly expressing the

[74] Geng Lin and Cui Jianyuan, How to treat indirect agents in the future General Provisions of the Civil Law, Journal of Social Science, Jilin University, Issue 3, p. 28, May 2016.

[75] Yin Tian, 2010; Yin Qiushi, On Principles of Renalism and Its Exceptions in Agency, Politics and Law, p. 84, January 2016.

[76] Yufen (2012).

[77] Thomson v Christie Manson& Woods Ltd and Others.

purchase order, and the auction is concluded.[78] There is a theory that the act of the auctioneer confirming the sale of the auction by dropping the hammer or other public expression of purchase is the expression of the intention of the commitment of the sale contract, which is generally accepted by the judicial decisions in mainland China.[79] Accordingly, the position of the auctioneer in the tripartite legal relationship should not be considered as an intermediary.

Although the tripartite legal relationship between the auctioneer, the buyer and the trustee cannot be regarded as an intermediary relationship when the auctioneer acts in his own name, the internal relationship between the trustee and the auctioneer can be regarded as an intermediary relationship. The auctioneer may, under the authority of the trustee, express an undertaking to the buyer. On the other hand, based on the agreement with the trustee, the auctioneer looks for potential buyers for the trustee, organizes the auction and promotes the sale contract between the trustee and the buyer, which is actually the "intermediary" in the intermediary relationship. Accordingly, the auctioneer has the obligation to truthfully report to the trustee, and the auctioneer also has the right to claim the remuneration when the transaction is established and the necessary expenses when the transaction is not established.

2.1.2 The Auctioneer Fails to Disclose the Legal Relationship of the agent's Will

In the auctioneer without exposing the will of the agent, on the one hand, the Anglo-American law system of the agents faithful relationship that range is very broad, "I do not open proxy allows any auction" three party's legal relationship with each other, that the auctioneer in does not need to under the condition of acceptance, the buyer and appointed person can agent appointed with the buyer at the same time.[80] However, this situation is prohibited by article 168 (2) of The General Principles of Civil Law in Mainland China, so the Anglo-American law of "I do not publicly represent" cannot be applied to the arbitrary auction legal relationship in mainland China.[81] On the other hand, The European law emphasizes whether acting in one's own name is known to the buyer, and the Swiss Debt Law also considers that the case where the auctioneer of an arbitrary auction fails to the agent. At the conceptual level, there are many similarities between the auction and any auction in which the auctioneer does not reveal the meaning of agency. For example, the trustee acts in his own name and in his own interests. However, there is still a great difference at the institutional level between the relevant provisions of the Contract Law of the People's Republic of China and the relevant provisions of the Auction Law of the

[78] Article 51 of the Auction Law of the People's Republic of China.

[79] Liu Yuanning, Research on Auction Legal System in China, p. 26, December 2008.

[80] See Footnote 42.

[81] Paragraph 2, Article 168 of the General Provisions of the Civil Law of the People's Republic of China: "An agent shall not perform civil legal acts in the name of the principal, except if the principal is agreed to or ratified by the parties".

People's Republic of China. First, article 418 (1) of the Contract Law of the People's Republic of China allows the trustee trader to sell the commissioned property at a price lower than the indicated price of the trustee trader, and the sales contract is established under the condition that the trustee trader makes up the price. However, paragraph 2 of Article 50 of the Auction Law of the People's Republic of China stipulates that an offer that fails to reach the reserve price (indicative price) does not become effective. Second, Article 419 clause 1 of the Contract Law of the People's Republic of China allows the auctioneer to become the buyer, but Article 22 of the Auction Law of the People's Republic of China does not allow the auctioneer to become the buyer. Finally, Article 421 of the Contract Law of the People's Republic of China stipulates that the auctioneer is directly liable for the contract concluded with the third party, but Article 40 of the Auction Law of the People's Republic of China requires the auctioneer and the trustee to bear the responsibility. In view of the differences in the above laws, any auction that the auctioneer fails to reveal the meaning of agency should be regarded as indirect agency and not as a trade record.

In summary, the legal relationship of arbitrary auctions in mainland China can be divided into two parts: who acts in the name of the auctioneer. The legal relationship of auctioneers acting in the name of trustee is roughly equivalent to direct agency in the European civil law system and public agency in the common law system. The tripartite relationship between the auctioneer, trustee and buyer should not be regarded as an intermediary relationship. The internal relationship between the trustee and the auctioneer may be considered an intermediary relationship. On the other hand, the auctioneer acts in his own name, and the legal relationship of arbitrary auctions in mainland China conforms to the determination of "indirect agency" in the European civil law system but does not conform to the determination of "disciplinary relationships". At the same time, there is a large gap between the "self-disclosure" agency in the Anglo-American law system, so it belongs to the indirect agency of no disciplinary law.

In addition, when the auctioneer acts according to its own name, from the angle of the surrogate directly constrains the parties, the provisions of mainland China have neither of the continental law systems to be agents such as form nor with the Anglo-American law system. Publically, but I am certain agents have certain gaps, so acting in the name of the person is the sole criterion for judging China's agent form. It should be noted that although arbitrary auction relationships can be constructed with the legal principle of "direct agency" and "indirect agency", it does not mean that such structures can be naturally incorporated into the current legal framework. Therefore, while clearly understanding the framework of auction legal relationships, it also needs to explain the provisions of the two legal relationships.

3 Self-reflection on the Application of the Law on the Legal Relationship of Arbitrary Auctions

3.1 Interpretation of the Internal Provisions of the Auction Law of the People's Republic of China

Article 40, Paragraph 1 of the Auction Law of the People's Republic of China stipulates that the buyer has the right to receive auction targets. The main doubt is that when the buyer fails to receive auction targets as agreed upon, the meaning of the breach of contract liability of both the auctioneer and the trustee is not clear. For example, according to the Interpretation of the Commission of Legal Affairs, it means that the auctioneer and the trustee form a contractual relationship with the buyer. Some scholars believe that Article 40 (1) of the Auction Law of the People's Republic of China is a special provision of Article 403 of the Contract Law of the People's Republic of China.[82,83] However, this article agrees with the interpretation of the Commission of Legal Affairs, that is, the provision is the expression of the basis of the buyer's right of remedy for breach of contract which distinguishes direct and indirect agency. That is, under direct agency, the buyer may request relief for breach of contract from the appointing party on the basis of this article. Under indirect agency, the buyer may request relief for breach of contract from the auctioneer in accordance with Article 40 of the Auction Law of the People's Republic of China and Article 403 of the Contract Law of the People's Republic of China or choose to request relief from either the trustee or the auctioneer. If the auctioneer fully discloses the information of the trustee and demands to assume the corresponding rights and obligations, it is in accordance with the provisions of the provo of Article 402 of the Contract Law of the People's Republic of China. The buyer can directly request remedies for breach of contract from the auctioneer, which does not involve the selection of the parties.

From the perspective of the types of debt performance obstacles, Article 40 of the Auction Law of the People's Republic of China stipulates the general state of debt non-performance, while Article 61, Paragraph 1 and Article 58 of the Auction Law of the People's Republic of China stipulate a state of incomplete debt performance. From this point of view, article 61 (1) and Article 58 can be regarded as special provisions of Article 40. In the relationship of direct or indirect agency, article 58 of the Auction Law of the People's Republic of China applies to the situation in which the buyer fails to obtain the auction target due to the defect of the right of the auction target. Where a buyer fails to obtain an auction target due to defects in the object of the auction target, paragraph 1 of Article 61 of the Auction Law of the People's Republic of China shall apply; Article 40 of the Auction Law of the

---

[82] Civil law office, commission of legislative affairs, National People's Congress, auction law book, Beijing: China commercial press, 1997, 93.

[83] Wu Teng, Contractual Relations and Agency Effect in Auction, Jurist, 2015 (003). 99.

People's Republic of China shall apply to other cases where the auction target cannot be obtained in accordance with the contract.

Through the interpretation of the above, although you can clear the auction law of the People's Republic of China "provision of the internal differences and doubt, but in the case of a specific and direct of indirect agency, the rules of the auction law of the People's Republic of China and the relevant provisions of the law of the People's Republic of China contract law still exists the phenomenon of incompatible, it is necessary to further explain and space.

3.2 Interpretation of Applicable Laws for Auctioneers Acting in the Name of Their Appointees

In the legal relationship of direct agency, the auctioneer acts in the name of the trustee in accordance with Article 162 of The General Principles of the Civil Law of the People's Republic of China, or the buyer is aware of the existence of the agency relationship in accordance with Article 402 of the Contract Law of the People's Republic of China, when the buyer cannot obtain the auction target in accordance with the contract, According to paragraph 1 of Article 40 of the Auction Law of the People's Republic of China and the general principle of direct agency, the buyer shall claim breach of contract against the trustee. However, article 61 (1) of the Auction Law of the People's Republic of China states that when the buyer suffers losses due to the auctioneer's violation of defect notification obligation or the trustee's violation of defect notification obligation to the auctioneer, the buyer can only claim compensation from the auctioneer. In the direct agency relationship of any auction, although there is no legal relationship between the auctioneer and the buyer, they should bear responsibility for the buyer. There are few studies on this issue in mainland China, but this paper argues that there are two ways to explain this issue.

First, although the auctioneer is not the opposite party of the buyer, according to Articles 51 and 52 of the Auction Law of the People's Republic of China, the auctioneer is the actual contracting party of the buyer. Therefore, according to the principle of good faith, the buyer enjoys trust interests in the contracting process with the auctioneer. At the same time, according to the appraisal right stipulated in Article 43 of the Auction Law of the People's Republic of China and the appraisal obligation stipulated in Article 6 of the Auction Regulations of Cultural Relics and Artworks issued by the Ministry of Commerce, the auctioneer has the possibility of being trusted by the buyer. In view of this, the auctioneer shall bear the liability of contracting negligence to the buyer according to Article 42 of the Contract Law of the People's Republic of China when the trust interests are harmed by defects in the false information of the auctioneer. It is important to note that the law of the People's Republic of China contracts law "article 42 as prescribed in paragraph 2, the premise condition that bears the contracting negligence is intentionally omitted to inform or provide false information, and stipulates the situation of the fault, but in" the auction law of the People's Republic of China "in article 61 (1) has not stipulated the auctioneer's subjective state accountability. In the practice of art auctions, for example, if the auctioneer fails to refer to an important document or fails to authenticate a key feature of the auction item, it is difficult to be regarded as intentional or to be bound by the liability for contracting negligence stipulated in article 42 (2) of the Contract Law of the People's Republic of China. However, if the act of failing to inform or providing false information due to negligence of the auctioneer violates the principle of good faith, it can be bound by article 42 (3) of the Contract Law of the People's Republic of China. The logic that the auctioneer, as the actual contracting party, should bear the liability of contracting negligence for infringing on the trust interest of the buyer is the reason for the auctioneer to bear the liability to the buyer in the absence of a contractual relationship.

On the other hand, the violation of defect notification obligation by the auctioneer under direct agency should be understood as the loss caused by the auctioneer to the buyer without contractual relationship due to his fault, which is very close to the interpretation of the third party liability case by experts.[84] The auction Law of the People's Republic of China and other laws provide the auctioneer with the possibility of practicing as an expert. At the same time, in art auctions, because auctioneers have the relevant knowledge and skills of art identification, they have also accumulated the experience of art identification due to their practice, which has become the realistic basis for art auctioneers to become experts.

From the perspective of experts' liability to the third party, the buyer establishes a sales contract with the trustee due to the trust of the auctioneer's appraisal opinion. When the auctioneer makes an incorrect appraisal conclusion based on a fault, the trust interest of the buyer has been violated, and the buyer needs to bear the corresponding responsibility. Regarding how to realize this responsibility, there are still two different paths. On the one hand, it can be handled according to the path of contractual responsibility, that is, there is a contract between the expert auctioneer and the trustee with the protection of the third party; On the other hand, experts can be held liable in accordance with article 6 of the Tort Law of the People's Republic of China. According to the provisions of article 311 (2) (2) of the German Civil Code, there is a legal debt relationship between the auctioneer (other party) and the buyer (one party) derived from the principle of good faith, so it can be dealt with in the way of contract. However, there is no relevant legal system for this kind of interpretation in mainland China, and since the practical circles in mainland China hold a cautious attitude toward the breakthrough of the relativity of contract, this kind of contract path is only discussed theoretically at present.[85] As for the path of infringement, we need to face the problem of how to solve the "pure economic loss" without compensation. There is still much room to discuss the problem that the auctioneer has to bear the liability of guarantee for defects in the object, although there is no contractual relationship between the auctioneer and the buyer when acting in the name of the trustee.

---

[84] Youjun (2013).

[85] Liming (2002).

3.3 *Explanation of Indirect Agency Relationship*

In the legal relationship of indirect agency, the auctioneer acts in his own name for the interests of the trustee. If the buyer fails to obtain the auction target according to the contract, the buyer shall claim breach of contract with the auctioneer according to the First paragraph of Article 40 of the Auction Law of the People's Republic of China and the general indirect agency law. This is consistent with most of the provisions of article 61, Paragraph 1 of the Auction Law of the People's Republic of China. However, if the appointee violates Article 27 of the Auction Law of the People's Republic of China, that is, he fails to inform the auctioneer of the defects and thus causes damage to the buyer, the buyer may request relief from the auctioneer in accordance with Paragraph 1 of Article 61 of the Auction Law of the People's Republic of China. At the same time, this situation seems to be similar to the conditions for requesting relief stipulated in paragraph 2 of Article 403 of the Contract Law of the People's Republic of China, but the effects of the two laws are quite different. Under indirect agency, the Auction Law of the People's Republic of China does not admit that the buyer can directly claim compensation for the defects of the consignor, but the Contract Law of the People's Republic of China grants the auctioneer the right to publicly appoint the consignor and the buyer the right to choose the consignor. In short, under the perspective of the Contract Law of the People's Republic of China, the buyer can conditionally claim direct compensation from the appointed party for defects in the goods. In this regard, some scholars have pointed out the tension between Article 61 of the Auction Law of the People's Republic of China and Article 403 of the Contract Law of the People's Republic of China, while others believe that Article 403 of the Contract Law of the People's Republic of China applies to "nondisciplinary indirect agency".[86,87] Therefore, it is necessary to further clarify the internal logic between the two articles.

This paper holds that in indirect agency, the issue of defects in objects should not apply to Article 403 of the Contract Law of the People's Republic of China but to Article 61 of the Auction Law of the People's Republic of China. This consideration is not based on the concept of "priority of special law" but on the fact that "failure of the trustee to inform the auctioneer of defects" in Article 61 of the Auction Law of the People's Republic of China does not constitute the provision of "cause of the trustee" in Article 403 of the Contract Law of the People's Republic of China. The reason is that if you think "appoint people to the auctioneer told defects" comply with the provisions of the "due to any reason attributable to appoint a person", so when appointed person due to the reason of not attributable to itself, such as their own lack of knowledge and skill, or by trading before hand to obtain enough flawless certificate) to be aware of the content on the flaw, thus did not inform or error told the auction, It is not fair to hold innocent appointees to account. Auctioneers themselves, on the other hand, have the right to identify items, and more have the duty to identify

[86] Yin Fei, On the Composition and Effectiveness of Hidden Agents, Legal Science (Journal of Northwestern University of Political Science and Law), No. 003, p. 113, March 2011.

[87] Yin Tian, Renalism and Development of Civil Agency, Tsinghua Law, p. 24, July 2010.

items in the art auction. If the state of the items is enough to cause the auctioneer suspicion, from the perspective of protecting their own interests, the auctioneer shall carry on the appraisal and on the basis of the appraisal conclusion to decide whether to change or cancel the appointment contract. Art auctions are simpler; according to the Ministry of Commerce "cultural relics and art auction procedures" article 6, the auctioneer has the obligation to appraise the lot, depending on the appraisal conclusion, to decide whether to terminate the contract. In other words, when an item appears in front of a buyer, it can be said that it is an item that the auctioneer has identified as suitable for sale. In this case, any defects in objects and damage to the third party should be attributed to the auctioneer's improper use of rights or improper performance of obligations, which is a manifestation of external relations in indirect agency and should not be confused with internal relations. In short, the trustee's notification of the auctioneer is a factor in the auctioneer's decision of whether to proceed with the auction and not a factor that prevents the auctioneer from performing properly to the buyer.

4 Summary

Auction activity has been developing in mainland China for a very short time, but it has already made great achievements. However, in the process of rapid development, various deficiencies and disputes have also been exposed. From the perspective of law, the construction of the legal system of arbitrary auctions has been basically completed through the promulgation and implementation of the Auction Law of the People's Republic of China and other regulations, but there are still some doubts to be clarified; otherwise, it will lead to ambiguity and abstraction in judicial practice. Therefore, at the macro level, the legal system of arbitrary auctions is in the position of completion but not perfection. At the micro level, many ancient sages have combed and clarified the legal relationship of arbitrary auctions, leaving valuable research results and greatly promoting the construction of the legal system of auctions. Through the analysis and reflection of this paper, I hope it will be helpful to perfect the macroscopic construction and further develop the microscopic construction of the auction legal system. Our main conclusions are as follows:

(1) For the question of who is the seller in commercial practice and judicial judgment of any auction and the determination of the legal relationship, the key point of this section is to clarify in whose name the auctioneer acts.
(2) Through the continental and Anglo-American law system comparison and analysis of the agent system, the auctioneer ACTS in the name of the appointed person, under the condition of China "the general civil law of the People's Republic of China" the 162nd and the law of the People's Republic of China contract law "article 402 any auction law of the identified close to essentially after abandoning the continental law and common law of direct agent; In the case of the auctioneer acting in his own name, the legal relationship of arbitrary

auction is similar to the indirect agency of nonofficial law in European law, but far from the private agency in common law.

(3) In combination with the current legal framework, since the auctioneer has the right and obligation to appraise the auction, in the case of direct agency, even if there is no contractual relationship, the buyer may claim relief from the auctioneer for the failure or improper performance of the precontractual obligations of the auctioneer. In the case of indirect agency, improper notification by the trustee does not become the cause that prevents the auctioneer from performing properly to the buyer, so the auctioneer cannot, in accordance with Article 403 of the Contract Law of the People's Republic of China, remove himself from the scope of the buyer's claims by disclosing the trustee.

Finally, we find that the two agency legal relations of arbitrary auctions must be identified before the medium can be integrated into the current contract law system. However, due to the long-term influence of the "nonfidelity clause", the research on appraisals in auctions is weak compared with other rights and obligations, and this is also the most likely dispute in auction practice. Therefore, research on arbitrary auctions needs to be further deepened to stabilize the order of the auction market and promote the further development of the auction industry.

References

Wang Shen, Gao Wanquan, Ding Xiaoyan. A Theoretical Review of Wu Tiesheng versus Shanghai Dekang Auction Company and Zhang Qi Auction Dispute Case [J]. Legal science, 2001 (7): 73–75

Huang Maorong. Sale Law [M]. Beijing: China University of Political Science and Law Press.2002:434

Hu Changqing. General Theory of Chinese Civil Law [M]. Beijing: China University of Political Science and Law Press, 1997:297

Yin tian Peking University. Civil agency doctrine and its development [J]. Tsinghua law school,2010,4(04):18-24.

Wang Zejian (2009a) The General Provisions of the Civil Law. Beijing: China University of Political Science and Law Press, p. 489

Wang Zejian (2009b) The General Provisions of the Civil Law. Beijing: China University of Political Science and Law Press, p. 449

Huo Yufen. Essentials of Auction Law [M]. Beijing: China University of Political Science and Law Press.2012:12

Zhou Youjun. The normative model and specific rules of experts' liability to the third party [J]. Contemporary law science,2013,27(01):98-104.

Wang Liming. Research on Contract Law, Volume 1 [M]. Beijing: China Renmin University Press, 2002

Chen Ziqiang (November 2018) The determination of the Modernization of the—Contract Act V. Taibei: New Xuelin Publishing Co., Ltd, p. 168

Edwin Peel (2015) Treitel on the Law of Contract, 14th edn. London: Sweet & Maxwell pp. 16–055

Brian Harvey and Franklin Meisel (2006) Auctions Law and Practice. London: Oxford University Press p. 345

Reynolds FMB (2006) Bowstead and Reynolds on agency. London: Sweet & Maxwell, pp. 9-016

Wang Zejian (2009ec) The General Provisions of the Civil Law. Beijing: China University of Political Science and Law Press, p. 419
Clive M. Schmitthoff (1969) The export trade: a manual of law and practice. London: Stevens & Sons, p. 136
Danny Busch (2005a) Indirect Representation in European Contract Law. The Hague: Kluwer Law International, p. 79
Danny Busch (2005b) Indirect Representation in European Contract Law. The Hague: Kluwer Law International. p 85
Dai Yongsheng (2016a) Swiss Debt Law. Beijing: China University of Political Science and Law Press, p. 189
Dai Yongsheng (2016b) Swiss Debt Law. Bei Jing: China University of Political Science and Law Press, p. 176

Chapter 4
Research on the Obligations of Art Auctioneers

The number of transactions in art auctions is rare, but the number is generally large, so the identification and evaluation information provided by art auction houses becomes particularly critical. Should the auctioneer bear civil liability for the wrong appraisal? Or under what circumstances? Although Chinese precedents have given preliminary responses to these problems and relevant laws and regulations have also expressed the obligation of adjudication, the response of these cases and the expression of laws and regulations are very abstract, and there are still some difficulties in answering these questions. Therefore, the system of the obligation of adjudication of art auctioneers urgently needs to be built. Research on art auctions focuses more on the discussion of public law, but the private law of art auctions is still blank. To date, no academic papers or monographs have been found to systematically discuss the appraisal or approval of artworks in auctions, which is worthy of academic attention.

1 Appraisal and Approval of Works of Art

1.1 The Right of Appraisal

Since the auction Law of the People's Republic of China was adopted at the 20th Meeting of the Standing Committee of the Eighth National People's Congress on July 5, 1996, although the law was amended twice in 2004 and 2015, the appraisal system, as article 43 of the law, has not undergone any changes in its content. Paragraph 1 of this article stipulates: "If an auctioneer deems it necessary to make an appraisal of an auction target, he may do so. "According to the legislative interpretation of the Legislative Work Committee of the National People's Congress, the auction Law does not require auctioneers to appraise auction targets, and it is necessary to appraise auction items that are difficult for the public to identify, such as cultural

Z. Zheng, *The Legal System of Art Auction in China*,
https://doi.org/10.1007/978-981-19-0128-7_4

relics, calligraphy and paintings, houses and so on.[1] The judicial judgment of some courts interprets this clause as an empowering norm, holding that the auctioneer has the right to choose whether to appraise the auction target, and cannot be held liable for failing to appraise the auction target.[2] Some scholars believe that China's appraisal market is in turmoil at present, and it is urgent to establish a comprehensive framework system from civil, administrative and criminal aspects.[3]

1.2 Administrative Supervision Over the Appraisal Power

With the development of the national economy, China's auction business is increasingly vigorous. In the process of the transaction volume gradually rising, some problems have gradually emerged, among which the "fake auction, fake auction, fake identification" is the most prominent problem but also has a direct connection with the art auction identification problems. To regulate auction behavior, maintain auction order and promote the healthy development of the auction industry, the Ministry of Commerce of China issued the Auction Administration Measures, and the Ministry of Culture issued the Art Operation Administration Measures accordingly to strengthen the management of art operation activities.

Article 27 (2) of the Measures for the Administration of Auction issued by the Ministry of Commerce and Article 8 of the Measures for the Administration of Operation of Works of Art issued by the Ministry of Culture both stipulate that auction enterprises shall not conduct false publicity and cause losses to buyers. Violators shall be subject to certain administrative penalties. The Measures for the Administration of Business operation of Works of Art also provides additional provisions on the due diligence obligations of art dealers (Article 10) and the provisions that art dealers should abide by when providing appraisal services (Article 11) for art transactions. Violators shall also be subject to administrative punishment. Some scholars believe that it is necessary to establish the supervision mechanism of appraisal, the access mechanism of appraisal institutions, and the accountability system of appraisal to improve the problem of artwork appraisal.[4]

The administrative supervision of appraisal rights is an important development of the appraisal system in artwork auctions. To a certain extent, this has broken the convention that auctioneers are not punished without appraisal in the Auction Law. Although these two administrative laws and regulations still regulate art auctions from the perspective of public law and have limited influence on private law, they lay a solid foundation for judicial attempts at appraisal obligations.

---

[1] Civil law office (1997, p. 98).

[2] Civil Judgment No.1571 (2013), Guangzhou Intermediate People's Court No.1571.

[3] Wu Bingheng: "Legal responsibility for the identification and valuation of ancient artworks" is listed in the Journal of Shanghai Institute of Political Science and Law (Legal Theory), No.04, 2012, p. 42.

[4] Liu (2011).

1.3 Disputes Over Appraisal Obligation

With the further prosperity of China'127s auction market, the number of counterfeit auction cases is also increasing. Whether the auctioneer should have the obligation of appraisal in the auction process has also become a focus of the judicial dispute over artwork auctions. Some opponents think that the current law does not clearly stipulate that the auction company should be responsible for the appraisal of lots, and in practice, it is impossible and unrealistic for the auction company to carry out the appraisal of all lots.[5] Some think: art business should be applicable to the buyer beware rather than the principle of seller attention, buyers should improve artistic accomplishment and identification ability, while maintaining a good state of mind[6]; Others believe that: according to the relevant provisions of the Auction Law (Article 62 (2) of the Auction Law), the law does not require the auctioneer to guarantee that the auction object must be genuine, which is also in line with the characteristics of the industry, especially the actual situation of art auction.[7]

Supporters believe that in view of the particularity of modern painting and calligraphy auctions, the appellee should carefully examine the source of modern painting and calligraphy auctions. In this case, the appellee used red font to describe the source of the auction in question, which was enough to cause the bidders to misunderstand the source of the paintings. However, the appellee did not carefully examine the source of the auction. Therefore, the court considers that the appellee has a great fault and shall bear the corresponding compensation liability.[8] Some people hold that the exemption clause set in Article 61 of the Auction Law cannot exempt auction companies from the obligation of examining and truthfully disclosing auction items in accordance with the Auction Law, nor can it become the protection of auction companies to know and sell fake goods. Strictly speaking, the nonguarantee or exemption clause of the auction company's defects refers to the situation in which the auction company does not know or should not know whether the authenticity and quality of the auction target is defective. If the auction company is grossly negligent in the examination and judgment of the auction items when soliciting the auction items, especially if it knows that the auction items have defects but does not make further verification and does not disclose the defects truthfully, the disclaimer of the auction company does not have legal effect[9]; Others believe that the premise of the obligation of defect notification is that the auctioneer knows the defect, and this "knowing the defect" should include two situations: one is that the trustee has informed the

---

5 Beijing Municipal High People's Court (2009) Gao Min No.3093.

6 Zhengzhou Intermediate People's Court (2015) Zheng Min 3 Final zi No.1385.

7 Civil Judgment No.11139 of Beijing No.1 Intermediate People's Court (2006) No.1 Intermediate People's Court No.1 Middle School.

8 Beijing No.2 Intermediate People's Court (2016) No.22 Civil Judgment No.225.

9 Beijing Municipal No.3 Intermediate People's Court No.3 Intermediate Court (2015) No.3 Middle School People (Commercial) Final Judgment No.08512.

auctioneer of the defect in advance;Second, although the trustee did not inform, but as an auction enterprise is fully capable and obligated to find defects.[10]

In addition, in 2017 released by the Ministry of Commerce on January 13, "the art of cultural relics auction procedures" article 6, specify the auctioneer to auction shall have the duty to examination and approval and audit, according to China association of auction of "cultural relic artwork auction target approved guidelines" article 4.3 and article 4.5 and article 6 of the regulation, assessment method and the purpose of appraisal is not.

2 The Purpose of the Work of Art Approval

2.1 Seeking Truth

From the perspective of sociology, artwork has a special status in the system of objects because of its authenticity. Walter Benjamin believes that "the presence of the original" is the prerequisite for the genuineness of the object itself. Even the most perfect copy, he argues, lacks one element: "its presence in time and space." Because each work of art is unique in time and space, whether it is the evolution of its position in the historical tradition or the physical changes produced over the years.[11] Jean Baudrillard also points out that in addition to symbolising nostalgia for origins, antiquities also have an obsession with authenticity such as provenance, age, authorship and signature. The charm of handmade products comes from the fact that it retains traces of human creative activities. Any creative activities are fleeting historical moments, but they can be retained in handmade products for an eternity.[12] Art appraisal is to try to find the time and space positioning of the artwork, describe its real context, and give it the correct meaning. This requirement for authenticity is also very important in the field of cultural asset preservation. In 1994, for example, the "nara declaration (also called nara document authenticity, Nara Documenton Authenticity)" refers to cultural heritage (cultural heritage) as its value judgment, whether it is based on "information source can be seen as a credible or real (information sources about these values may be understood as credible or truthful)".

However, authenticity is usually an abstract, vague, ambiguous word meaning, which is not as easy to recognize and test as the words describing size, size, color and other physical attributes.[13] Moreover, the concept and requirement of authenticity will vary from culture to culture, and it is almost impossible to establish a fixed criterion of judgment.[14] What is more difficult is that it is very difficult to reconstruct

---

[10] Suzhou Intermediate People's Court (2014) Suzhong Shang Final Judgment No.00632.

[11] Benjamin and Xudong (1998).

[12] Baudrillard and Zhiming (1997).

[13] Chen (2001).

[14] Fu (2002).

the real scene when it was created with only the object in front of you. Even for works of art unearthed from archaeological sites, there are many factors that can affect their authenticity.

Therefore, what art appraisal pursues is "discovery the truth", similar to judicial trials. In the criminal procedure, judicial trials aim to explore the "substantial truth". Under the principle of argument, the purpose of civil action is "truth in form". The main difference between the two is that substantial truth refers to objectively constant fact itself, and any possible evidence that helps to discover it is the object of investigation. Formal truth is to focus on civil litigation is to solve the dispute of private rights, factual evidence is known to be advocated or proposed by the parties, the court only on the facts advocated by the parties to form psychological evidence, therefore, the truth sought by the civil procedure may not be consistent with the truth of the facts.

Ideally, artwork examination attempts to present the real context of artwork completely, which is similar to the purpose of pursuing substantial truth in criminal proceedings. Sometimes in order to clear the authenticity of a work of art, art history scholars to invest enormous time and energy, in contrast, in contrast, efforts to search the textual research, different times and in different parts of the scholars, even still continually on the same artwork for a new clues and evidence, try to restore the truth of the work.

In practical applications, art appraisals sometimes must take the form of truth similar to the pursuit of civil litigation. Because some works of art do not necessarily have the value of in-depth study, the examination and approval process of some works of art must strive for time limitation, especially the art waiting for the transaction on the art market, considering the cost and profit, cannot allow the examination and approval process for too long. More importantly, the examination and approval of artwork correct probability of existence, often end up with civil litigation evidence of "absolute majority advantage (preponderance of the evidence)" principle, to do judgment. As the law pursues, it is a measure of legal interest with social significance. The authenticity found in the examination of works of art can only be regarded as the conclusion under the weight of evidence.

2.2 Evaluation

Another important purpose of examining and approving works of art is to give proper evaluation to works of art. By judging the importance of a work of art, it can properly allocate resources, provide market reference and give play to the social and economic functions of a work of art.

The expression of art value can be divided into qualitative value judgment and quantitative value judgment. The former, as the collection of cultural relic grading standards in our country, can distinguish between the level of cultural relics, secondary, tertiary cultural relics such as grading standards, as well as the cultural asset preservation law in Taiwan, the antiquity grading login specified and abolished censorship method "to distinguish the national treasure, important antiquities, general classification of antiquities, is based on text to illustrate the value, and value in a way that is grade difference between high and low; The latter, known as an appraisal or art valuation, expresses value by number and determines whether it is worth more or less.

Value judgments will try to be measured by "standards", but standards are artificial definitions, and inevitably, there will be subjective judgments.

The qualitative standard of value judgment, for example, in our country, "the collection of cultural relics and grading standards," art can be divided into level cultural relics, secondary, tertiary cultural relic, the difference of standard, there is a special important value, have important value, and has a certain value as a three level standard, some abstract words such as the other as such as size, defects presence of discriminant conditions. In the "cultural relics collection grading standards" in the annex, still on pottery, porcelain, bronze, gold and silver ware[21] the reference standards for listing the types of artworks, such as pottery, include: 1.2. It can represent a certain cultural type with a special shape and intact shape; 3. Beautiful shape, bright color and complete shape in tricolor. In these three standards, in addition to the unearthed site, dating standards, complete shape and other objective and clear description, the rest, such as special shape, beautiful shape, bright color and other conditions, are dependent on the examiners free heart certification and professional quality.

Another example is the examination criteria for "national treasures" stipulated in Article 4 of The Examination Measures for Designation and Abolition of Classification and Registration of Antiquities in Taiwan: "1. They have special historical significance or can express traditional, ethnic or local cultural characteristics; 2. History has been handed down for a long time or historical events have deep origins; 3. It has special characteristics of the times, technologies and schools and has special artistic attainments or scientific achievements. Excellent quality and rare quantity; Having special historical, cultural, artistic or scientific value. "Article 3 criteria for the examination of "important antiquities" are as follows: (1) they are of historical significance or can express traditional, ethnic or local cultural characteristics; 2. It has important historical origins; 3. It has important characteristics of the times, technologies and schools; 4. Have important artistic attainments or scientific achievements; 5. Excellent quality and rare quantity; Having important historical, cultural, artistic or scientific value. "The main difference between them lies in the fact that national treasures must have "particularity", "long history" and "extremely rare quantity". However, there is room for subjective judgment as to what degree is special, how long is long, and how much is rare.

The legislative purpose of such standards is obviously to avoid rigid provisions limiting the judgment of experts and scholars. More importantly, values themselves have the characteristics of different people. Because "justice" is relative, the value judgment of works of art cannot be absolutely accurate, and the grading cannot fully and truly reflect the value of works of art collection. In fact, it is only a means to facilitate the strengthening of management in a certain management system.[15] Therefore, the focus of system design is not to formulate an immutable iron law but to focus on how participants can supervise and cooperate with each other, construct objectivity through mutual subjectiveness, and legitimize the way of evaluation.[16]

The subjective criteria of value judgment can also be seen in quantitative value judgment, i.e., appraisal. Since there is no net value or fair market value for works of art, its price can easily change from time to time, from place to place and from person to person. Artists, for example, decide prices based on their motivation and willingness to sell, galleries take costs and profits into account, and collectors set prices based on their personal finances and taste judgment.[17] For example, although the market price of a work of art can be measured by money, it sometimes has historical or aesthetic value that money cannot replace. Other factors, such as the intrinsic quality of the artwork, the reputation of the artist, the number of works, the amount of market demand, the brand image of the gallery, the money, time, manpower and material resources spent making and promoting the artwork, are also factors affecting the price.[18]

Although the appraisal of art works is very subjective, practitioners in the art market still have certain practices, including absolute price, relative price, strategic price and other appraisal methods. Absolute prices mainly appear in rare treasures, as long as buyers and sellers agree. Relative prices are calculated from the quantity, age, size and other conditions of similar works in a simulated way. A strategic price is the seller's business strategy to raise or lower the price. In addition, different practitioners will adjust their own prices.[19]

To reduce the subjective scale of standards, practitioners also refer to art indices or public records of art auctions over the years. For example, Mei/Moses Fint Index of the United States, Artron Index of China, AMI Zhongyi Index of China Art Network, ArtPrice.com database of France, Chinese auction Yearbook, And sales records from Sotheby's, Christie's and other major auction houses. Although these data may be manipulated, priced or hyped, due to the large sample size and long sampling time, some risks are relatively apportioned.

Because of the interest involved, the examination and approval cannot be directly converted to qualitative value judgment, and sometimes it is even excluded from the examination and approval of works of art. In particular, if art appraisal experts work in museums, they still have to be regulated by the ethical regulations of museum professionals and are strictly forbidden from appraising prices for private collections, so they will naturally avoid engaging in appraisal activities. Such views are mainly based on the consideration of interest avoidance.

In addition, the market has many fine business professional knowledge and skills and can study art appraisals of experts and scholars at the same time. The work of

---

[15] Yuan (2006, p. 29).

[16] Lin (1999, p. 61).

[17] Li (2005, p. 86).

[18] Guo (1990).

[19] Huang (2008).

examination and approval and giving attention to two or more is easy to question because experts from colleges may be able to distinguish the authenticity of works of art but do not know the value of the market.

If it is found that the truth is the "inside" of art approval, then the value judgment can be said to be the "table" of art approval. The starting point of art appraisal is to clarify and discover the authenticity of the artwork and then judge whether the artwork is valuable. However, in the restoration and preservation of cultural assets, the study of art history, transactions in the art market and other fields, the value of artwork, and how much contribution can be made to the above fields depend on how much recognition and disclosure of the information carried on the artwork. However, the specific process of art approval is still subject to some limitations, so it is objectively difficult to achieve the ideal state. Specifically, the uncertainty of artwork attribution will affect the process of discovering truth. The asymmetry of the authentication information will affect the value judgment of artworks.

3 Contents of the Obligation of Examining and Approving Works of Art

According to the Stipulation of Auction Regulations of Cultural Relics and Artworks issued by the Ministry of Commerce, the auctioneer shall have the obligation to examine and approve the auction target, but the stipulation of the Ministry of Commerce does not specify the content of the obligation. In view of the present situation of theoretical research in China, there are many gaps in both legislative and interpretive theories. Need to fill.

In view of the above analysis of the legal relationship of auctions, we can clarify the position of the appraisal issue in art auctions in China's civil law system. On the one hand, appraisals in art auctions may exist in commission contracts and sale contracts, so their core lies in the basic theory of the contract. It is bound by direct agency in general Principles of civil Law and entrustment in Contract Law. In detail, the obligations related to the appraisal include the obligation to comply with the instructions of the client, the obligation to inform the client, and the obligation to deal with it in person.[20] On the other hand, based on the rule that the special law is superior to the general law, the examination and approval in art auctions will also be bound by the relevant provisions of the Auction Law. In detail, the contents of the obligation related to the examination and approval include the obligation of keeping the target and the obligation of confidentiality.[21] However, reading these laws, we can still feel that, on the one hand, China's laws on the content of the obligation of approval in art auction is very rough, no targeted; On the other hand, these provisions are too principled and difficult to operate.

[20] Section 396-423 of the Contract Law.

[21] Section 10 of the Auction Act.

From the perspective of the development of foreign legislation and cases, in the case of appraisal errors, the auctioneer should assume certain duty of care to the trustee. It is necessary to assume certain express guarantee obligation to the buyer.

3.1 The Duty of Diligence of the Auctioneer Toward the Trustee

According to article 398, paragraph 2, of the Swiss Debt Act, the auctioneer shall be diligent in his appraisal work. Whether the auction house experts or third-party experts, their duty of care is mainly determined by analyzing the express or implied consent of each party.[22] For example, by mutual consent, experts are asked to consult only specific archives without scientific identification or to investigate only entries in catalogs that rely on specific artists and not other possible entries.

Once an entrustment contract is formed, "the trustee is entitled to rely on the auctioneer's good faith and judgment."[23] This duty of care goes beyond the usual standard for two reasons. First, the duty of care standard expects auctioneers, like other professionals, to exercise their "own best judgment" and show rationality or reasonable judgment.[24] Second, although the auctioneer may be held liable, the duty of care standard still expects the auctioneer to use his or her special abilities in carrying out the valuation.[25]

Thus, the determination of the responsibility of an expert depends on his specific qualifications and abilities: if the expert claims to have special knowledge and skills, he can apply those knowledge and skills, and not just be limited to the minimum standards of his profession.[26] Failure by an auctioneer to apply his or her knowledge or skill adequately, or lack of the necessary minimum knowledge, may result in a breach of duty of care.[27] In the event of a breach of duty of care, the auctioneer loses the right to claim compensation for the services rendered.[28]

There are also cases where an appraisal of a work of art goes beyond the knowledge of the auction house, for example, by lacking information about the artist or by lacking the necessary appreciation of the period or period in which the work was created. In this case, the auction house may consult a third party expert or not accept the

---

22 Dai (2016, p. 179).

23 Bullock (1988–1989, p. 369).

24 See Footnote 23.

25 Cristallina S.A.v. Christie, Manson & Woods Int'l, Inc., 117A.D.2d284,294, 502 N.Y.S.165,172 (1st Dept.1986).

26 Lerner (2005, p. 604).

27 The scholar distinguishes between four different negligence situations that lead to the breach of the duty of diligence, first, the expert lacks the necessary knowledge; second, the expert's knowledge is only a "belief"; third, the expert neglects his knowledge; fourth, the expert does not use his knowledge appropriately. Karlen (1986).

28 7 Am. Jur. 2d Auctions and Auctioneers, paras.67, 78.

commission. In general, unless the expert responsible for the identification could not have ascertained authenticity, even after careful examination, based on current scientific knowledge, he or she could not successfully claim exemption for lack of skill, experience or knowledge.[29] At the same time, the auction house cannot claim exemption of negligence due to its own reasons.

When performing the duty of diligence, different countries follow different standards, such as the "reasonable auctioneer standard" adopted by most countries, such as Switzerland and the United States. Britain has a unique code of conduct for auctioneers.

3.1.1 Reasonable Standards of Care for Auctioneers

If the parties have not agreed on the duty of diligence, the duty of diligence should be defined according to objective standards, that is, the degree of diligence a person with professional knowledge should have under the same circumstances. The responsibility labeling of duty of diligence needs to be analyzed on a case-by-case basis, including the difficulty of art appraisal, the reasonable time limit necessary for appraisal and the importance of the artwork. An expert's duty of care is higher if his reputation creates a reasonable expectation that the client will pay for it. Some legal scholars believe that in the case of an artist, or a well-known expert specializing in the art of a particular period or period, the client may expect an expert with special skills and knowledge to provide an opinion befitting his or her status and thus superior to that of the average expert. At the same time, these experts are liable for negligence that ordinary experts might be excused from.

The duty of care is intended to determine whether the expert carried out the assessment seriously, whether important elements or information was missed in the process, rather than whether the expert's opinion was accurate. This purpose also applies to auctioneers who identify and appraise items before the auction begins. That is, what obligations of care can be foreseen by the auctioneer who performs an appraisal and valuation when considering certain facts, performing certain appraisal techniques, or adopting different appraisal strategies?

The same rule could apply in cases where an auction house misidentified an item. If the auction house can prove its identification process is with the same condition other auction houses expected is consistent with the industry level, and until the auction on the same day, the level of expectations and diligence degree still generally accepted view for everyone, so even if the conclusion of the identification error, it would not be adverse to the auction house.[30] Conversely, if the auction house is proved to have failed in its duties, it will be liable for breach of its principal-agent obligation, which is equivalent to a breach of the agency contract. The court will also determine on a case-by-case basis whether the auction house ignored factors or indicators in the appraisal process that could raise doubts about the accuracy of the appraisal.

---

[29] Chappuis (2007).

[30] Federal Court Ruling 93 II 19, 21.

In general, the determination of the necessary duty of care plays a vital role in the determination of an auctioneer's responsibility.[31] Therefore, large auction houses that have, or claim to have, a high level of expertise should assume a duty of care commensurate with their expertise.

However, auction houses may claim that the sheer volume of goods they receive makes it difficult, if not impossible, to conduct a thorough study of every lot for sale. In accordance with the contract of entrustment and the commercial terms binding upon the trustee, the trustee shall warrant to the auctioneer that all information provided on the property, including any information relating to the appraisal, is accurate. However, in the case of false appraisals, the consignor and the buyer usually have little or no knowledge of the authenticity and valuation of all their works of art.[32] They rely entirely on the expertise of the auctioneer or surveyor to appraise and value the commissioned property. The duty of care requires auctioneers to give their clients some standard of scrutiny before an art sale begins. Therefore, the auctioneer should not rely solely on the information provided by the client but should verify the reasonable expectations of the client in accordance with the auction house's examination standards.

In Reale v. Sotheby's, Inc., on the sale of 74 rare U.S. coins, the New York court of Appeals rejected the plaintiffs' argument that Sotheby's had been negligent in allowing consulting experts to estimate the value of the coins before they were sold without examining them.[33] Because the plaintiff could not prove that failure to inspect the collection would result in lower valuations or other harm.[34] In addition, the court held that Sotheby's had not breached its duty to its client or to professional standards after the client indicated that he did not want some coin experts involved in the identification of his coins.[35] The auction house did not breach its obligations by ignoring the principal's instructions, as the commission contract gave Sotheby's absolute discretion to decide whom to consult.

Instead, the trustee must prove that the auctioneer's lack of care in preparing and selling resulted in harm to the trustee. The auctioneer has a specific obligation to obtain the best price at auction. This does not mean that he must guarantee the outcome of the auction. For this purpose, the auctioneer may determine the reserve price of the entrusted property in advance. In practice, the obligation involves the auctioneer setting reasonable underestimates and overestimates of prices that are most likely to motivate bidders and encourage them to bid high.[36]

According to Cristallina v. Christie's, the New York State Court of Appeals, the auctioneer was held to have an "implied duty of good faith to use his best efforts to sell

---

[31] Federal Court Ruling 127 III 328, 331.

[32] See Footnote 31.

[33] Reale v. Sotheby's, Inc., 278A.D.2d119, 718 N.Y.S.2d37, 2000 WL1868592, 2000 N.Y.Slip Op.11338.

[34] Reale v. Sotheby's, 278A.D.2d119, 120-121 (2000), 718 N.Y.S.2d37.

[35] Reale v. Sotheby's, 278A.D.2d119, 120 (2000), 718 N.Y.S.2d37,38.

[36] The estimated price represents the "price range where the lots may be sold", but does not predict the actual sale price of the lots. Lerner (2005, p. 434).

the consignor's products."[37] In particular, in this case Christie's failed to give proper advice on the attractiveness of commissioned paintings and the setting of reserve prices and estimated price ranges. Ahead of the sale, Christie's used promotional campaigns to promote the sale and consigned paintings and said it expected to sell at a price below the valuation range previously agreed with the consignor. Christie's also proposed selling the painting at a public auction. The risk of public auction is essentially that the failure of the auction depends on the disclosure of information, thus negatively affecting the marketability of the auction.

In the Cristallina case, almost all of the commissioned paintings were not sold and were therefore bought by the auction house. Two Christie's experts negotiated and were separately responsible for the preparation of the sale. One of them had expressed concern about the appeal of the painting and their chances of getting a given valuation. However, these concerns were not enough to persuade Christie's experts to recommend private sales or withdraw paintings from sale before printing catalogs. Therefore, it can be inferred from the ruling that the auction house has an obligation to properly inform the principal about the sale, the type of reserve price and valuation and other considerations in accordance with "a standard of care of special skill commensurate with local industry standards" in order to market the entrusted property in a suitable manner.[38]

Basically, if an auctioneer misidentifies a consigned property, all efforts to further promote a successful sale are lost. A misjudged lot does not reach its full potential because its actual value is misrecognized in the first place. In addition, if accurate identification could lead the auctioneer to place the item in a sale that would attract potential interested buyers or to contact potential interested buyers, then missing such an opportunity could result in a breach of the obligation to promote the sale of the trustee's property.

In conclusion, when a trustee enters into a contract of trust with an auctioneer, he has the right to expect the auctioneer to appraise and appraise his property, taking into account all the same factors that can reasonably be considered by an equivalent auction expert. In the case of a misidentified auction, whether the auctioneer fulfils this standard must be examined on a case-by-case basis.

3.1.2 Distinguish Standards of Care at the Auction House Level

The commission contract for the provision of services under section 13 of the Supply of Goods and Services Act 1982 contains a hidden clause that "the supplier will perform the services with reasonable care and skill". For auctions, the duty of diligence of the auctioneer is mainly reflected in the responsibility for the goods in his possession, including the loss or damage of the goods and the accurate description of

[37] Cristallina S.A.v Christie Manson & Woods, International Inc., 117A.D.2d284, 502 N.Y.S.165 (1st Dept. 1986).

[38] Cristallina S.A.v Christie Manson & Woods, International Inc., 117A.D.2d284, 294, 502 N.Y.S.165, 172 (1st Dept. 1986).

the property responsibility. The auctioneer's obligation to accurately describe property is reflected in the tort law and Contract Law provisions as "in order to ensure an appropriate price, the service provider must carefully describe the property in its possession". In other words, it is the auctioneer's responsibility to accurately identify the attributes and values of the entrusted property.[39]

The description of the property shall be made by the auctioneer in accordance with the express or implied description of the property unless the commission contract permits the auctioneer to do so himself. In the general consignment contract or the auction rules of the auction house, the auctioneer will stipulate in advance that the appraisal of the entrusted property and the auction catalog shall be described by the auctioneer himself. In the absence of such a clause, the auctioneer may breach its obligation to misdescribe the trustee's property, thus causing the trustee to be liable to the buyer. In this case, the auctioneer must compensate the trustee for his loss.[40]

In addition, "the auctioneer may directly cause loss to the trustee by failing to describe the goods as being in the best condition". Although auctioneers have stipulated in their commission contracts that they can describe the goods themselves, they still have to describe the goods carefully and accurately to their potential to attract the right bidder or the best price. Otherwise, the auctioneer may be liable for negligence.

In the case of false appraisal, the auctioneer made mistakes in both the description of the property and the appraisal of its value. Generally, the misattribution is related to the attributes of the artwork, such as the creator, date, provenance and so on, and auctioneers offer and sell misidentified artwork at inappropriate prices. This price segment will appeal to a completely different kind of collector or art dealer. People who highly value and respect art and antiques and are willing to buy them are less likely to bid on art, which describes a huge discrepancy in price. Therefore, although the auctioneer has a clear right to appraise an artwork, the auctioneer may be liable for breach of duty of care by failing to accurately describe the best advantage of the artwork.[41]

The auctioneer's standard of care "will depend on whether the auction house is a general practice auction house or a professional auction house." By adopting the distinction between medical malpractice cases between different qualified physicians, case law determines the obligation distinction of auctioneers according to the actual skills and knowledge of the auction house.[42]

(1) Standard of duty of care for general licensed auction houses

In luxMoore-May v Messenger-May Baverstock, the specific application of the concealment clause contained in section 13 of the Supply of Goods and

[39] Reynolds, Francis, Bowstead and Reynolds on Agency, Sweet & Maxwell, 2006, 403.

[40] Meisel, Frank. "Auctioneers and Misdescriptions: Between Scylla and Charybdis." Modern Law Review 732,010,125.

[41] Harvey and Franklin (2006, p. 278).

[42] Mackay, James, Halsbury's Laws of England, vol. 2(3): Auction, 4thed. Butter worths Lexis Nexis, 2003, p. 255.

Services Act 1982 in cases of mistaken identification was analysed. The original owners, Luxmoore-May, commissioned Messrs Messenger May Baverstock, a local auctioneer, to arrange the sale of two paintings of fox terriers. The auctioneers showed the paintings to art advisers and came up with a verdict worth between £30 and £50 each. On the advice of the auctioneer, the consultant gave the two paintings to Christie's for £50 each. The paintings were examined quickly and freely by Christie's, who concluded that the appraisal and valuation were reasonable. The consultant's valuation range and appraisal opinion are therefore relayed in the auction catalog. The paintings were successfully sold for £840 on October 10, 1985 and were sold again at Sotheby's just five months later. Sotheby's identified the paintings directly as the work of the artist George Stubbs, rather than making vague statements such as "authenticated by George Stubbs." The catalog also said the estimate was 18,000–24,000 pounds each. Art trading company Spinks successfully sold the two works at auction for a total of £88,000.[43]

On September 2, 1986, after Sotheby's sale, the Luxmoore-May couple filed a lawsuit against the auctioneer, claiming that he had breached his duty of care in the appraisal and evaluation of commissioned works. In the auctioneer's opinion, the Luxmoore-May couple should have been judged by the standard of care required of a general practising auctioneer rather than a professional auctioneer. The trial judge found the defendant's valuation negligent and ruled against the plaintiff that the auctioneer had failed to "recognize and inform the potential value of the two foxhound paintings. "Therefore, the responsibility of the auctioneer for failing to recognize the potential of the painting and to carry out the necessary further research on the work is very slight. The plaintiff protested and appealed.

The appellate court reversed the first decision, and the appellate court's decision established a fundamental principle that is still valued today. The appeals court held that the auctioneer had an obligation "to express a well-considered opinion and to provide further appropriate advice" on the sale value of the foxhound painting. However, the court did not find liability for wrongly identifying works of art. Instead, the court held, "The standard of duty of care allows the agent to present a different point of view, even a false one, if the agent does not present any point of view that is a true breach of duty of care."[44]

The high court merely examined whether the auctioneer could be held liable for failing to find that the painting might have been painted by George Stubbs. In theory, if hidden properties are discovered, auctioneers will usually investigate further. To determine whether the auctioneer was likely to have been aware that the painting had been painted by George Stubbs, the high court assessed the extent to which the auctioneer had exercised his duty of care in appraising the painting and whether that had complied with legal standards. In this assessment, the High Court did not review the accuracy of the findings because "an assessment is a statement of opinion and

[43] Luxmoore-May and another v Messenger-May Baverstock (afirm), Court of Appeal, Civil Division,19901AllER1067, 19, 901 WLR1009CA1989.

[44] Luxmoore-May and another v Messenger-May Baverstock (afirm), Court of Appeal, Civil Division, [1990] 1AllER1067, 1076b.

judgment, and this statement is controversial most of the time." As Lord justice Mann argued, "the question of whether the dogs were in fact painted by George Stubbs... There is no need to answer... Identification must remain a mystery." Instead, the high court considered whether, through consultants, the auctioneer had inadvertently failed to spot that the painting might have been painted by George Stubbs.[45]

The High Court first accepted the auctioneer's claim that it qualified as a general practising auctioneer, thereby establishing the scope of the standard of duty of care to which a trustee was entitled to expect. Second, the court held that the auctioneers' advisers should have asked their experts to look at the painting when they displayed it at Christie's appraisal counter, because those experts were more likely to discover that it was actually painted by GeorgeStubbs.[46] In the end the court of Appeals held that no one could expect additional artistic knowledge from a local auctioneer, especially if that knowledge was supported only by his own artistic adviser. The trial judge's opinion was that an unreasonably high standard of care was imposed on the auctioneer. To expect Christie's to provide an expert opinion for every piece of art on display, given the large amount of pro bono appraisal it provides, is also to impose an unreasonably high standard of care on the auctioneer. Of course, there is no clear ruling that Christie's is not liable to the requestor of the valuation when such a free valuation is carried out, but it is liable if such a free valuation is not carried out. In summary, the standard of care of an auctioneer in general practice is differentiated according to the expertise he or she provides.

Moreover, "compliance with the required standards is judged on the basis of the actual situation faced by the actual evaluator in the actual situation, not on the basis of ex post facto interests".[47] The diligence of the auctioneer must be determined by whether a professional body supports the auctioneer's opinion. In luxmore-may v. Messenger-May Baverstock, the reason the judge held that the evidence was insufficient to show that "a qualified appraiser could find two foxhound paintings by George Stubbs" was that there was a wide range of opinions among experts at auction.

Although the ruling was in favor of local auctioneers, the case caused consternation among auctioneers because it showed that, in some circumstances, a false identification could constitute a breach of an auctioneer's duty of reasonable care. Nor did the ruling address the circumstances under which local auctioneers might be held liable for faulty appraisals.

In addition, some scholars argue that Luxmoore-May v. Messenger-May Baverstock is a special case that does not have universal applicability.[48] On the one hand, some scholars argue that there is no comparison between the appraisals of local auction houses and the free appraisals of large auction houses, because the latter

---

[45] Luxmoore-May and another v Messenger-May Baverstock (afirm), Court of Appeal, Civil Division, [1990] 1AllER1067, 1083b.

[46] Luxmoore-May and another v Messenger-May Baverstock (afirm), Court of Appeal, Civil Division, [1990] 1AllER1067, 1078d.

[47] Luxmoore-May and another v Messenger-May Baverstock (afirm), Court of Appeal, Civil Division, [1990] 1AllER1067, 1081a.

[48] Mackay, James, Halsbury's Laws of England, vol. 2(3): Auction, 4thed. Butter worths Lexis Nexis, 2003, p. 238.

are aimed at attracting potential customers rather than other auctioneers who may bring legal liability.[49] On the other hand, according to auction practice, auctioneers usually do not disclose to their clients the advice of experts or consultants during the appraisal process, and in this case the defendant auctioneer did so. Technically, expert consultants are the auctioneer's agent, not the trustee's. Therefore, the auctioneer is not vicariously liable for the negligence of the expert consultant.[50]

From a judgment standpoint, LuxMoore-May v. Messenger-MayBaverstock May represent a trend in which litigant owners of potentially valuable art or antiques are more likely to be expected by law to seek the help of a professional auction house than a general licensed auction house.

(2) **Duty of care standards for professional auction houses**

As mentioned above, Christie's performs free inspections of lots, and with over the counter valuations, it is generally considered that this may not constitute a trust relationship. Without considering the bona fide donation in the service and the auctioneer's bona fide performance, the standard of the duty of diligence of the auctioneer must refer to the similar professional behavior of professionals with professional skills. The commonality of such professional behavior is that the professional behavior performed by the auctioneer is trusted by the inquiry.

Unless the auctioneer states, "the inquirer, after consulting with a person of special skill, is free to reject its conclusion in its entirety". The auctioneer may be liable for negligent misrepresentation due to economic loss caused to the information-seeking party even if the information is truthfully disclosed, whether orally or in writing. In such cases, the standard of care may be required to be lower than in the provision of normal services, or the burden on the auctioneer providing off-site valuations may be too heavy.

When both parties sign an entrustment contract, the auction house shall assume contractual obligations to the principal. Any breach of this obligation can be evaluated against the same criteria as local auction houses. That is, "whether the auction house gave an opinion to the principal, and whether this opinion was consistent with it, is a rational and competent opinion that other valuers working for international auction houses should have made based on the same information available to them in similar circumstances." Under the Luxmoore-May judgment, clients can expect a higher level of care from international auction houses. In some cases, however, the standard of this obligation may be difficult to determine.

In Thwaytes v Sotheby's, the Crown Court of the British High Court attempted to impose a standard of care on international auction houses. In the case, sotheby fell out with his client Lancelot Thwaytes when it sold an oil painting called "the carders sharps" for £42,000 in 2006. According to the client's instructions, the auction house. The painting is by Michelangelo Merisida Caravaggio disciple. In fact, however, the painting by Michelangelo Merisida Caravaggio himself was worth 10 million pounds

[49] Harvey and Franklin (2006, p. 278).

[50] Luxmoore-May and another v Messenger-May Baverstock (afirm), Court of Appeal, Civil Division[1990] 1AllER1067, 1081a.

at the same time. In its judgment, the Royal Court cited the Luxmoore-May argument that Sotheby's had a higher duty of care than local auction houses.[51]

The High Court, the Royal Court, held that a higher standard consisted of three elements: first, someone who submitted a work to an international auction house could expect it to be evaluated by a higher-quality expert, meaning three things: first, expertise in art history; Second, I am familiar with the styles and works of different artists. Finally, connoisseur's "eye". Second, an international auction house should properly examine the consignor's items and devote enough time to reach a relatively firm conclusion. The royal court also found that the local auction house in luxmoore-May had conducted only a cursory review, far short of what was required of Sotheby's. Third, it is unlikely that an international auction house "should not pay attention to the potential value of a painting because of its less than optimistic condition". This was also a factor in the negligence of the auction houses that the Court of Appeals found in LuxMoore-May.[52]

In Thwaytes v. Sotheby's, the Royal Court also acknowledged that given the current duopoly of auction houses, the implementation of the above standards is very difficult, "at least in the case of old master works, only Sotheby's and Christie's." (atleast as regards Old Masters namely Sotheby's and Christie's). 'Just because Christie's and Sotheby's can act in a particular way does not mean it is not negligent,' the court said after examining sotheby's actual appraisal and valuation process for commissioned paintings. 'Greater protection of client interests must be considered.' As a result, the court highlighted the difference between art appraisal practice and legal standards. Although the court was concerned about the protection of the interests of the parties, it ultimately ruled that the auction house had not taken unreasonable measures. In a later special case, the court legalized the auctioneer's appraisal process.[53]

In Coleridge v. Sotheby's, the UK High Court heard an action brought by the plaintiffs against the defendants for the misvaluation of the gold necklace "Coleridge Collar". In this case, Supt believed the gold necklace was made in the late seventeenth century and advised his client, Sir Coleridge, to sell it privately to interested buyers for 35,000 pounds. Sir Coleridge agreed and commissioned Sotheby's to sell the necklace for that price. The necklace later reappeared at Christie's auction, estimated at £200,000 to £300,000, and sold for £260,000 with the hammer down. So Sir Coleridge argues that Sotheby's wrongly identified the necklace as late seventeenth century and wrongly sold it for a private sale of £35,000 rather than auction it. Sir Coleridge argues that the color and workmanship of the necklace's gold was the standard used before 1576 and that Sotheby's would have drawn the right conclusion if it had exercised its duty of care.[54]

---

[51] Hedley Byrne v. Heller [1964] AC465 at 486, 502.

[52] Lancelot Thwaytes v. Sotheby's, [2015] EWHC36(Ch), Case No: HC-2012–000, 042, para.76.

[53] Lancelot Thwaytes v. Sotheby's, [2015] EWHC36(Ch), Case No: HC-2012–000, 042, para.79.

[54] Coleridge v. Sotheby's, [2012] EWHC370(Ch) Official Transcript, 2012 WL608706. para.53.

A curious detail of the Coleridge case about the standard of care expected of international auction houses is that after the gold necklace was sold to a private buyer, the buyer was appraised and valued by another international auction house, which considered the necklace to be a more valuable Tudor work. Christie eventually accepted the more valuable conclusion. Will the auction house's standards of appraisal and valuation become the standard of care expected by international auction houses? According to Coleridge v. Sotheby, the answer is "not necessarily". In fact, an appraisal by an auction house may not automatically be carried out in accordance with statutory standards of care.[55]

In the Coleridge case, the court avoided taking Christie's appraisal and valuation standards as an expected standard of care. Instead, Sir Coleridge had to prove sotheby's was wrong to date the necklace to the late seventeenth century. In addition to providing evidence of error identification, Sir Soon must also according to the principle of "advantage evidence (the balance of probabilities)" proof in the position of the consultant experts on any kind of appraiser, Coleridge Collar was or could have been made before 1576.

Ultimately, based on expert evidence presented at the trial, the court found that Sotheby's had not breached its duty of care by concluding that the necklace was seventeenth century.

Although Sotheby's appraisal did not breach a duty of care, the court further examined whether another competent Sotheby's auctioneer's estimate of the sale price for a private sale was appropriate. During the trial, the auctioneer made it clear that if she had been asked to submit a private sale price, she would have followed Sotheby's practice of offering double the lowest auction estimate and that she had offered £50,000, £15,000 more than she had told Sir Coleridge. The court accepted the figure sotheby's would have reported if it had acted as it was supposed to. As a result, the court found that Sir Coleridge was entitled to an understated sum of £15,000.[56]

In conclusion, in judging whether an international auction house has fulfilled its duty of care, case law has established the following standard: the auctioneer is expected to perform the duty of care when performing an appraisal under the same circumstances. Courts have consistently held that an auctioneer needs to exercise a duty of care only if other qualified experts are able to reach the same conclusion. In other words, if the standard assumes that the academic community agrees on some or all of Coleridge Collar's attributes, the court in the Coleridge case will adopt a scheme that takes into account the interests of all parties when reviewing the reasonableness of auction house appraisals.

[55] Coleridge v. Sotheby's, [2012] EWHC370(Ch) Official Transcript, 2012 WL608706. para.57.

[56] Coleridge v. Sotheby's, [2012] EWHC370(Ch) Official Transcript, 2012 WL608706. para.58.

3.2 The Auctioneer's Express Guaranty Obligations

Case histories in both the United States and the United Kingdom include cases concerning the liability of a broker, auctioneer, or dealer who sells a work of misidentified art.[57] The legal theory behind these cases encompasses both tort law and contract law. Disappointed buyers often Sue sellers for fraud and misrepresentation or breach of "express warranties" given to buyers by sellers.[58,59] Courts rarely clearly distinguish between these theoretical bases based on the concepts of tort and contract.

Jendwine v. Slade, perhaps the earliest case on the subject, established the traditional approach to the problem.[60] The defendant sold the plaintiff two paintings which he claimed to be originals but which were in fact reproductions. The plaintiff sued for fraud, and the court resolved the question of whether the appearance of the artist's name in the catalog constitutes an express warranty or a description and opinion by the buyer for reference only. The court held that the catalog did not constitute an express warranty because the artist had long since died, and it was impossible to determine whether the paintings were originals. The catalog indicates only the seller's opinion that the work is original and that the buyer's independent judgment is required. The court concluded that "if the seller stated only what he believed, he may not have committed fraud."[61] Therefore, the Jendwine case focuses on whether

---

57 Although the terms Broker, Dealer and Auctioneer are often appear synonymous in everyday life, their legal meanings are different. An auctioneer, as defined by Black's Law Dictionary, is an "a person authorized or available by law to sell other land or articles at public auction and receive commissions or remuneration from others." (The same below) the difference is also made between the auctioneer and the broker, the former only has the right to sell, and the latter can both buy or sell. A trader is "a person who buys for sale, not one who buys for hold or makes to sell. "Finally, a broker is defined as" an agent employed to trade and contract to be paid".Bryan A. Garne. Black's Law Dictionary 11th Edition. New York: Thomson Reuters West.2019.P.304 Auctioneers and brokers are bound to the law of agency. The term "seller" is used in this article to refer to "trader," "auctioneer" and "broker".

58 Common-law fraud actions generally require proof of several elements that are stated differently in different judicial judgments. These elements include: (1) defendant had a statement of material facts; (2) defendant's statement was false; (3) the judge was convinced that the statement was untrue; (4) the judge was convinced that plaintiff acted on the false statement (also called scienter); (5) plaintiffs proper reliance on the agent prejudiced plaintiff; and (6) plaintiff did not know that the statement was false and had reason to believe it was true. False representation is an integral part of the fraud; Harvey and Franklin (2006, p.189); However, the term is often alternating with fraud, depending on the different decisions of the court.

59 In the United States judgment, the use of the term "express security," because the main point of controversy in the suit usually gives to the seller exactly the express warranty, or the mere opinion. Black's Law Dictionary defines an express warranty as "a promise or agreement by the seller to have a certain quality to the goods sold or a good title to the seller. "A court also held that" the express warranty amounts to a promise that if the facts prove to be untrue, the express security compensates for any damages to the promisor… it is to relieve the express guarantor from the burden of finding the truth himself." Bryan (2019).

60 Harvey and Franklin (2006, p. 276).

61 Harvey and Franklin (2006, p. 276–277).

the seller makes an express guarantee to the buyer or merely represents an opinion. The court held that if the statement was an opinion, the seller was not liable for any fraud as long as the seller actually believed the statement to be true.[62]

In two later decisions, Lomi v. Tucker and DeSewhanberg v. Buchanan, the court held that if the seller's representations formed an express warranty, the buyer could rescbe the sale or retain the painting and pay the seller only what the jury thought the copy was worth.[63,64,65] In Pennell v. Woodburn, "the seller expressly guaranteed the painting to the buyer and the buyer resold it to a second buyer, who sued for recovery of costs against the first buyer of the guarantee." Through the second buyer's lawsuit, the first buyer is allowed to recover all costs from the seller.[66]

Finally, in Power v. Barham, the court held that it was up to the jury to decide whether a judgment constituted an express warranty or expression of opinion.[67] In this case, the seller issued a receipt to the buyer that read: "Four Paintings, Scene of Venice, Canaletto, 1601". The jury found that a contract had been entered into between the buyer and the seller for Canaletto's oil painting and that the receipt was therefore an express warranty, not merely an explanation or statement of opinion. The buyer's written receipt supports the express warranty, although it is issued to the buyer at the end of the sale. This result differs from the Jendwine case, where an auction catalog for buyers to study before an auction does not constitute an express warranty.

The court distinguished between the results of Power and Jendwine because in Power, the artist had recently died, so the seller should have been able to determine the provenance of the painting. In the Jendwine case, however, the artist died much longer, making it impossible to determine the provenance of the painting. Therefore, to obtain common-law relief, the disappointed buyer must prove that the seller's representation constituted an express warranty, not merely an expression of opinion, and that the seller knew at the time of sale that the representation was false. These early English decisions summed up the common law basis for distinguishing representation from express warranty.

62 Harvey and Franklin (2006, p. 278).

63 Kendall (1997, p. 326–328).

64 Hodge M. Malek., ed. Phipsonon Evidence, 17thed. London: Sweet & Maxwell/Thomson Reuters, 2010, p. 256.

65 Kendall (1997, p. 278).

66 Philip (1995).

67 Francis V. O'Connor. "Authenticating the Attribution of Art–Connoisseurship and the Law in the Judging of Forgeries, Copies, and False Attribution." In Ronald D. Spencer: The Expert versus the Object–Judging Fakes and False Attributions in the Visual Arts, New York: Oxford University Press, 2004, p. 79.

3.2.1 Express Guarantee System in Statutory Law

New York is recognized as the art capital of the Western Hemisphere and is home to many of the largest and most prestigious auction houses. Because of the frequency of accidents and the apparent inadequacy of common law contract and tort theories concerning the practices of various art auction houses and dealers, The State of New York hopes to regulate the conduct of art auction houses and dealers through statute law. New York state now has a comprehensive statutory system that attempts to regulate several aspects of the art market.

The New York Sales Act was perhaps the first written law to regulate the art market. In Weisz v. Parke-Bernet Galleries, Inc., the court considered the two paintings' express warranties of authenticity.[68] Mr. Weisz and Mrs. Schwartz bought paintings in 1961 and 1964, respectively. The paintings are listed in the auction catalog of parke-bernet galleries as works by RaoulDufy. A few years later, the district attorney's office discovered that the paintings were fakes and notified the buyers. The buyer sued Parke-Bernet, claiming that the auction catalog listing constituted an express warranty under the New York Sales Act. Parke-bernet argues that the auction rules in the catalog include exceptions for authenticity and authorship. Therefore, two questions are raised: whether the plaintiff knew or should have known about the existence of the exemption clause and whether the clause is valid if the plaintiff knew or should have known.[69]

The trial court concluded that Mr. Weisz was unaware of the disclaimer because he lacked the relevant knowledge to be bound by the terms of the contract. In contrast, the court found that although Mrs. Schwartz did have actual knowledge, the terms were invalid because Parke-Bernet had intended the plaintiff to rely on its superior knowledge and experience, and the design of the catalog auction catalog encouraged the plaintiff to believe in the authenticity of the items. The court found that Parke-Bernet had failed to adequately declare and emphasize this disclaimer, particularly because the auctioneer had not separately listed the specific disclaimer at the beginning of the auction. The court held that this was consistent with "an act consistent with the law as a whole, which reflects the growing need for fair dealing between parties with fundamental inequalities in knowledge, expertise, or economic power."[70] The trial court placed an almost absolute burden on the auction house to compensate the buyer because it was theoretically in a position of superior knowledge to determine the authenticity of the work of art, and the buyer relied on that expertise. Although Parke-Bernet believed the works to be authentic at the time of the sale, absolute responsibility remains.

However, the Court of Appeals reversed this decision for three main reasons. First, neither the common law nor the law of sale in force at the time of an auction recognizes that the seller's representations create an express guarantee of authenticity or copyright. Second, Parke-Bernet expressly disclaims any express warranty, express

---

[68] Ormrod (2008, p. 237).

[69] See Footnote 68.

[70] See Footnote 68.

or implied, as well as any representation of the authenticity of the painting as the work of an artist. In the end, the court found that the auctioneer did not commit fraud or misrepresentation because Parke-Bernet did not knowingly deceive; it is the buyer who bears the risk that the appraisal may be wrong. The court found that "buyers who failed to act with caution when they entered into the wrong contract will be dismissed."[71] This decision largely follows the common law analysis of Jendwine v. Slade, which focuses more on the distinction between express warranties and statements of opinion and on the theory of caveat emptor.

In Vom Lehn Astor Art Galleries, Ltd. In this case, the court sought to avoid the common law theory of deception and misrepresentation and to provide some relief to plaintiffs when the circumstances were particularly unreasonable.[72] In this case, the plaintiff agreed to pay $67,000 for 20 jade carvings that the seller stated were hand-carved from the Ming Dynasty. In fact, the carvings have none of those features and are worth approximately $15,000. The court rejected the plaintiffs' claim of fraudulent misrepresentation because they did not require a complete description of the engraving on the sales and appraisal documents. Under section 2-302 of the UCC, the court dismissed the defendant's claim to execute the remainder of the contract and demand further payment on the ground that the price charged was unreasonable. However, the court cannot award any damages under this clause.

Nonetheless, the court held that under New York's Door-to-door Sales Act, the plaintiffs could reject the entire sale and recover their deposit and costs. Since the defendant did not notify the buyer of its right to rescind, the court holds that the buyer may cancel the transaction at any reasonable time by giving notice to the seller. Therefore, the plaintiff rescinded the contract entirely without any claim of fraud or misrepresentation. However, the door-to-door sales Act provides limited precedent or protection for buyers who rely on the seller's representations (whether express warranties or expressions of opinion) to judge the nature and quality of works of art, subject to the seller's restrictions on auctions outside their place of business.

The UCC represents a comprehensive legal framework governing the sale of goods. While there are no published cases explaining the specific circumstances in which the UCC does not apply to the sale of art, there is considerable disagreement among legal scholars as to whether the UCC provides adequate protection to purchasers of false or counterfeit art. One view is that UCCs' express warranty protects consumers of art from sellers who knowingly pass off a fake as original and art dealers who naively sell what they believe to be genuine.[73] The other view is that UCCs do nothing to help buyers when they are in trouble.[74]

---

[71] See Footnote 68.

[72] Eric B. Rasmusen and Ian Ayres. "Mutual and Unilateral Mistake in Contract Law." Journal of Legal Studies 22, no. 2.P332–333.

[73] Herbert E. Nass., etal. "Art Law: Rights and Liabilities of Creators and Collectors." Womans Art Journal NO.9.11989; Feldman, Franklin and S. E. Weil. "Artworks: law, policy, practice." Ztschrift Für Allgemne Mikrobiologie NO.10., 8.1970.

[74] Hobart, A Giant Step Forward-NewYork Legislation on Sales of Fine Art Multiples, Art &The Law NO.261, 1983.

The protection of UCC for consumers is mainly reflected in the express guarantee clauses in sections 2-313, the implied express guarantee clauses in sections 2-314 and 2-315, and the exemption clauses stipulated in sections 2-316. UCC believes that the basis for the protection of art buyers lies in the confirmation of the purpose and motivation of consumers who purchase art works and the existence of relevant express warranties. section 2-313 of UCC provides that an express warranty can be established in three ways. One is that "the seller makes a confirmation or promise to the buyer of the facts relating to the goods, and such confirmation or promise forms the basis of all or part of the transaction". The second is "any description of goods forming the whole or part of the basis of the transaction"; the third is "the sample or model that forms the basis of all or part of the transaction".[75] However, the application of these provisions in the art trade has encountered some problems.

The first question that requires interpretation is whether the buyer must rely on the seller's representation to prove the existence of an express warranty. On the other hand, the problem requires the clause to say that the auctioneer's promise or description of goods is "part of the basis of the transaction". There are large differences in whether this expression requires the buyer to actually rely on the seller's description to complete the transaction or whether the UCC eliminates the requirement of "dependability". It appears from commentary 3 to sections 2–313 that the dependency requirement is eliminated.[76] However, several cases and scholars have argued that "transaction basis" is a redefinition of the "dependent nature" of the UCC prior to the law.[77] Support for this conclusion comes mainly from the explanation in remark 1 that the express guarantee "relies more on each consensual 'compromised' aspect".[78] If relying on the seller's representation is a necessary element of the buyer's claim, then some professional buyers, such as museums, galleries and major collectors, have relatively equal information access and relatively equal bargaining position with the seller of the art, so they cannot establish an express guarantee.

Whether reliance is an element of an express guarantee, disappointed buyers also have larger hurdles to overcome. Article 2-313 (2) states: "A mere confirmation by the seller of the value of the goods, or a mere opinion or appraisal of the

75 American Law Society, United States State Law Committee: United States Unified Commercial Code and its Official Review (Volume I), Sun Xinqiang, Beijing: Renmin University of China Press, 2005, p. 94.

76 American Law Society, American United State Law Committee: The American Uniform Commercial Code and its Official Review (Volume I), translated by Sun Xinqiang, p. 95.

77 For example, DuBoff believes that the buyer can not rely on the seller's statement only in face-to-face negotiations, but the buyer must show a knowledge of the seller's statement. Leonard D. DuBoff. "Controlling the Artful Con: Authentication and Regulation." Hastings L.j.NO.27.1975.P.247; Hobart argues that UCC section 2-313 eliminates the certification requirement of fraudulent intent to defraud sellers, commit intentional fraud, and buyer trust. Hobart, A Giant Step Forward-New York Legislation on Sales of Fine Art Multiples, Art &The Law NO.261, 1983 P.336.

78 American Law Society, United States State Law Committee: United States Unified Commercial Code and its Official Review (Volume I), Sun Xinqiang, Beijing: Renmin University of China Press, 2005, p. 95.

goods, shall not constitute a guarantee."[79] Under the latter part of this clause, the description of the seller's comments and judgments with respect to the goods does not in fact constitute an express warranty. Unfortunately, this oversight seems to go back to the common law distinction that Jendwine and Power considered. Any seller may attempt to evade responsibility for the authenticity of a work of art by claiming that the determination of the author is an opinion rather than an express warranty. Although the description of a painting as "Picasso" would normally constitute the dominant description, ambiguous statements in the auction catalog, such as "attributed to Picasso", may not create an express warranty that the painting is by "Picasso". Since it can never be absolutely certain that the work of a deceased artist was created by the artist himself, any statement by the seller can be characterized as a statement of opinion.[80] Of course, there are also scholars who believe that when the seller's statement increases the purchase price of the artwork, even if the statement is considered only an opinion, if the opinion turns out to be incorrect, the seller should be held responsible.[81] Nevertheless, there is considerable disagreement as to whether such an analysis of sections 2-313 will ultimately apply to the sale of works of art.

Second, the implied warranties of marketability in sections 2-314 May have limited applicability to the sale of works of art.[82] Although the implied express warranty applies to the seller, do not know the art of any defects can also be applied to art failed to meet vendibility standard but the seller fails to find defects, but if the works of art in the art market made a deal for a long time and did not find its lack of authenticity, it may be no longer applicable implied express warranty terms.[83] At the same time, the implied express guarantee also limits the scope of applicable subjects, that is, the seller must be "a merchant engaged in certain goods transaction". Therefore, private collectors or museums engaged in piecemeal sales of works of art would not be eligible, and the subject of the provision might even be limited to art dealers or auctioneers who regularly deal in works of a particular period or artist. The more important question is how to judge whether the goods are "used for ordinary purposes."[84] If the purpose of owning a work of art is to enjoy its general aesthetic value, rather than the special value of owning a particular work of art by a

---

79 See Footnote 79.

80 Leonard D. DuBoff. "Controlling the Artful Con: Authentication and Regulation." Hastings L.j.NO.27.1975.P.247.

81 Robert M. Jr. Kincaid, The Uniform Commercial Code Warranty Provisions and the Theory of Strict Liability in Tort as Solutions to Art Counterfeiting in Painting: A Critical Analysis, St. Louis U.L.J.NO.201976.P.189; Houseman, L. Currentpractices and problems in combatting illegality in the art market. Seton Hall Law Review, 12(3), 1982, P.178; Lawrence S. Bauman."Legal Control of the Fabrication and Marketing of Fake Paintings." Stanford Law Review 24.51972.P.267.

82 Uniform Commercial Code Warranty Solutions to Art Fraudand Forgery, 14 Wm. & Mary L. Rev.409. https://scholarship.law.wm.edu/wmlr/vol14/iss2/8.

83 Leonard D. DuBoff. "Controlling the Artful Con: Authentication and Regulation." Hastings L.j.NO.27.1975.P.247.

84 American Law Society, American United State Law Committee: The American Uniform Commercial Code and its Official Review (Volume I), translated by Sun Xinqiang, p. 95.

particular artist, then even misidentified or falsified works of art may be suitable for the common use of these commodities.[85]

Third, the implied warranties of specific use listed in sections 2-315 also rarely apply to the sale of works of art, since specific use does not mean that the buyer wishes to acquire a specific work of art by a specific artist. The "specific use" requirement is met only if the purpose of the purchase is to make a specific investment or complete a specific collection.[86]

At the same time, the UCC also stipulates and limits the exemption clause of goods sellers for express guarantees. Section 2-316 (1) of the exclusionary express warranty states that "words or acts that deny or limit an express warranty shall be void where such words or acts cannot be reasonably explained."[87] The basis of the express warranty can be said to be the "core description" or "the performance of the seller must conform to the sales claims of the underlying quality". Such an express warranty cannot be repealed even if the seller has acted in good faith but is unaware of the forgery or misidentification. The inspection of goods by the buyer does not exclude an express warranty. However, a work of art with obvious flaws, or a seller asking a buyer to inspect the work, may cause the buyer to notice that he or she bears the risk of defects in the work. Even so, this limitation on the exclusion clause would appear to deprive the buyer of additional protection, since it would be difficult to determine the seller's representation and cause express warranties.[88]

Finally, article 2-316 (2) of UCC once again protects the buyer by limiting the seller's exemption of implied terms by adding specific expressions and having to be conspicuously indicated in the exemption clauses.[89] The limitations of this section on implied express warranties may apply to the sale of works of art, like the sale of other goods, if the buyer can determine that an implied express warranty exists. If there are pure economic losses, the UCC also allows both parties to reach an agreement limiting the extent of the damage. For example, the buyer's remedies may be limited to returns and refunds.[90]

In 1966, New York issued a comprehensive "law of art and cultural affairs (New York ArtsandCultural Affairs Law)" to supplement the UCC, and according to the specific problems of industry of the art market, the solution was put forward.[91] Michigan subsequently enacted a regulation that was broadly similar to New York's

---

[85] Robert M. Jr. Kincaid, "The Uniform Commercial Code Warranty Provisions and the Theory of Strict Liability in Tort as Solutions to Art Counterfeiting in Painting: A Critical Analysis".

[86] Lawrence S. Bauman. "Legal Control of the Fabrication and Marketing of Fake Paintings".

[87] See Footnote 84.

[88] Leonard D. DuBoff. "Controlling the Artful Con: Authentication and Regulation. "Hastings L.j.NO.27.1975.P.247.

[89] See Footnote 84.

[90] American Law Society, American United State Law Committee: The American Uniform Commercial Code and its Official Review (Volume I), translated by Sun Xinqiang, p. 238.

[91] 《New York Arts and Cultural Affairs Law》 section 11.01-15.21。https://codes.findlaw.com/ny/arts-and-cultural-affairs-law/aca-sect-12-01.html.

Arts and Cultural Affairs Act in regulating the art market.[92] The first difference between the New York statute and the UCC is the creation of an express warranty. Section 13.01 (1) of the arts and cultural affairs act makes it clear that whenever an art merchant gives a buyer who is not an art merchant a written document as to the authorship of a work of art, that document is presumed to be part of the basis of the transaction and gives rise to an express warranty.[93] The Michigan statute takes the definition of an express warranty a step further by removing many of the ambiguities involved in determining whether a seller's statement constitutes an expression of opinion or an express warranty. The New York statute provides documentation to determine express warranties, even if the seller does not want to do so or maintains that it is "merely the opinion of the art dealer."[94] The most important thing about the Michigan statute as it relates to express warranties is that a "written document" includes not only a sale order or memorandum but also "a written or printed auction catalog or other prospectus to be sold."[95]

Notwithstanding the existence of an express warranty disclaimer in New York and Michigan statutes similar to section 2-316 (1) of the U.C.C., such disclaimer must be deemed reasonable and must be used in the specified language and be conspicuous.[96] Under The New York statute, an escape clause must clearly tell the buyer that "Seller assumes no risk, liability or obligation for the material facts stated." Furthermore, the immunity clause is invalid if the work of art is a forgery; 2. The relevant information provided on the sale date or delivery date is false, misleading or erroneous.[97] However, auction houses can circumvent this situation to some extent because they limit the conclusions of an artist or period through a complex system of art terminology that limits their liability in the event of misidentification.[98] One might wonder how well potential buyers understand these terms. Sophisticated buyers who need the least protection are most likely to benefit the most from differences in these terms, while less sophisticated buyers are unlikely to benefit unless they are already well informed about the information. Although the intent of these laws is clearly to clarify the application of UCC express warranties in the sale of works of art and to

---

92 《Michigan Compiled Laws》 sectios 442.321 to 422.325 http://www.legislature.mi.gov/(S(gyvoueb1xbb5zjbknl5ck21q))/mileg.aspx?page=GetObject&objectname=mcl-600-2155.

93 《New York Arts and Cultural Affairs Law》 Article 13.01, wherein the term art merchant is expressed in section 11,01 (2) of the Act as a person specializing or not specialized in art or art reproduction, or who believes he has the knowledge or skill unique to such work, or has such knowledge or skill because of an employed agent or other intermediary.

94 《Michigan Compiled Laws》 sections 442.322 (2) (a).

95 《Michigan Compiled Laws》 sections 442.321(1)(f).

96 《New York Arts and Cultural Affairs Law》 sections 13.01(4)(b)(i).

97 《New York Arts and Cultural Affairs Law》 sections 13.01(4), It is noteworthy that section 2 of section 4 (b) imposes a very strict burden upon the art merchant under which his exemption will be deemed unreasonable if the art is proved fake and not clearly shown in the description of the work; but article 3 of section 4 (b) provides that the parties intended that the information of the goods was false and only by proving that the merchant provided incorrect information on the date of the sale or exchange. In contrast, art merchants are not liable if the false information was not determined after the transaction. From this view, section 442.323 of the Michigan statute had a similar effect.

98 《New York Arts and Cultural Affairs Law》 sections 13.01(2).

make such applications more effective in protecting consumers, some scholars also say that these laws are a duplication of UCCs, and some even argue that they hinder the normal operation of the art market.[99,100]

The New York state statute was used only once to more accurately explain the application of the UCC to the issues raised by art exchanges. In Dawson v. G. Malina, Inc., the plaintiff purchased eleven pieces of Chinese ceramics and jade carvings from the defendant. After consulting with experts who doubted the authenticity of one of the pieces, Dawson tried to rescind the purchase. The defendant agreed to return some of the items, but the disposition of five of them remained in dispute. At the heart of the case is whether the defendants breached express warranties for the sale of the five disputed items. Dawson believed that g. Malina, Inc. constituted an express warranty on the goods by the description of letters, invoices and sales receipts sent to him by G. Malina, Inc.[101] Dawson, providing the legal basis of general commercial law (New York General Business Law): 219-c is New York, "from New York commercial code (New York Commercial Code) interests" in section 2-313 a.[102] The court interpreted this statute to remove the uncertainty as to whether any art dealer's statement of authorship constitutes an affirmative of fact, so that the UCC provisions can be applied to determine whether there is an express warranty or merely an expression of opinion. In fact, the New York statute is very clear that the defendant acknowledges that the description of the item constitutes an express express warranty, and the other issue in this case is whether the description given is manifestly incorrect and thus constitutes a breach of an express warranty.

To determine whether an express warranty has been violated, the court must decide the appropriate standard of proof and determine which party bears the burden of proof. Dawson argued that he could only show that the artwork did not in any way fit the description given and that the defendant argued that the applicable standard should take into account the various imprecisions inherent in artwork identification. The court found that the plaintiff had the burden of proof and held that the standard of proof at the time the defendant made the statement whether it was incorrect should be weighed by expert testimony at trial. Using the testimony of expert witnesses submitted by both parties, the Court concluded that three of the five express warranties for the disputed items were not actually justified and that the defendants had therefore breached those express warranties.

---

99 DuBoff argues that New York State statutes are more comprehensive in consumer protection than the UCC, particularly reflected in limiting the ability of art merchants to reject an express warranty, Leonard D. DuBoff. "Controlling the Artful Con: Authentication and Regulation."; Peter Barry maintains that the express warranty provision of the New York State statute shifts the burden of proving authenticity from buyer to seller, eliminating the uncertainty created by the UCC, Skolnik. "Art Forgery: The Art Market and Legal Considerations." Nova L.j (1983), 339–351.

100 Akst argued that UCC is very similar to New York State statutes in regard to consumer protection, except that the latter is easier for art merchants to waive express guarantees, Akst (2019).

101 David Ormrod. "The Art Tradeandits Urban Context: England and the Netherlands Compared, 1550–1750.".

102 《New York Arts and Cultural Affairs Law》 sections 13.01.

The Michigan arts code is almost identical to the New York arts act, and it has a similar application in Lawson v. London Arts Group. In this case, the plaintiff purchased $29,000 in chalk art, which the defendant identified as an original work by Frederick Remington. A few years after the sale, the buyer began to doubt the authenticity of the work and sued after experts confirmed their suspicions. At the time of the trial, Frederick Remington's original work was priced between $150,000 and $170,000. The court settled three issues in the lawsuit. First, the court held that the defendant's statement: "The Indian brave… An original work identified as having been painted by Frederick Remington in 1901" constitutes statutory express warranty. Second, the court affirmed the jury's verdict that the defendant knew or should have known that the painting was a copy but failed to authenticate it, so the express warranty was false. Because the express warranty was false, the plaintiff was entitled to full restitution of damages, in which case the jury awarded damages of $140,000.[103]

The third and most complex issue is which statute of limitations applies. The court qualifies the dealer's express warranty standard as quality or fitness and applies a four-year period of proof. Therefore, the calculation does not begin until the plaintiff begins to doubt the authenticity of the work. The relief of damages and the long period of proof give the purchaser important additional protection and, in the absence of legal requirements, a significant departure from the accepted practice of dealers and auction houses. Dawson's case shows that although the UCC itself may not be able to deal with the problems existing in the art market in full, in view of the art market after the special legislation, such as New York and Michigan's existing law, UCC may to clarify the auctioneer or traders to make a major contribution on the responsibility of the buyer, especially in the case of express warranty and false statements.[104]

In short, the common law protections available to consumers in the UCC alone are very limited. Such protection depends on the distinction between making an opinion and making an express undertaking. Sellers of art have generally succeeded in claiming that their statements about authenticity and authorship are merely opinions and not express warranties. Although UCC has been adopted in almost every state, it does not go beyond common law provisions in this particular area, requiring statutory or enactment to raise issues requiring additional consumer protection.

3.2.2 Theoretical Analysis of the Regulatory Path of the American Art Market

Due to the agency and trust relationship between the auctioneer and the original owner or trustee of the artwork, the interests of the owner are properly protected by law. However, it appears that buyers of works of art purchased through intermediaries do not receive equal protection. Because the auctioneer is the agent of the owner or

[103] William (2002).

[104] David Ormrod. "The Art Tradeandits Urban Context: England and the Netherlands Compared, 1550–1750".

principal, he has no special obligation to the buyer. If the buyer's representation is inaccurate, the most common law and statutory law require the buyer to prove that the seller provides an accurate express warranty. Only regulations in New York and Michigan that clearly go beyond UCC are particularly faced with the particular problems and difficulties posed by art market practices.[105]

Although the terms "dealer" and "auctioneer" may be used interchangeably at the beginning of this article, the traditional distinction between these terms may need to be introduced at this point. Art dealers typically buy works of art from the owner or artist for a certain price and then sell them to the purchaser in their own name, rather than on behalf of the original owner or artist. Works of art sold in this way are usually thought to fetch a higher price than they would in a public auction. Although the dealer as owner has a clear financial interest in the artwork, he or she also has a higher standard of obligation to ensure the title and authenticity of the artwork. This may be seen as an offset against higher prices, in exchange for which buyers can count on and reasonably expect greater protection from dealers.

Auction houses, on the other hand, generally do not buy works of art, so they have no direct financial interest in the work. Its financial interest is based entirely on the commission it earns from selling the item, but the commission will be higher if the item is sold at a higher price. The price may be lower than if the same item were sold through a dealer, but the buyer takes a greater risk on the authenticity of the artwork.

This dichotomy can also be reflected in considering whether the term "merchant" used in the UCC applies equally to dealers and auctioneers. Section 2-104 (1) of the UCC defines "merchant" as "a person engaged in the business of trading in a certain class of goods or otherwise demonstrating by professional connection that he has expertise or skill in the goods or practices involved in the exchange". One question raised by this definition is whether dealers or auctioneers can be regarded as dealers associated with all types of works of art and antiquities or just those of a particular period or genre. More important, however, is whether an auctioneer is considered an art dealer—that is, an art dealer with special knowledge or skill in art—or simply an art dealer familiar with auction practice, according to the UCC definition.[106]

Nevertheless, this distinction between dealers and auctioneers disappears for several reasons. First, the differences between the way dealers and auction houses do business are blurred by several changes in accepted practice. Auction houses buy works of art for resale under their own names and thus take a direct financial interest in the sale, although they must notify potential buyers before the sale. Dealers and galleries, on the other hand, provide them with consigned items that operate in a similar system to auction houses. The New York and Michigan statutes acknowledge this fact, explicitly applying their standards uniformly to the generic term "art dealer", which includes dealers, galleries and auction houses. These developments

---

[105] Meyer, Fora National Art Registry, N.Y. Times, July 30, 1986, at A22, col.1.

[106] Whether this liability is based on identifying Sotheby's actions as fraudulent and false statements, and perhaps in violation of the New York City's ordinance regulating the auction houses for, or on higher tariffs cannot be determined.

have led at least one commentator to conclude: "Auction houses must be regulated in the same way as dealers and galleries.

This subdivision of the practical distinction between dealers and auctioneers is reflected in the elimination of the legal distinction between the consequences applicable to their respective roles. As discussed before, the court in Cristallina and Rothko two ruling of remedial measures, involving dealers and auctioneers, buyers and all the people, is basically the same, that is to say, the court give the injured party to choose remove or fully expected damage compensation, and according to the value of art appreciation or depreciation for these damages. A comparison of all four decisions suggests that the relationships between dealer and owner, dealer and buyer, and auction house and owner should follow the same legal framework. The only missing piece in this quartet is the relationship between the auction house and the buyer. The Abrams case may have clarified that relationship, but not because of an out-of-court settlement. However, the judge's opinion in granting the preliminary injunction may indicate a willingness to impose a specific obligation on the purchaser of the auction house.

The emergence of these judgments, together with the narrowing of the actual differences between dealers and auctioneers, may lead to the development of a single theory of potential liability that applies equally to dealers and auctioneers and will regulate the relationship between dealers and owners and buyers of works of art. Several such theories may be presented, and the strengths and weaknesses of each will be discussed in turn.

The first theory is based on the agency principle. As previously considered, the auction house, acting as the owner's agent, has a clear fiduciary duty to all. This theory also describes the relationship between art dealers and buyers as agency. Therefore, the art dealer will act as an agent for both parties. The main objection to this agency relationship is that there is considerable potential for conflicts of interest if the auctioneer is both the owner's agent and the buyer's agent.

The answer to this objection might be that buyers often rely on the expertise and reputation of the auctioneer, regardless of whether the law recognizes a formal agency relationship. Of course, in the sale of real estate, brokers who are identified as the seller's agent under traditional legal principles usually act on behalf of both the buyer and the seller, regardless of whether the law grants legal recognition of this dual relationship. However, recent decisions now recognize this duality, when the buyer effectively treats the broker as his or her agent, by imposing an agency relationship on the cobroker. The California Court of Appeals further characterized brokers as having a positive duty to investigate and disclose to buyers because of fiduciary obligations. In some unusual cases involving the art market, the auctioneer, the broker, and other employees of the auctioneer are also considered agents of the buyer. Extending such liability to art dealers in the form of fiduciary obligations would offer several advantages.

The second theory is strict liability based on corporate liability tort and best cost avoider theory. Policy considerations for the development of this theory are based on the unequal bargaining position between manufacturers or other individuals who place goods in commercial circulation and consumers of particular products. This principle also justifies the manufacturer's ability to avoid losses or absorb and apportion the inevitable costs of losses. Although this theory can solve some problems, a major difficulty lies in the nature of strict liability in tort theory. The judicial tendency is to limit its application to defects inherent in the product and unreasonable hazards involving personal injury or property damage, where pure economic losses would be regulated by commercial sales laws.

However, there is precedent for enforcing strict tort liability for pure economic loss caused by a misrepresentation made by a seller on movable property. The main source of this strict liability can be found in section 552D of "Tort Restatement (second)".[107] This is alongside sections 402A, which deals with defective products, and 402B, which deals with misrepresentations resulting in personal injury. However, such a precedent may provide inspiration for the development of a strict liability theory for misrepresentation in the sale of chattels in the context of the art market.

The policies that underlie this theory of strict liability will rely on the superior knowledge and expertise of art dealers. The premise is that merchants can be more sure of the authenticity of a work of art than purchasers can—whether through scientific testing, research, questioning ownership, or simply avoiding dubious claims about authenticity and attribution. In cases where a merchant makes a mistake (even if there is none), the merchant is better able to spread the cost across all buyers rather than imposing the full cost on a single buyer. Case and Menzelv Weiszv Parke Bernet Galleries, Inc. In the List, the lower court basically relies on the theory for the plaintiff, and risk is added to the auction house or dealer. The theory of strict liability may be particularly suited to solving problems in the art market because of the high degree of uncertainty involved in art appraisal. Professional skills are required to conduct appraisals, while the ultimate uncertainty of appraisals may put merchants putting art in the commercial stream in the best position to take the risk of error, avoidable or not, and spread those costs across all purchasers. When applied to the art market, this strict principle of liability therefore applies only to transactions between art dealers and nontraders. One could adopt the definitions laid out in the New York and Michigan statutes, perhaps with some modifications, to determine which buyers are considered art dealers.

This liability depends primarily on express warranties as defined in the New York and Michigan statutes. These statutes provide that express warranties are created by any mark or description of a work of art given in writing by the merchant of the art and are not denied or limited; however, this extension seems to apply only to authorship claims and not to other elements of the attributes of the work of art, such as the date and provenance of the object. It seems that this limitation should be eliminated under the strict principle of liability.

These regulations also allow merchants to include the term... in this express warranty As well as the customs at the time and place of sale and the use of the trade term.... The meaning of. The merchant is therefore responsible for explaining the technical terms and transactions used in the art market. The policy concept on which

[107] False representations of material facts are made to the public concerning the nature or quality of the chattel sold by advertising, labels or otherwise, even if not by fraudulent or negligent purchases.

the principle of strict liability is based appears to be better, as imposing an obligation on art dealers to interpret these provisions or simply using simple language, rather than imposing the responsibility on nontraders, in order to understand technical terms and trade practices.

A final important question that must be resolved is whether such guarantees can be denied or limited. It seems clear that disclaimers or disclaims containing instructions or qualifications should not be valid. Disclaimers or restrictions, for example, which could easily be incorporated in the instructions but appear at the front of the auction catalog, should be regarded as unreasonable and should not disclaim any express warranties arising from the instructions themselves.

The New York and Michigan statutes also hold that exceptions are invalid if the artwork is a forgery; 2. The relevant information provided on the sale date or delivery date is false, misleading or erroneous. Strict liability is therefore imposed only in cases where the artwork becomes counterfeit. If the appraisal is incorrect, the art dealer is liable only if it has previously established such inaccuracy. Nevertheless, one might think it reasonable to extend the strict liability for incorrect attribution when it is relatively easy for an art dealer to qualify identification with "maybe" or "maybe."

The main objection raised by this theory is fairness and economic utility in the context of the art market. In particular, auctioneers may argue that buyers are able to buy works more cheaply at auction, thus taking on the additional risk of misattribution of works of art. When a buyer buys work from an owner from a dealer rather than a commission and the agent acts on its own behalf as a seller, the buyer pays a premium and transfers the risk to the dealer. By limiting the auctioneer's liability, a system of choice can be preserved: buyers who are risk averse can buy from dealers, while buyers who want to bargain can take risks and buy from the auction house.

However, this dichotomy is breaking down, and even realistic case law often fails to draw a clear line between dealers, brokers, galleries and auction houses in regard to the art market. Furthermore, the truly immature buyer may not even know about this theoretical option when deciding to buy at auction. In these circumstances, it seems reasonable to impose strict express warranties on merchants of art.

3.2.3 Enlightenment of the Explicit Guarantee System of Art Auctions in China

Through the comparative study of the Anglo-American law system, we can find that the supervision of the Anglo-American law system on the art trading market mainly comes from two ways. One is to establish a special legal relationship between the auctioneer and the buyer by building a trust relationship. This path has something in common with the liability of experts to the third party. However, in the existing legal framework of China, the buyer needs to bear the burden of proving that the expert has made mistakes, and such mistakes reach the burden of proof that damages the interests of the third party, which is undoubtedly very difficult for some inexperienced buyers.

Another way is to give the auctioneer strict express guarantee liability, specifically, that is, the auctioneer to any nonprofessional buyer to make a written statement form the basis of the transaction contract, thus constituting an express guarantee. This approach is applied to the existing legal system of our country, which essentially clarifies the scope of application of Article 615 of the Civil Code. First, at the subject level, if the economic status of the seller shown in this article is significantly higher than that of the buyer, a relatively loose standard should be adopted in determining the "quality description" made by the seller. Second, the quality description made by the seller should include any written description.

Of course, both expert liability to third parties and breach of express warranties provide considerable protection to immature buyers participating in the art market. These two theoretical models can also be criticized for being fundamentally inconsistent with market reality. In the words of the New York Appellate Court in Weisz v. Parke-Bernet gallery, the buyers were "told that if they did not exercise caution despite all the warning signs, their deal would fail." According to this view, anyone committing to the arcadia of the art market—at high prices and with scant information—must assume the risks inherent in such exchanges.

Nevertheless, these very similar circumstances should prompt people to recognize that the art market is a lively and important part of the business transaction and that it needs to develop a flexible and realistic model to protect those consumers who enter the market.

References

Jean Baudrillard. The System of Things [M]. Trans. Lin Chi-ming. Taipei: Times Culture Press, 1997:84

Walter Benjamin. Enlightenment. Selected Writings of Benjamin [M]. Translated by Zhang Xudong and Wang Ban. Hong Kong: Hong Kong Oxford University Press.1998:218

Bullock, Reginald Jr. "Imposing the Underwriters' Duty of Care on Art Auctioneers." Cardozo Arts & Entertainment Law Journal 7 (1988–1989)

Fu Chaoqing. International Historical Preservation and Preservation: Charter, Declaration, Resolution and Proposal [M]. Taipei: Taiwan Architectural Culture Press, 2002:367

Chappuis, Christine, Authentication of work sofart: responsibility of the expert and qualification of the contract in Swiss law. Art Law vol. 19, 2007, 56

Chen Y X. Research on the appraisal function of art museums -- Taking the Palace Museum, Shibo and Hongxi as examples to discuss the appraisal function of art museum collections [D]. Institute of Museology, Tainan University of the Arts, 2001, 15–16

Civil Law Office, Legislative Affairs Commission, National People's Congress, et al. Auction Law Book [M]. Beijing: China Business Press. 1997:7–198

Garne, 2019.Bryan A. Garne. Black's Law Dictionary 11th Edition. New York: Thomson Reuters West.2019

Harvey and Meisel, 2006.Harvey, Brian W. and Franklin Meisel. Auctions Law and Practice. 3rd ed. Oxford: Oxford University Press, 2006

Lin Jiazhang. Research on comprehensive quality assurance System of criminal authentication-Analysis of the development model of criminal laboratory certification System [D]. Institute of Criminal Police research, Central Police University, 1999

Jisheng, 1990.Guo Jisheng. Art History and Art Criticism [M]. Taipei: Shulin Publishing Co., LTD., 1990:322
Karlen, 1986.Karlen, Peter H. "Fakes, Forgeries and Expert Opinions." Journal of Arts Management and Law 16, no.3 1986, P9–10
Kendall, John. "the Expert Determination: Its Use in Resolving Art and Antiquity Antiquity." [J] Art Antiquity and Law 2, No. 4 (December 1997)
Lerner, Ralph E. and Judith Bresler. Art Law -- The Guide for Collectors, Investors, Dealers and Artists. 3rd ed. New York City: Practising Law Institute, 2005
Leslie Kaufman Akst. "Regulation of the New York Art Market: Has the Legislature Painted Dealers in to a Corner?" Journal of Oral Surgery 30.2019, 78
Mold, 1995.Mold, Philip. Sleeper-In Search of Lost Old Masters. London: Fourth Estate, 1995. P89
Yuan Nanzheng. A review of the classification of cultural relics in mainland China [R]. Chiayi: International Symposium on The Classification of Antiquities.2006
Ormrod, David. "The Art Trade and Its Urban Context: England and the Netherlands, 1550 – 1750" [J] In Auctions, Agents and Dealers -- The Mechanisms of The Art Market 1660-1830, Edited by Jeremy Warren and Adriana Turpin, 11 -- 19. London: The Wallace Collection, 2008
Eric B. Rasmusen and Ian Ayres. "Mutual and Unilateral Mistake in Contract Law." Journal of Legal Studies 22, no. 2.P332–333
Wankang, 2005.Li Wankang. Introduction to Art Marketing [M]. Shanghai: Fudan University Press, 2005:15–17
Wenhe, 2008.Huang Wenhe. Decoding of Art Market and Investment [M]. Taipei: Artist Publishing House, 2008:14–31
William W. Stuart "Authenticity of Authorship and the Auction Market." Maine Law Review. NO. 54, 2002, p. 86-88
Liu Yajian. Analysis of problems and Management countermeasures of antique art appraisal Industry [J]. Collectors Circle, 2011 (2):113–115, 127. (in Chinese)
Dai Yongsheng. Swiss Debt Law [M]. Beijing: China University of Political Science and Law Press, 2016:32–257

Chapter 5
Exemption System of Art Auction Contract

Among many disputes involving art auctions, one kind of dispute is relatively large, involving the liability of defect guarantees of auctioneers and trustees, which is called a nonfidelity clause in the industry. This paper discusses this issue, including three parts: first, it introduces the legislation, industry regulations and typical cases of nonfidelity clauses; second, several theories related to nonfidelity clauses are expounded. Finally, several factors affecting the validity of nonfidelity clauses are analyzed, including the legal status of auctioneers, auction legal relations and the classification of bidders/buyers.

1 Commercial and Judicial Practice of Exemption System

1.1 Interpretation of Disclaimer Clause

According to paragraph 2 of Article 61 of the Auction Law, if an auctioneer and a trustee declare before an auction that they cannot guarantee the authenticity or the quality of an auction target, they shall not bear the liability of guaranteeing defects. This clause is the "nonfidelity clause". According to this paragraph, for the auction of works of art, as long as the auctioneer in a certain way (such as in the auction catalog to make a statement) cannot guarantee the authenticity or quality of the works of art as the auction target, do not have to assume the guarantee responsibility for the defects of the works of art. The purpose of this paragraph is to strike a reasonable balance between the rights and obligations of auctioneers because of the complexity and professionalism of art appraisal and evaluation. At the same time, however, if the application of the paragraph is not strictly restricted, it can become a shield for auctioneers to evade their responsibilities. Is the liability for guarantee of defects in this paragraph equivalent to the liability for guarantee of defects in the Contract part of the Civil Code (hereinafter referred to as "Contract Part")? Is it fair for the buyer to bear the entire risk of any flaws in the authenticity or quality of the work being sold?

Z. Zheng, *The Legal System of Art Auction in China*,
https://doi.org/10.1007/978-981-19-0128-7_5

Will the regulation encourage auctioneers to act irresponsibly, knowingly sell fake works, collude with their clients to sell fake works, or be indifferent to the quality of works of art? After the nonfidelity clause has the above legal basis, the major auction houses in the industry have refined it, mainly regulating it from the following three aspects. First, they stated that they will not bear the liability of warranty for defects. Second, bidders are required to confirm that they have understood and accepted the status quo of the artwork at their own risk and responsibility; Third, make it clear that the auction catalog does not constitute a guarantee of its contents.

1.2 The Nature and Dimension of Artwork

The works of art traded in the auction house, including but not limited to two large contents: one is the works of art under the "Works of Art Management measures", refers to the painting works, calligraphy and seal cutting works, sculpture works, art photography works, installation works, arts and crafts works and the limited copies of the above works; The other is art relics.

The essence of art consists of three levels. In the first place, a work of art belongs to a totality, that is, to the total works of the author. There are striking similarities between many of the works of an artist. Second, artists and their works are not isolated but belong to contemporaneous and contemporaneous art schools or art families. Third, the artistic family is also included in a broader overall, that is, its era or society. To understand a work of art, an artist, a group of artists, one must relate it to the spirit and customs of its time. Danner concludes, "The object of a work of art is to express some principal or projecting feature, that is, some important idea, more clearly and completely than the actual thing; To do this, a work of art must be a totality composed of many interconnected parts whose relations are systematically changed."

Art has three dimensions. The first is its original dimension. Traced back to the source, art is the artist's inner expression, using certain skills, combined with specific materials, the artist's mind to express the view of the world. The original attribute is concerned with the inner ideological, artistic and social nature of the artwork. The second is its economic dimension. Goods are not works of art, but works of art may be goods. When an artist creates a work of art, he or she may pursue economic or other purposes. Regardless of the purpose, once the artwork enters the circulation field, that is, there are buyers and sellers, and the circulation is carried out in society, then the economic attributes of the artwork will appear. Most works of art do not have a fair value, but some works of art, often traded on the auction market, produce an economic value that can be expressed through auction prices. The third is its legal dimension. Works of art should have material materials as the carrier, and these material materials themselves are the objects in the property law, existing owners, protected by law. After the creation of a work of art, in addition to ownership, there are other rights such as copyright. The legal attribute focuses on the civil and commercial subjects related to art works, their rights and obligations.

1.3 Authenticity of Works of Art

There are three terms associated with the authenticity of works of art, each with different meanings. First, authenticity means that the internal characteristics of a work should be consistent with the information expressed externally. In this sense, authenticity often corresponds to forgery. When viewing, the audience will of course assume that the artwork is the work of the artist himself. The beauty, perception and value of the work of art are greatly diminished by the knowledge that it has been created by someone else pretending to be the artist. Authenticity should be determined by the market, not the courts. Second, originality, as a concept of copyright law, means that a work originates from a particular author and is an original rather than a copy. From the point of view of copyright law, originality means that the work was originally created by the artist rather than copied from others. Third, attribution refers to the assignment of a work of art to a particular artist, period or geographical origin. The complexity of attribution lies in the fact that misattribution of artworks is not necessarily untrue, but misattribution can bring huge legal and economic impacts.

The Oxford English Dictionary defines forgery as a "fictitious invention" or "false production". Art theorists tend to describe forgery. One might describe the characteristics of forgery as (1) imitating something and (2) intending to deceive someone, or capable of deceiving someone, about the provenance of the work. Taking painting as an example, forgery may involve a job of copying an existing painting as far as possible or even copying the original artist's signature. In most cases, the person who created the work intended to convince others that the copy was in fact the original. This type of forgery can be called "deceptive copying". However, people who copy do not always want to cheat. Another type of forgery can be called "honest reproduction". For example, the poster is a copy, the museum that made the poster does not have the intention to deceive, and no one can mistakenly think that the poster is the original painting. The poster is "fake" because it is not "real", but no one expects it to be real. Because "fake" is less pejorative than "counterfeit," we can use the word "fake" as an abbreviation for honest reproduction and "counterfeit" as a shorthand for deception. Thus, it can be seen that the "fake" in true and false focuses on the fake copy, and the fake copy (that is, "fake") is obviously different from the honest copy (that is, "fake"). Forgery is immoral and violates moral and legal norms.

To appraise art and antiques, experts use three main attributes: visual judgment, historical documents or provenance, and scientific analysis. No tool is perfect enough by itself. Instead, they complement each other. The results based on connoisseurs' opinions should therefore be supported by archival evidence or scientific reports.

1.4 Typical Cases

Although there is no unified legislation, in judicial practice, there have been a number of cases involving the nonfidelity of auction houses.

In the appeal of the auction contract dispute between Su Minluo and Xiao Fuyuan et al., the plaintiff bought an oil painting pond by Wu Guanzhong at the hammer price of 2.3 million yuan, but it was later found that the painting might be a forgery. Then, the plaintiff found the painter himself, and the painter to draw inscribed "which is not what I do, is a pseudograph", etc., therefore the plaintiff for the auction and client filed a lawsuit, think two defendants in the case of knowing is a fake picture for auction, its behavior constitute fraud, request to cancel the auction contract, the defendant return auction price and commission, etc. The court held that in not confirmed should an auctioneer and a trustee shall be known in advance litigation strains pseudograph of cases, the auctioneer in litigation from the auction items the authenticity of defects make the disclaimer bidders to know, and through the law's auction display program effectively guarantee the bidder can fully understand the reality of litigation items before bidding condition, In addition, in the introduction of the contested auction items, there is no description of the authenticity or false publicity that can overturn the disclaimer statement, so the disclaimer statement made by the auctioneer on the authenticity or falseness of the contested auction items shall have the effect stipulated in the second paragraph of Article 61 of the Auction Law. On this basis, all of the plaintiff's claims were dismissed.

In the case of Xu Hansheng v. Xiamen Special Economic Zone auction house calligraphy and painting auction contract, the plaintiff who bought liu Haisu and five other calligraphy and painting was later identified as forgery and sued the auctioneer to the court. The court held that the plaintiffs should have judged the authenticity of the items before they were sold. However, after the auction, the disputed object was sent to an appraisal committee for appraisal, which the court did not identify, and there is no legal appraisal institution for Chinese calligraphy and painting to authenticate it. The plaintiff cannot prove that the auctioneer did not inform the auctioneer of all that was known about the work and that the auctioneer committed fraud. Where it is difficult for the buyer to show that the auctioneer has not made an explanation of the situation of the auction target known to him or her, and it is difficult to show that the auctioneer has not fulfilled the obligation of disclosure, and the auctioneer has expressly declared that he or she is not liable for the defects of the auction target, the buyer shall bear the adverse consequences of the fake auction by himself.

In wu Tie sheng sues Shanghai de kang to auction the case such as company, plaintiff passes auction, with the price of 40 thousand yuan buys annatto to rush day ganoderma taishi chair 4, show according to brochure, chair material is annatto, time is republic of China. Later, the plaintiff learned from other ways that the article was fake, and its age was not the Period of the Republic of China but was made by special technological means. Therefore, the plaintiff sued the court, asking the trustee and the auctioneer to refund the auction money and compensate for economic losses. The court held that the auctioneer's statement in the brochure was sufficient to convince the bidder that the auction object in question was made in the "Republic of China".

Therefore, the trustee and auctioneer in the performance of the auction behavior from time to time defects, namely, the payment of four mahogany chutian Ganoderma Taishi chairs, not the "Republic of China" period production, but "modern antique mahogany furniture". According to the plaintiff's claim, the auction and sale relationship between it and the two defendants should be terminated.

2 Disclaimer of Defects

2.1 The Meaning of Warranty Liability for Defects

The liability for guarantee of defects is originally the liability borne by the seller of the sales contract under the contract compilation, including the liability for guarantee of defects in property and rights. There are different interpretations in Chinese academic circles. Some scholars believe that the liability for guarantee of defects should be included in the framework of liability for breach of contract. Some scholars believe that the two should exist independently, which is a parallel relationship.

General view is that the auctioneer of the liability for guaranteeing the drawbacks are similar to the contract provisions, including flaw guarantee of property rights and for guaranteeing the drawbacks, the legal relationship in an auction, an auctioneer has the delivery of the auction, should guarantee the rights intact and no does not conform to the stipulations of the law or agreed by the parties to the quality requirements, the drawbacks of loss caused by reducing its value or utility.

However, if we look closely at the liability in Article 61 of the Auction Act, which relates to the authenticity or quality of the auction object, it seems on the surface that it is only related to the guarantee of defects of the object, not the guarantee of defects of specified rights. The defect of the object refers to the fact that the quality of the object delivered by the seller does not conform to the standard stipulated by the contract or the law, resulting in the loss of the purpose and value of the object. The constitutive criteria of such liability include the following: the subject matter must be defective; The defect must have existed when the risk of the subject matter was transferred to the buyer; The buyer is in good faith and without gross negligence; The buyer must timely fulfill the defect notification obligation.

No provision does not mean that there is no warranty for defects of right. The guarantee of the right defect is hidden behind the legal relation of auctions and certainly exists. If the artwork auctioned is genuine, but there is a burden of rights, then it is very likely to lead to the successful bidding buyer, and finally because the right holder of the artwork (usually the security right holder) exercise the right to lose the ownership of the artwork, and ultimately lead to the failure of the purpose of bidding. The reason why there is no right defect guarantee stipulated in Article 61 is that the subject of the right defect guarantee should be the trustee rather than the auctioneer. From the perspective of cost-effectiveness, it is cheaper and more efficient to disclose the problem of whether there is any defect in rights to the consignor. However, it is impossible for the auctioneer to have the energy and time to investigate every piece of art submitted for auction, and there is no way for the auctioneer to determine whether there is any defect in rights.

In practice, it is common practice for auction rules to include clear disclaimers of defect guarantees, such as Clause 1 of Article 5 (Defect guarantee) of Chapter 1 (General Provisions) of China Guardian Auction Rules and Clause 9 (Guarantee Statement) of Part 1 (main provisions on bidders and purchasers) of Xiling Seal Association Auction Rules. Beijing Auction Rules chapter 1 (general) Article 4 (warranty of defects) Clause 1.

Experts have pointed out that the disclaimer of warranty for defects is not absolute; otherwise, it will cause an imbalance in the interests of bidders, so it should be strictly interpreted. According to Article 18 and Article 27 of the Auction Law, the information of the auctioneer on the defects of artworks is derived from the obligation of the trustee to inform and the right of the auctioneer to inquire. If the trustee informs or the auctioneer of the defects and fails to inform the bidder, the auctioneer shall bear the responsibility. In other words, the auctioneer shall bear joint and several liabilities only when he knowingly carries out the auction without timely disclosure of the defects entrusted by the trustee.

2.2 *Disclaimer Notes*

Three aspects should be considered when understanding the liability of defect guarantees of auctioneers.

First, is the authenticity of the artwork a defect of the object? Objectively, the defect of the object refers to the fact that the delivered object does not conform to the usual nature and objective characteristics of the object. Subjectively, the defect of the object is that the delivered object does not conform to the agreed quality of the parties, resulting in the reduction or loss of its value or utility. Both subjective and objective theories are adopted in the contract compilation of China's Civil Code.

There is a point of view that the exemption of warranty for defects should be limited to the quality of the auction target but should not be extended to authenticity. The idea behind it is that authenticity is difficult to judge and that auctioneers cannot make accurate and objective judgments about the authenticity of all works of art within the bounds of their experience/knowledge. That is true. Authentication of authenticity is a very complicated problem in practice. Some courts even hold that it is impossible to authenticate works of art.

The above views are debatable. On the one hand, authenticity appraisals are necessary, and the appraisal conclusion is directly related to the appeal of the parties. If this problem is left unchecked, it will encourage the proliferation of fakes and condone counterfeiting. Factual truth and legal truth, on the other hand, are two different issues. Some works of art are so old that it is difficult for professionals to distinguish their authenticity, not to mention nonprofessionals such as courts. However, it is possible for courts to pursue legal truth. In other words, the main job of the court is to determine the authenticity of works of art through rules of evidence. For example, the court can entrust professionals to make an appraisal, and the appraisal conclusion obtained through legal procedures can be regarded as a legal solution to the problem of authenticity.

What needs to be further considered is whether, under certain circumstances, the court has the obligation or responsibility to intervene in the authentication of authenticity, whether the intervention of the court is necessary or better, how the court can intervene in the authentication of authenticity, and whether the appraisal conclusion after the dispute can overturn the auction result.

Second, the auctioneer is not the seller in the sales contract, and the liability for guaranteeing defects comes from the trustee. The client shall have the right of ownership or disposal of the artwork submitted for auction and shall be aware of such information as the author, age, material and style of the artwork. The principal bears the most direct liability for warranty of defects. Only in the auction activity is a sale contract divided into several auction contracts (entrusted auction contract, bidding contract and transaction confirmation, etc. According to article 18 of the Auction Law, the auctioneer has the right to ask the trustee to explain the source and defects of the auction target. An auctioneer shall explain the defects of an auction target to the bidder. Article 27 stipulates that the trustee shall explain to the auctioneer the origin and defects of the auction target. If the consignor does not inform the auctioneer of a defect, the auctioneer has no way of knowing about the defect, let alone telling the bidder about it. However, the failure of the trustee to do so does not relieve the auctioneer of his obligation to explain the defect to the bidder, even though the auctioneer was indeed unaware of the sale. Under article 61, an uninformed auctioneer may, after assuming responsibility to the buyer, recover from the trustee who has failed to do his duty of disclosure. These terms state that the principal is ultimately liable for warranty of defects.

The nonfidelity clause can protect the interests of subjectively well-meaning auctioneers to some extent; that is, the auctioneers can apply the nonfidelity clause only when the authenticity and quality cannot be determined due to the subjective cognitive level and objective testing conditions. If, through any means, the auctioneer has prior knowledge of defects in the artwork (both the object and the rights), the auctioneer is obliged to disclose such information. The question is to what extent the auctioneer is obliged to seek information about defects from the trustee; Whether the boundary of this obligation shall be limited to the content provided for in the above article; How to judge the circumstances under which the auctioneer should know the defect information, thus increasing their burden and responsibility.

Finally, we should pay attention to the use of contract and auction law. As one of the sales contracts, auction contracts should be preferentially applied to auction law according to the special law rather than the common law, but the general rights, obligations and responsibilities of auction parties cannot completely exclude the application of the contract provisions of the Civil Code. If the auctioneer intentionally falsifies or sells fake goods but declares disclaimer at the same time, such contradictory statements constitute fraud and will result in invalid statements. Therefore, the auctioneer shall bear civil liability instead of exemption according to relevant provisions of the contract.

3 Emptor

3.1 Implications of Caveat Emptor Principle

From another point of view, the essence of article 61 (2) of the Auction Law is the application of the caveat emptor principle in auction activities. In the early stage of sales law, the principle of the caveat emptor was widely applied by the courts. The buyer's sole responsibility principle means that the seller has no obligation to disclose defects of the goods, and the buyer relies on his own judgment at the time of purchase rather than on any express or implied statement made by the seller. According to the principle, the buyer has his own eyes and should be allowed to judge the quality of the goods and bear the consequences of his choice. If the buyer is unsure about the quality of the goods or the seller's ownership of the goods, the buyer's remedy is to consult someone else or obtain appropriate guarantees from the seller.

If the seller intentionally misrepresents the nature or quality of the goods or the ownership of the goods, the buyer may Sue for tort of fraud. If the seller not only states the facts but also guarantees their truthfulness in express terms of warranty, the seller shall be liable for fraud. Although the existence of a contract is an important factor in the establishment of a guarantee liability, it does not necessarily mean that the guarantee should in fact be a term of the contract. In short, the seller's guarantee liability is not contractual liability but tort liability; that is, the seller made a false statement and deceived the buyer into signing the contract. However, in the absence of fraud, the seller's statement of fact alone is not enough to make it liable for the falsity of the statement unless it makes an express guarantee of truthfulness, that is, the seller uses the word guarantee to establish the cause of action.

In the nineteenth century, the sale by description and the sale of specific objects appeared as opposites. The principle of buyer confidence has different requirements on the buyer according to the certainty of the information available to the buyer. In an 1868 case, the judge highlighted the difference between the sale of a particular thing, in which the buyer is able to inspect the goods for himself and does not require an implied guarantee, and the sale by description, in which the buyer has no opportunity to inspect the goods for himself and therefore relies on the skill and judgment of the seller.

For a contract to be a sale by description, descriptive statements must be relied upon as terms of the contract, not merely as inducements to enter into the contract; that is, external inducements should be distinguished from internal commitments. In the sale of a particular item, the goods already exist and are specified, and the buyer can inspect them himself. The specific goods sales contract should be signed when the goods are physically designated and physical inspection is available, which means that the goods have been determined, conform to the agreement between the two parties, and should be the only goods in reality.

The principle of caveat emptor allows the buyer to take great risks and provides a reasonable excuse for the seller to evade responsibility. It is precisely because the risk is too great to protect the inexperienced buyer, so the development of the law, from "buyer beware" to "seller obligation", that is, the law imposed more obligations on the seller, such as requiring the seller to bear the liability of warranty for defects.

3.2 The Application of the Caveat Emptor Principle in Art Auctions

Art auction is the sale of a specific thing. Before a sale, the auctioneer arranges a preview so that potential bidders have plenty of time to look at the artwork. However, due to the limited time and the technology and cost of detection methods, it is impossible for bidders to form objective evaluations or conclusions by their own naked eye observations. In other words, this type of trading is also called "delivery as is".

Auctioneers generally exempt themselves from liability in this way (buyers and sellers acknowledge the goods being sold as they are, and buyers accept all defects, whether present or future), so there are very few cases of conflict over the quality of the work. At the same time, the court adopted the principle of buyer confidence, which means that the buyer has the responsibility and sufficient time to check and confirm the quality of the artwork in advance. However, the defect of quality is most likely to occur between the successful bid and the buyer's receipt of the lot.

In one case, a total of seven works were successfully auctioned. One painting, by Glackens, was claimed by the buyer as a fake and sued the auction house for breach of warranty. Auction houses insist on disclaimers based on sales slips signed by buyers that they are not liable. The memorandum of Sale contains the following statement: All properties sold are subject to the principles of "without warranties, warranties, etc." The court held that this disclaimer of authenticity was valid because the buyer had actually signed the sales order in very clear and unambiguous language and there was nothing in the Contract Law to prevent such disclaimers. Since then, similar disclaimers have been widely accepted by the courts.

Under the United States Uniform Commercial Code, a "disclaimer" provided by an auctioneer is invalid if the statements contained therein are not sufficiently clear and consistent. An important issue related to the caveat emptor principle is the terms of sale. Traditionally, buyers have made bids based on the principle of "buyer caution" and a broad understanding of the conditions of sale and the guarantees offered by the auction house. However, as the auction market continues to change, auction houses are increasingly appealing to clients based on their interest in owning art rather than their legal experience and business literacy, resulting in a large number of new bidders, including many who are not familiar with the rules and practices of the auction industry. Not only are such people unaware of the technical issues and terminology of auctions, but many members of the general public are barely able to tell the difference between the sales jargon used by various auction houses. The difference between the sales terms can be clearly contrasted with the difference between the warranties or guarantees provided by each auction house.

Sotheby's and Christie's are typical auction houses that offer strong protection to buyers. Such auction houses deal with most buyers' concerns about the authenticity of a lot, including factors such as timing and provenance. Sotheby's defines "copyright" as the term "creator, period, culture and origin" and states it in the conditions of sale: it guarantees a catalog or other accurate and authentic description of the quality of the lot, with a few exceptions, such as works dating before 1870. Related terms are highlighted in bold. Christie has also set similar rules for authenticity guarantees, but only for the statements highlighted in capitals in the first line of the catalog. In addition, both Sotheby's and Christie's have stipulated some restrictions on the performance of authenticity guarantees, such as the buyer's claim of return within five years from the date of auction and return according to the original condition at the time of auction, and the buyer shall provide written opinions of more than two experts recognized by both parties. Even though these are the auction houses that provide strong protection for buyers, they still have viewing obligations in their rules of business.

In China's auction practice, the auctioneer's auction rules mostly contain the content of buyer's confidence/review responsibility, for example, Chapter 1 (General) Article 5 (Warranty for defects) Clause 1 of China Guardian Auction Rules, "Beijing Auction Rules" chapter 1 (general) Article 4 (warranty of defects) paragraph 2 and Chapter 3 (about bidders and buyers) Article 32 (bidder's review responsibility). In the traditional sense, the principle of buyer confidence is still used in the art auction applicable to the sale of specific objects, and its main content can be summarized as follows: requirements or emphasis on bidders to personally check and express satisfaction with the status quo, fully understand and accept the defects of the auction objects. Assume legal responsibility for their own auction behavior. Voluntarily assume the risk and waive the right to dissent.

4 The Catalog is Uncertain

4.1 Auction Catalog and Statements Thereof

The term "auction catalog" refers to electronic or text materials that are distributed by the auctioneer to unspecified objects before the auction day to introduce the auction target. Art auctions generally have pictorial images and text descriptions of the two content types. A pictorial image, merely a presentation of the appearance of an auction object, cannot say anything about its intrinsic quality, nor its age or its author, but only that the object will be auctioned. Therefore, as long as there is no obvious and significant difference between the appearance of the auction target and the image, the image is generally not legally meaningful. Text description, among which author, material and age, is most prone to disputes. The key question is under what conditions the text description on the auction catalog constitutes a deterministic description. The judgment premise is whether there is an obvious and strong cutoff judgment wording in the specific expression.

According to the "cultural relics art auction procedures" article 8, before the auction activity is held, the auctioneer should make an auction map so that the relevant parties understand the auction activity and the basic situation of the auction target. The auction catalog generally includes the following contents: the name of the auction activity, the time and place of the preview and auction, the auction rules and other contents that should be known by all parties involved in the auction, the authorized text of the entrusted bidding, the contact information of the auctioneer and other information, the basic information and special instructions of the auction target. The basic information includes the name of the auction target, author and date of birth, age, form, texture, size, seal, inscription and postscript, reference price and so on. The contents of the auction catalog shall conform to the examination opinions of the administrative departments of cultural relics of the people's governments of provinces, autonomous regions and municipalities directly under the Central Government. For auction targets prohibited from leaving the country and those without retentive prices, the auctioneer shall make special marks in the auction catalog. At the request of the bidder, the auctioneer may provide a report on the status of the auction object as a supplement to the auction catalog. All auction targets should be published in the auction catalog and can be attached with pictures as needed. Pictures should be as accurate as possible to reflect the actual situation and quality of auction targets.

In general, auction catalogs do not constitute a guarantee for bidders/buyers. However, whether to constitute a guarantee, the most crucial is to see the auction map for the description of the artwork, especially the text part, whether it is clear to provide guarantee, in other words, whether the text description has a reasonable foundation in fact, whether it is enough to let the bidder/buyer to produce a substantial judgment of the authenticity of the artwork.

4.2 Cases Related to the Uncertainty of Catalogs

In one case, the plaintiff bought several paintings labeled paintings by Raul duffy at a public auction but later discovered they were fakes and took the auctioneer to court to have the contract revoked. In the first instance, the court held that the auctioneer's disclaimer was inadequate because it failed to draw the plaintiff as buyer's attention to the particular conditions of sale and implicitly indicated the attribution of the work, leaving the plaintiff to believe in good faith that the author of the work was the tagged artist. Based on this, the court of first instance decided in favor of the plaintiff. In the defendant's appeal, the Court of Second Instance held that the auction catalog describing and explaining the paintings at auction contained an exemption for any express or implied warranty or representation of the authenticity of the paintings by the alleged artist; In no intention deliberately fraud cases, the buyer for the following risks, namely, in identifying paintings belong to the artist's original work, and participate in the bidding, they may be wrong, so the buyer under the condition of the principle of the buyer's ego exert cautious, not through litigation claims that this is a bad deal.

Another case involves the sale of seven Chinese artworks. After receiving pottery and jade carvings, the plaintiff suspected that a vase did not belong to the Song Dynasty as claimed by the defendant and sued to revoke the contract. The court held that, first, in determining whether a work of art is consistent with the description given by the seller to the defendant, the standard to be applied is whether the seller's statement to the plaintiff about the work of art can be said to have had a reasonable basis in fact when it was made. Second, with respect to a particular item, the evidence in this case shows that there is no reasonable basis in fact for the seller to attribute a particular item to a particular period. Accordingly, the plaintiff's claim is upheld, the contract is rescinded, and the defendant restitutes the price with interest to the plaintiff.

In another case, plaintiffs bought works labeled Salvador Dali, a famous painter, and then sued the seller (an art gallery in Hawaii) on the grounds that the paintings were not authentic. After hearing it, the court held that if the statement of truth or falsity was made without factual reasonable basis, the buyer was entitled to a remedy under the express warranty of violation of Hawaiian law; In the case of a work of art certified as genuine by an expert in the field or by a merchant engaged in business, the certificate of authenticity constitutes an express guarantee.

There are other cases of conflict over auction catalogs. In one case, bidder Jendwine won two oil paintings, one by Claude Lo and the other by Terness. The auction catalog vouched for authenticity because the bidder thought the author's name was printed on it. However, the auction house argues that the name printed in the catalog does not constitute a guarantee that the work is indeed by the artist. In the dispute, the court said the auction house was right because the art was so old that the auction house could not be sure whether the work was truly by the artist they believed it was. The result of the case became a general rule for the description of auction catalogs, namely, that catalogs represent the opinions of sellers and nothing else. In addition to auction catalogs, there are other forms of attribution. In another case, the seller provided a receipt indicating the name of the author of the work purchased. The court held that the description of an official receipt constituted an explicit guarantee at the time of sale and not merely the opinion of the seller.

In practice, the auctioneer's auction rules usually contain the uncertainty of the catalog, such as Article 32 of Chapter 3 (uncertainty of catalog) of China Guardian Auction Rules and Article 3 of Part 1 (main provisions on bidders and buyers) of Xiling Seal Association Auction Rules. In addition, "Beijing Auction Rules" chapter 3 (about bidders and buyers) article 30 (auction catalog). The auction catalog or written description, other than making a clear and strong closing judgment or statement, shall be used for reference only and shall not be a reasonable basis for the transaction because of the uncertainty of its judgment or statement and shall not constitute a security for the auction transaction. However, the statements contained in receipts and other documents or notes may also be considered an explicit statement of attribution because they are more formal than the auction catalog and thus constitute a guarantee of the authenticity of the transaction.

5 Summary

In practice, the nonfidelity clause has developed into a series of clauses that constitute the auctioneer's exemption system for disputes over the authenticity of artworks. To protect their own rights and interests, auctioneers will try their best to make use of this clause and the exemption system behind it to avoid the risks caused by disputes over the authenticity of artworks. For the auction industry, this is a rational choice, reasonable and legal. However, the nature of the nonfidelity clause and its advantages and disadvantages need to be thoroughly and carefully examined. It is better to assign the risk of authenticity ultimately to the client. In the course of an auction, the auctioneer is also liable if he or she acts in subjectively bad faith (for example, if he or she knows a fake and fails to give a hint). In addition, the assumption of risk should be determined in individual cases, since the world of commercial law is not black and white and is analyzed in combination with various factors. For bidders/buyers, it is suggested to draw on the concept of financial consumers and distinguish between ordinary bidders and professional bidders. For the latter, let them assume the risk as much as possible and use their own judgment; For the former, more protection should be given and adequate relief channels provided. The essence of a nonfidelity clause is the inherent mechanism of industry development. On the basis of inheriting tradition, we should consider the principle of fairness so that intentional counterfeiters, those who know about counterfeits and sell counterfeits, those who know about counterfeits and do not report have no way out, and vulnerable counterfeiters and those whose rights are infringed on are protected.

Chapter 6
Blockchain Technology and Research on Informed Consent Rules in Art Auctions

With the development of society and the economy, the application scope of informed consent rules is also expanding. Important applications of informed consent rules can be found in many fields, such as national politics, consumer protection and the use of personal information. In the field of art auctions, informed consent rules also have a great influence. Generally, in the traditional art auction process, the informed consent rule is hidden in the "auction rules" formulated by the auctioneer, which provides support for the effectiveness of some provisions in the "auction rules" (such as "exemption clauses"), thus reducing the obligations of the auctioneer and increasing the risks borne by the buyer. More importantly, with the continuous development of the new generation of information technology, blockchain technology has a trend of deep integration with the traditional art auction market. For example, in July 2018, Christie cooperated with Artory, an art technology supplier, to use The Ethereum private chain The Registry as The medium. The successful application of blockchain technology in the art auction market has been realized.[1] It can be predicted that art auctions will become more intelligent under the support of blockchain technology. Supported by consensus mechanisms and code, "auction rules" will become more complex, which may lead to the further weakening of informed consent rules behind "auction rules". Informed consent rules themselves, therefore, should become the starting point for reflection, what is "knowledge", what is a "yes", this principle from the first, to continue to expand, what is behind the theoretical basis, the present art auction of informed consent is separated from traditional cognitive rules, and may be given new connotation or explain path. In fact, theory and legal rules have objective regularity, but there are no pure legal technical rules divorced from social changes. Any legal rules will be combined with social facts and legal concepts and then can be objectively understood and properly applied. Taking this as the starting point, this paper attempts to explore the theoretical basis of informed consent rules, cope with the impact of block chain technology on the art auction market, and build

[1] https://www.sohu.com/a/260025813_100285263, 2020年12月21日.

Z. Zheng, *The Legal System of Art Auction in China*,
https://doi.org/10.1007/978-981-19-0128-7_6

a new interpretation framework of informed consent rules to further improve the institutional system in the art auction market.

1 Theoretical Basis of Informed Consent Rule in Art Auctions

1.1 Informed Consent Rules and the Principle of Good Faith

The informed consent rule of art auction consists of informed consent and consent. The so-called "informed" means that the buyer is aware of the information disclosed by the auctioneer. In practice, such information may be required to be disclosed by the auctioneer, as stipulated in Article 46 of the Auction Law; It may also be voluntarily disclosed by the auctioneer, such as an escape clause. The so-called "consent" means that the information disclosed by the auctioneer can produce certain effects through the consent of the buyer (generally, signature in practice), such as the items stated in the auction reaching the buyer or the buyer recognizing the exemption clause. Through the above analysis, we can easily find that both the behavior of the auctioneer disclosing necessary information and the behavior of the buyer's consent seem to be related to the principle of good faith in the Contract Law.

As a German judgment shows, "During the contracting process, the parties have the obligation to inform the other party of the facts of importance to the other party which may hinder the purpose of the contract, and the scope of which is in good faith... Shall prevail.[2] In the interpretation and application of private law, the principle of good faith is the highest guiding principle to achieve fairness and justice, so it is also called "emperor clause".[3] Some theories subdivide the specific function of the principle of good faith into specific function, limiting function, supplementary function and correction function.[4] Among them, the supplementary function refers to the various ancillary obligation groups created in addition to the main obligation under the contract in order to ensure the realization of the purpose of the contract without obvious change in nature.[5] If we understand the act of the auctioneer disclosing necessary information and the consent of the buyer as a kind of collateral obligation, the informed consent rule can indeed be regarded as a supplementary function of the good faith principle in the absence of clear legal provisions. Derived from.

Although the informed consent rule can be implemented through the good faith principle of a word, the connotation of the good faith principle is highly abstract, open and uncertain. Informed consent rules still need further argument involving the

---

[2] BGH NJW 1979, 2243; 1974, 849.

[3] Congfu (2008).

[4] Yao Zhiming: Principles of Integrity, The Taiwan Law Review, Issue 76, 2001, p. 113–115.

[5] Zejian (2001).

theoretical basis and look at more specific guidelines or more persuasive reasons for reference to maintain the stability and predictability of the law.

1.2 Informed Consent Rules and Independent Decision and Self-responsibility

Similar to the medical field, in the application scenario of art auctions, informed consent rules can also strengthen the independent decision of the buyer. Specifically, auctioneers sacrifice their own space of private law autonomy to use some information and disclose this information to buyers. As a result of receiving this information, the buyer may make a more prudent decision on whether to trade or not. Conversely, the buyer has to bear the consequences of this decision. Therefore, can informed consent rules be derived from the theory of autonomous decision and self-responsibility? Self-determination and self-responsibility are also called substantial freedom of contract, including "agreement does not give rise to illegal" (VolentiNonFitIniuria).

And "correctness guarantee" (Richtigkeitsgewahr). We will examine the relationship between informed consent rules and these two contents.

1.2.1 "Consent Does not Produce Illegal"

The case of the German Federal Constitutional Court points out that "the core of the autonomy of private law is the individual's independent decision in legal life".[6] Through the expression of meaning of legal act, personal meaning determines the establishment and content of legal act. Under the Volenti Non Fit Iniuria requirement, the law is generally required to respect the will of the individual, even if his will is objectively incorrect or irrational. Therefore, individuals have the right to decide and satisfy their economic requirements responsibly and on their own. In general, the legal order believes that individuals are capable of making the best decisions about which interests to pursue in which ways and that individuals, in turn, should be held accountable for their decisions. Therefore, self-determination and self-responsibility are two sides of the same coin, influencing each other, and both theories also give one party reason to believe that the other party will faithfully perform the contract agreed upon by both parties.

Although "consent is not illegal" is one of the main contents of autonomous decision and self-responsibility, there is a premise that individuals are capable of making the best decision for their own interests or needs; otherwise, the autonomy and self-determination of the content of the contract and responsible for it will become an empty talk. This does not mean that individuals should always be able to make the best decisions, but it does mean that individuals are better at understanding

[6] Secretariat of the District of the Judicial Court of Taiwan: Selection of the Federal Constitutional Court of Germany (13), Taibei: Cailin Co., Ltd., 2011, p. 743.

the decisions they are about to make and the benefits they are about to gain than others. Even if there are moments when bad decisions are made, the average rational individual learns from them to make better decisions in the future.

Self-determination and self-responsibility are strongly associated with art auctions. On the one hand, auctioneers often have to sacrifice their control and use of certain information and take responsibility for it. For example, Weisz v. Parke-BernetGalleries, Inc. In the case of", the first-instance court decided that the defendant should bear the responsibility for auctioning the fake works.[7] According to the verdict, the first-instance court said: "In theory, the accused possesses superior knowledge and skills in determining the authenticity of artworks... The design of the auction catalog encourages the plaintiff to be confident that the items are authentic. Therefore, the defendant is liable for the plaintiff's reliance on him."[8] On the other hand, the appellate decision on Weisz reveals the relationship between self-determination and self-responsibility and the buyer. The Appellate court in Weisz reversed the first-instance court's finding that the auctioneer was liable, holding that "the court will not deny the wrongful contract entered into by the purchaser who, despite being informed of the transaction, conducted it imprudently in a dangerous environment."[9] This view was repeated in later practice and eventually formed a convention in art trading called "caveat emptor".

1.2.2 Correctness Guarantee

A contract is the result of mutual consultation and compromise between the two parties. With the help of the substantial freedom of contract, both parties "give and take" each other in the negotiation to achieve the balance of interests, so there are certain "correctness guarantee" (Richtigkeitsgewahr) in the contract mechanism and the substantial freedom of contract.[10] In the process of concluding a contract, although one party needs to safeguard its own interests, it also needs to consider the position of the other party. Through continuous consultation, both parties harmonize their interests and reach contract terms acceptable to both parties. Social norms need to be consistent with the proper order of the whole society, but the contract is not consistent with the order between the individual parties, and sometimes there may be situations beyond the proper order of the individual. The law generally recognizes an adverse outcome provided that the adverse party agrees to accept it and can expect to recover from other benefits. It can be seen that the contract formed through negotiation not only includes the subjective will of the parties but also includes some elements of objective order such as legal stability, clarity or transaction security. Similarly, the concept of "correctness" in correctness guarantees, on the one hand, should be based on the negotiation between the two parties; on the other hand, it

[7] Weisz v. Parke-Bernet Galleries, Inc. 67 Misc. 2d 1077, 325 N.Y.S. 2d576 (N.Y.Civ.Ct. 1971).

[8] Gerstenblith (1988).

[9] Weisz v. Parke-Bernet Galleries, Inc. 77 Misc. 2d 80, 351 N.Y.S. 2d 911 (N.Y.Misc. 1974).

[10] Yi Jun: The Meaning of the Basic Principles of Civil Law, Law Studies, No. 6, 2018, p. 60.

also includes the subjective evaluation of the parties and the objective elements of the contract.

If the contract concluded between the parties wants to meet the requirements of correctness guarantee, it needs to be based on the ability of both parties to reconcile interests. In practice, due to the gap in social or economic status between individuals, most people may not be able to identify their own interests and pursue their own interests responsibly. Therefore, it is not easy to realize that all contracts meet the requirements of correctness guarantees.

From the perspective of the correctness guarantee of contracts, we find that the realization of substantial freedom of contracts is based on the correctness of contracts. The correctness of the contract depends on the correctness of the agreement of both parties. The correct agreement between the parties shall be based on their full understanding of the relevant conditions of the contract. If one party's intention is flawed due to a lack of necessary information, subsequent negotiations may not result in a correct contract. Therefore, some scholars believe that complete information (Vollstandige Information) is crucial to the expression of parties' intentions. Only with complete information can the parties make perfect decisions (Perfekte Entscheidung) and conclude correct contracts.[11]

Under the theory of complete information added, we can find that the validity of the contract guarantees associated with informed consent also has specific rules, namely, the informed consent rule to bridge the information asymmetry between the parties and improve the validity of the sale contract. At the same time, the winner of information, namely, the buyer, will have the ability to self to safeguard their own interests. Therefore, some scholars have also asserted that "under certain circumstances, informed consent can constitute a necessary functional condition for realizing the substantial freedom of contract".[12]

1.3 The Expansion of the Theory of Self-determination and Self-responsibility

As mentioned above, under the principle of good faith in contract law, the theoretical basis of informed consent rules in art auctions can be derived from the theory of freedom of contract substance, that is, the parties' self-determination and self-responsibility theory. However, subject to correctness guarantees, the application scope of informed consent rules is quite narrow. With the further development of theories and theories, the theory of self-determination and self-responsibility presents a trend of expansion, and situations that may not be within the range of the theory of self-determination and self-responsibility are gradually accepted, among which a typical example is information defizit.

[11] Günther Hönn, Kompensation gestörter Vertragsparität, 1982, S.163, 257.

[12] Klaus Hopt, Nicht Vertragliche Haftung außerhalb von Schadens-und Bereicherungsausgleich, AcP183, 1983, S.502f.

As mentioned above, an important content of the contract correctness guarantee is that the information possessed by the parties must be complete. However, this theory does not discuss whether the contract concluded by parties with incomplete information meets the correctness guarantee. Generally, the parties involved in economic transactions will have certain knowledge and skills to make better decisions or satisfy their own interests. Responsible for, be responsible for the implementation of the theory of although to be on the premise of the necessary information, but this theory is also not clear how much information, what information the need not reach the level of "necessary", in addition, request the parties to the absolute after complete information collection to trade is not viable, so some scholars advocated is not on the essence of the contract freedom set high threshold, Otherwise, it "will become a freedom subject to objective reason"[13]; Some scholars hold that the "objective and rational standard" freely imposed on the essence of the contract "is not the result of the independent development of individual personality in law".[14]

Some scholars try to return to the theory of freedom of contract substance to explain the problem of lack of information. The theory holds that "There are dual attributes of self-determination and self-responsibility in the freedom of contract, which are related to the risk of contract failure. On the one hand, self-responsibility makes the other parties to the contract trust the effectiveness of the contract; It is also an incentive for the person to determine whether he wants to enter into a particular contract, or what kind of contract."[15] According to this view, the lack of information can be incorporated into the theoretical system of self-determination and self-responsibility, and if the contract is often invalid, the parties will have difficulty properly and appropriately controlling their own behavior. When a party does not have complete information, his behavior can also be determined by himself because the completeness of information is related to the preparation and collection of information in the early stage of the contract. In normal transactions, parties can decide for themselves what information to obtain and at what cost. If the parties concerned stop collecting information for the consideration that the value of information is less than the cost of collecting information, the decision made in the absence of such information also meets the requirements of self-determination theory. Therefore, some scholars pointed out: "In principle, the parties can abstractly judge whether it is necessary to continue contracting and taking risks in the absence of information."[16]

From the perspective of legal stability and clarity, some scholars argue that the negation should be arranged differently according to the intellectual differences of the parties concerned, that is, denying the absolute "waffengleichheit" of the parties concerned. The opinion points out that "not all inferior intellectual knowledge leads to the loss of information, and even if the loss of information leads to the loss of

[13] Manfred Wolf, Rechtsgeschäftliche Entscheidungsfreiheit und vertraglicher Interessenausgleich, Mohr Siebeck, 1970, S.82.

[14] Lorenz Fastrich, Richterliche Inhaltskontrolleim Privatrecht, C.H.Beck, 1992, S.41.

[15] Manfred Wolf, Rechtsgeschäftliche Entscheidungsfreiheit und vertraglicher Interessenausgleich, Mohr Siebeck, 1970, S.82.

[16] Gebhard M. Rehm, Aufklärungspflichten im Vertragsrecht, C.H. Beck, 2003, S.123.

information, it does not automatically make the party with the loss of information entitled to the possibility of canceling the contract".[17] In principle, the information necessary for the free exercise of consciousness is difficult to be objectively defined and can only be determined by the parties concerned. In addition, some scholars argue from the compromise between Willens Theorie and Erklarungs Theorie that "in civil law norms, although autonomous decision should be respected, not every situation that interferes with autonomous decision will affect the validity of the contract."[18]

2 Summary

In summary, we can briefly sort out the theoretical context of informed consent rules in art auctions. First, the informed consent rule in art auctions can be summed up as "derived from the principle of good faith" in a word, but this statement is too vague and abstract, which is not strong enough in persuasion and operation. Second, the informed consent rule in art auctions can also be derived from the theory of self-determination and self-responsibility, that is, the substantial freedom of contract theory, which is restricted by the two theories of "consent does not give rise to illegal" and "correctness guarantee". Finally, with the development of the theory of self-determination and self-responsibility, the situation of information deficiency has been brought into the range of the theory, that is, the contract does not naturally produce adverse effects due to the parties' lack of information.

It is worth noting that with the particularity of art and auction gradually exposed by the academic community; The growing prosperity of business practices; With the rapid development of science and technology, some new theoretical and practical problems challenge the informed consent rule in art auction under the traditional theory.

3 Challenges to Informed Consent Rules in Art Auctions

With the development of the social economy, trading to the technicalization and specialization of the social division of labor has become the norm, the extent of unequal information is gradually intensified, an information disadvantage trading risk becomes increasingly large, and parties under the traditional theory of informed consent in art auction rules are also facing many challenges. First, with the support of emerging technologies represented by block chain, informed consent rules in art auctions will be formalized, which will deviate from the essence of contract certainty and stability under the recognition of maintaining legal order. Second, professional art auction procedures and professional art auctioneers bring about discussions on

---

17 Lorenz Fastrich, Richterliche Inhaltskontrolle im Privatrecht, C.H. Beck, 1992, S.73.

18 Qiyang (2010).

consideration and expectation of professional roles, which limit the scope of the substantial freedom of contract theory to a certain extent, thus affecting the role of informed consent rules.

3.1 *Formalization of Informed Consent Rules*

Informed consent is considered a natural principle in art auctions, but it is generally difficult to judge the extent to which individuals are aware of "informed" content. Generally, what standard should be used to measure whether an individual knows or not, whether it is the cognitive standard of the general rational person or the differentiated cognitive standard of "thousands of faces"? It is also an extremely complex issue. Practice, most people probably do not think it necessary to or interested to understand the auction rules in an auction is a related terms concerning the connotation, more will not go to refer to or take the initiative to understand the related risk, because the participation and the received one item to them have little impact, as long as agreed or accepted, the intended use can be achieved. However, "informed consent", as a kind of behavior, is similar to a "gate". As long as the behavior of "informed consent" and "consent" is made, it will have a corresponding effect in law and thus produces the conflict between the form and substance of individual "informed consent". Prophesying, people usually discussed, informed consent is a kind of form or behavior in the sense of "informed consent" appearance, but often not meaningful informed consent, because people's subjective meaning are represented only by behavior, thus emphasize the form of informed consent and there is nothing wrong with this, just on the behavior of informed consent, The separation of "formal knowledge" and "substantive knowledge" is more obvious.

Such informed consent may become a mere formality in many aspects, regardless of the subjective understanding of individuals or the objective activities of art auctions combined with block chain technology in reality. Therefore, some critics oppose the principle of informed consent. For example, some theorists believe that since data processing in modern society has difficulty defining a clear purpose in advance, if the informed consent principle is rigidly applied, data activities cannot be carried out, and the data economy will struggle.[19] Some theorists believe that informed consent is no longer just a "personal decision". Through big data technology, "individual decisions" will be transformed into "individual-collective decisions" that will inevitably have a direct impact on others. In this understanding, personal decisions become a new moral responsibility, and we have a moral obligation to consider how the decision will affect others like us before making it.[20] This view is close to the characteristics of the data age and the nature of data utilization to a considerable extent. However,

[19] Lin Huanmin: The Dilemma and Way out of Informed Consent Principles in Personal Information Protection, Journal of Beihang University (Social Sciences), No. 3, 2018, p. 15–16.

[20] Huang Baiheng: The New "Personal Decisions" and the "Informed Consent" in the Era of Big Data, Philosophical Analysis, Issue 6, 2017, p. 108–109.

if individuals do not know their own risks when they provide informed consent, how can they consider the impact on others? Such a sense of moral responsibility is worthy of affirmation, but it may be too far beyond the objective reality and urgent needs of the present stage and is impossible to reach.

From the perspective of risk, the informed consent principle seems to have space and possibility for further refinement. In terms of risk awareness, the objects of informed consent can be divided into known risks and unknown risks. In terms of the subject acquiring and holding information, it can be divided into the initial acquiring subject and the subsequent transfer subject, and the majority of individuals may not know who the latter transfer subject is, or it is impossible to know, depending on which subjects the initial acquiring subject will have necessary commercial or noncommercial contacts with. What is certain is that individual information may be at risk of uncertainty. Thus far, it is basically clear that informed consent can be stratified from the perspective of risk and risk control, namely, informed consent for known risks and informed consent for unknown risks. Informed consent was obtained from the initial acquisition subject and the subsequent transfer subject. However, the passive characteristics of informed consent are reflected. At the same time, there is also a certain contradiction, that is, how individuals can give informed consent to unknown risks and uncertain and unknown subsequent subjects. This is one of the main reasons why informed consent is always considered both necessary and ineffective.

3.2 *Commission System and Consideration*

3.2.1 Consideration (Entgelt Gedanken)

Of thought on the theory of informed consent, is based on the economic attributes of information, the adjustment of competitive information risk allocation, the contracting consultation and the nature of the contract, on the basis of considering that informed consent for information property right and cause economic problems, as well as the contract for the parties competing interests in order to meet the demand of legal function.

The nature of informed consent is to change the risk allocation of auction information in the contract. In addition to legal adjustment, the distribution of contract risk can also be changed by express or implied agreement of the parties. Under consideration, informed consent is justified if the information provider can obtain some form of compensation for the information providing behavior to compensate it for taking the information risk on behalf of the other party, that is, the arrangement that implies some implied agreement or behavior expectation. This work of art auctions is reflected in the auctioneer to the buyer's commission system. Although some scholars believe that the commission charged by the auctioneer is the consideration for the service provided by the auctioneer to the buyer (such as renting the venue and preparing the auction), rather than the consideration for providing information[21]; However, opponents believe that the auctioneer provides services such as venue and the audience is all bidders participating in the auction, but the object of commission charged by the auctioneer is only the trustee or the highest bidder, so they do not agree to understand the commission as the consideration for the services provided by the auctioneer to the buyer.[22]

Starting point of value ideas, that is, information disclosure will be regarded as one of the parties of the informed consent to pay the object, which is from the other party in return for some sort of payment of remuneration, information can be available in the information disclosure by reward, for their willingness to an important cause of production information, also by the information of price internalize externalities.

Therefore, under consideration, the premise of informed consent is essentially paid. In the framework of civil law, paid or unpaid is often a demarcation point between the degree of liability. Therefore, informed consent, as an additional liability beyond contractual payment, can also be based on the compensatory basis in the civil law system. However, the requirement of consideration does not mean the equilibrium of equivalence because it is very difficult to directly evaluate and trade information, and complete equivalence is not an inherent requirement of civil law, so equivalence is not the connotation of consideration.

3.2.2 Information Risk Allocation of Artwork Auction Contracts Under the Commission System

For the allocation of information risk, from the perspective of the self-interested understanding of the freedom of contract and the competitiveness of the contract negotiation, in principle, the parties should bear the risks related to the conclusion of the contract and the realization of the contract objectives. It may also be distributed by law or by express or implied agreement of the parties. Specifically, the nature and purpose of contracts are the keys to guiding the risk allocation of contract information. In general, in interessen Gegensatzlicher Vertrag (such as a contract of sale or lease), the parties treat the benefits accordingly and offer their own benefits, usually without obtaining additional consideration for the provision of payment information; In interessen Wahrnehmender Vertrag, for example, a contract for legal services or medical treatment, the consideration received by a party usually includes the furtherment of the interests and objectives of the other party.[23]

If, artwork auction contract is a contract of the pure conflict, then the auctioneer a commission behavior can be understood as: the auctioneer to use its information advantage of art, has concluded a commission for treatment of payment of the contract, the auctioneer does not get extra payment at the same time, there is no need

[21] Xinsheng (1989).

[22] Liu Ningyuan: Auction Law on Exemption of Defty Liability, Law, No. 1, 2000, p. 39–40.

[23] Johannes Köndgen, Selbstbindung ohne Vertrag: zurHaftungausgeschäftsbezogenem Handeln, Mohr Siebeck, 1981, S.246.

to bear the risk of information. However, with the continuous development of the auction industry, the interest status of auctioneers and buyers has undergone some subtle changes. In the situation of the interests of the two parties opposing each other, the new situation of auctioneer protecting the interests of buyer has gradually emerged. Outside decision points out, the auctioneer shall safeguard the interests of the customers, for customers to rule out the art value of information is missing, at the same time, even if the auction for the customer provides the free their own professional knowledge, can also from the commission, the property value of goodwill (Good will) sources such as reward, therefore, the auctioneer need to bear the risk of information.[24]

3.2.3 Expectations of Proper Behavior for Professional Roles

Legitime Verhaltenserwartung is a problem in reliance. In short, simple de facto trust is not enough to rationalize the reliance liability. From the perspective of legal norms, the decisive factor is not whether there is de facto trust, but whether the party with inferior information should trust the other party, that is, whether there is a specific expectation of proper conduct for the other party.[25] The liability for culpability in contrahendo therefore presupposes that reliance on the expectation of conduct (Vertrauenaufeine Verhaltenserwartung) is justified on the basis of the transactional view (Verkehrsauffassung) or otherwise, Vertrauen durfen is the decisive factor of trust responsibility, and simply claiming the existence of a simple trust relationship is not enough to rationalize such expectation.[26]

The expectation of proper behavior of professional roles refers to the expectation of proper behavior inspired by professional roles, socioeconomic status or professional status, which should be trusted and protected. The professional role as a kind of right, representative and personal status of specific behavior expectation, connected or career is usually a conflict of interest by the behavior expected of the parties shall be coordinated and see if there is no such rights table, decisions made by the parties will be different, trust and protection for the standard form of legal act, the average, is an exception.[27]

For art auctions, if the auctioneer informs the necessary information to arouse the professional role's expectation of proper behavior, then the content of informed consent will also be affected by the responsibility of trust. Auction contract concluded by the parties, in other words, behavior can also be regarded as a kind of trust investment, therefore, the obligation of one party how can blame to cause it to the other party that the objective facts of trust, has become an important factor decided

[24] Cristallina S.A.v. Christie, Manson & Woods International, Inc., 117A.D.2d 284 (N.Y. App. Div. 1986).

[25] Klaus Hopt, NNicht Vertragliche Haftung außerhalb von Schadens-und Bereicherungsausgleich, AcP183, 1983, S.641.

[26] Gebhard M. Rehm, Aufklärungspflichten im Vertragsrecht, C.H.Beck, 2003, S.198.

[27] Franz Bydlinski, System und Prinzipien des Privatrechts, Springer, 1996, S.69.

to protect the content of the informed consent or not, the trust on the specification or justified expectation, besides can borrow from business practices to be specific, It can also be determined by the legal principle of the allocation of areas of responsibility or risk in information, and of course, the circumstances of the case are also relevant to the decision to rely on facts. The express or implied behavior of the auctioneer can also generate legitimate expectations of information disclosure. From the point of view of the information economy, the information party has incentives to obtain information only when it can make use of information, and information is also used in transactions, such as principal or secondary payments in the contract. Accordingly, the buyer at the auction house purchase paid the price of gold is usually higher than in general stores or private, the higher the price can be used as the auction house consumers better advice or information should be provided the implied requirement of reflection, professional to provide their professional pay the higher prices, can produce its should be more looking forward to that on the norms of behaviour.[28] Therefore, it can also serve as a theoretical basis for informed consent rules that the parties engaged in the conduct of related fields in their business, and that the other party will trust their expertise, so as not to further explore.[29]

3.3 Summary

In summary, emerging technologies, professional trading processes and professional traders, on the one hand, improve the trading efficiency and transaction amount of art auctions; on the other hand, they also challenge some basic theories of art auctions. Emerging technologies represented by block chain technology have gradually made informed consent rules in art auctions a mere formality. The modern transaction process under the commission model and the emergence of professional auctioneers, which can arouse the expectation of buyers' proper behavior, make the application of informed consent rules increasingly complicated. It has become increasingly difficult to explain informed consent rules through the traditional theory of freedom of contract substance.

The reasons for the abovementioned problems can be attributed to the limitation of the theory of substantial freedom of contract. Specifically, the substantial freedom of contract is based on the premise that the cost of obtaining information between the parties is not significantly different. This premise leads to two consequences: first, there is little difference between the economic status of the parties, there is no ideological "weak party", and there is no need for special intervention by laws or policies; second, there is no special trust relationship between the parties who need information and the parties who can provide information. Therefore, the informed

---

[28] Gebhard M. Rehm, Aufklärungspflichten im Vertragsrecht, C.H.Beck, 2003, S.195f.

[29] Eike Schmid & Josef Esser, Schuldrecht. Band I Allgemeiner Teil. Teilband 2. Durchführungshindernisse und Vertragshaftung, Schadensausgleich und Mehrseitigkeit beim Schuldverhältnis. C.F.Müller, 2003, S.145.

consent rule in art auctions can be adapted to the theory of freedom of contract substance. In contrast, the business practices of modern art auctions greatly add to the cost of the buyer for real information. On the one hand, auction houses and their subordinate group mastery part buyers do not have professional skills and knowledge, and the professional skills and knowledge both in real information involve the arts, such as identification technology, and promote auction transaction security, such as block chain technology, which makes the economic status of auctioneers and buyers increasingly different. On the other hand, due to the lack of knowledge and the gap in economic status, choosing to trust the auctioneer has become the most economical way for the buyer to obtain real information, so there is a certain degree of individual dependence between the buyer and the auctioneer. Therefore, in the commercial practice of modern art auctions, the traditional theory of freedom of contract substance is not enough to explain the new connotation of informed consent rules.

4 Reconstruction of Informed Consent Rules in Art Auctions

4.1 Relaunch of Informed Consent Rules

With traditional contract theory, real freedom to the key to explaining the rules of informed consent in information costs does not differ substantially between parties and modern economic society, ecological existence, growing disparity of the economic status of gaps between parties, and buyer dependence on auctioneer statements also increases increasingly; therefore, informed consent rules in art auctions should also imply trust and trust. As some theorists say, what is decided by individual informed consent is not only a reflection of individual self-determination and self-responsibility but also a manifestation of "otherness" to a considerable extent. The transformation of such personal decisions and informed consent from "self involved" to "other involved" is the essence of big data technology and the requirements of its application results. Based on the involvement and operation mode of big data technology, it is possible for people to consider the impact on others when making personal decisions and providing informed consent.[30] However, neither strengthening nor relaxing individual self-determination reduces the risk, and only strengthening the responsibility of those who know and control the risk is more feasible.

After the informed consent of the buyer, a large part of the transaction is beyond their knowledge and control. In fact, such consent is more like an act in the sense of procedure than an act in the sense of substantive private law, but it produces legal

[30] Huang Baiheng: The New "Personal Decisions" and the "Informed Consent" in the Era of Big Data, Philosophical Analysis, Issue 6, 2017, p. 110.

consequences in the sense of substantive law. If we regard the informed consent of the buyer in art auctions as a technical rule and the content of informed consent often exceeds the cognition of the buyer, this rule will inevitably be questioned because conflicts and contradictions between the systems may be completely impossible to resolve. Judging from the current discussion, it is difficult to find other solutions that can reasonably replace informed consent rules.

When the buyer's informed consent is examined again, it should not be regarded as an isolated legal act but should be examined in the objective law of the development of things. Therefore, we need to explain or structural principle of informed consent, not just the simple one form sense "confirmation", but a trust to protect the dialectical unification of informed consent and trust responsibility, based on trust and the corresponding risk control by the auctioneers, an auctioneer and based on this kind of trust and at the same time engaged in an untrustworthy trading activities.

4.2 Informed Consent Rules Based on Reliance Liability Theory

Evidence of a buyer's need for confidence can be found in cases of misrepresentation and interruption of consultations.[31] In the case of violation of the obligation to explain, the right of claim based on contractual negligence is often used as a remedy.[32] Therefore, in art auction, in order to protect the trust of the buyer on important matters related to the conclusion of the auction contract, the informed consent rule can also be derived from the trust responsibility. In addition, from the perspective of Redlichkeit Erwartung des Rechtsverkehrs, the more information the parties obtain, the less friction they will have in the process of the transaction. As much information as possible is in the interest of both parties.[33]

From the perspective of legal effects, the types of reliance liability can be divided into positive reliance protection and negative reliance protection, which have different purposes. The former can satisfy the parties' trust; the latter can compensate for the loss of broken trust. The trust contained in the informed consent rule should belong to the category of active trust protection. The effect of positive reliance protection is to make one party bear the restriction of legal action. In art auctions, the effect is that the auctioneer is bound by his or her own flawed expression of intention. In general, this is an adverse consequence that requires special justification. Trust of the counterpart is only a necessary condition, not a sufficient one. Because the factor of trust can only answer why the trustor is worthy of protection and why it is given a claim, it cannot answer why the consequences of trust should be borne by the other party, which needs to be solved by the principle of liability.

[31] Franz Bydlinski, System und Prinzipien des Privatrechts, Springer, 1996, S.74.

[32] Stephan Lorenz, Der Schutz vor dem unerwünschten Vertrag, C.H.Beck, 1997, S.388.

[33] Lehmann Michael, Vertragsanbahnung durch Werbung, C.H.Beck, 1981, S.307.

4.3 The Imputation Principle of Active Reliance Protection

There are three theories about which imputation principle should be adopted in positive reliance protection. One is the inducement principle, which holds that whoever leads to the occurrence of the trust fact should be responsible for it, without examining whether it is subjectively at fault. It is worth noting that until the middle of the twentieth century, the doctrine was in a dominant position. The second is the fault principle. It is not enough to think that a person merely causes the fact of trust to bear the responsibility of positive trust, and only when he or she is at fault in this regard will the law give positive trust protection to the counterpart. In the late twentieth century, the fault principle gradually gained its dominant position. Third, the risk principle. Canalis is representative of what needs to be said. The so-called trigger principle, he thought, the result liability principle was actually another kind of expression, and the result liability principle in modern civil law is not the true sense of the imputation principle. Trust responsibility, if using this principle, is to abandon the "blame" of the elements so that trust responsibility is lost as the basis. Trust responsibility, on the other hand, also should not be commonly use fault principle, need to adopt the principle is based on the ethical necessity "trust responsibility", other trust responsibility responsibility responsibility should not be using this principle, especially the right to representation and risk principle should be used, because the risk principle is advantageous to the transaction security, in line with the right image responsibility of special purpose.[34]

As a matter of fact, positive reliance protection applies to a wide range of cases, so it is not necessary to adopt a unified principle of liability. In the field of legal act systems, positive reliance protection can be generally summed up in two situations: one is to make defective legal acts effective; the other is to make the effect of legal acts belong to someone. The first case is the typical case of active trust of the buyer protecting "informed consent" in art auctions, which cannot adopt the unified principle of liability. For example, in the case of false expression of intention, if the buyer is given positive confidence protection and the auctioneer's right of revocation is limited, the principle of imputation is obviously inconsistent with that of positive confidence protection in the case of retention of true intention. The latter requires the auctioneer to be intentional, while the former cannot be intentional; otherwise, there is no mistake—unintentional meaning does not coincide with expression. From the perspective of the fairness principle, if the error is caused by the serious fault of the auctioneer, the auctioneer should bear the adverse consequences by himself and cannot transfer them to the buyer. In this case, it is obviously not enough to require the auctioneer to bear the liability of negative trust interest compensation. The buyer should enjoy stronger positive trust protection; that is, the expression of intention cannot be revoked, and the auctioneer should perform the obligation according to its promise. In the first draft of The German Civil Code, in accordance

[34] Yang Daixiong: Active Trust and Protection in the Legal Behavior System—and Several Issues in the Formulation of the General Provisions of the Chinese Civil Code, Law between Chinese and Foreign Countries, Issue 5, 2015, p. 1161.

with the provisions of articles 99 (1) and (3), if a demonstrative error occurs due to the gross negligence of the demonstrator, the demonstrator shall not claim that the demonstrative error is invalid unless the counterpart knows or should know that the demonstrator has made the demonstrative error. Such a provision is worthy of affirmation, but it was deleted in the second draft of the German Civil Code.[35]

As far as the legal act with formal defects is concerned, if the auctioneer defrauds the buyer with respect to the formal elements of the legal act, he shall not claim that the legal act is not established on the grounds of formal defects. In such a case, the buyer should have the option of either claiming that the legal action was disallowed or that the legal action was upheld. The reason for this is as follows: from the point of view of the fraudster, if it is allowed to claim that the legal act is unjustified on the grounds of formal defect, it is equal to allowing it to profit from the fraud that causes formal defect, which obviously goes against the principle of good faith. From the point of view of the defrauded party, it mistakenly believes that the legal act is valid because of being defrauded, so it has trust in the legal act. If the legal act is not valid because of form defects later, it does not conform to the principle of trust protection. In short, the binding force of the defective legal act may require that one party intentionally create the reliance fact, or it may only require that it is seriously negligent in this regard.

In summary, active reliance protection should adopt multiple imputation principles. For defective legal acts, positive reliance protection should be based on one party's intention or serious negligence.

References

Chen Congfu: The Theory and Practice of the Principles of Integrity, The Political University and Law Review, No. 104, (2008), p. 20

Qiao Xinsheng: Brief on the legal nature of Auction, Hebei Law, No. 4, (1989), p. 10

Patty Gerstenblith, Picture Imperfect:Attempted Regulation of the Art Market, William&Mary law Review,Vol. 29,3, 1988, P.506-507

Wang Zejian (2001) The General Provisions of the Civil Law. Beijing: China University of Political Science and Law Press, p. 597

Shi Qiyang (2010) The General Provisions of the Civil Law. BeiJing: China Legal Affairs Press, p. 243–244

[35] Kommission zur Ausarbeitung des Entwurfs, Entwurf eines bürgerlichen Gesetzbuches für das Deutsche Reich. Erste Lesung, De Gruyter, 2013, S.23.

Chapter 7
Policy Argumentation on Records of Artwork Authentication

1 Introduction

1.1 Introduction to the Record System of Artwork Authentication

The art authentication system is the focus of solving the dispute over fake works of art itself. It is different from the trust mark, authenticity label or origin mark that Australia, New Zealand, the United States and Canada try to make for traditional handicrafts. The policy vision of art authentication is to prevent the spread of fakes by regulating the circulation of works of art and making the provenance of works of art transparent through the recording of transactions by government departments. Therefore, it is similar to other countries' examination systems for cultural relic exports, such as France's Export Certificate, South Korea's confirmation of noncultural property, China's cultural relic exit permit and other management methods. It is similar to the international network system established to solve looting and theft, such as the Lost Art Internet Database set up by the German government to assist in the search and return of looted cultural relics during the Second World War. The Art Loss Register (ALR) was established by private organizations in the United Kingdom and the United States to stop cultural theft. The management of art circulation is bound to be quite difficult because there is no urgency to maintain public security for movable goods such as automobiles and firearms, and there is no incentive for public transactions. This paper will discuss the implementation scope, expected effect and policy inducement of the policy.

Z. Zheng, *The Legal System of Art Auction in China*,
https://doi.org/10.1007/978-981-19-0128-7_7

1.2 Overview of Policy Arguments

Policy argument is a term used in the field of policy analysis. It can be traced back to Aristotle's rhetorical syllogisms of Ancient Greece—a way of reasoning from "premises" to "conclusions". Modern scholars use such principles to further design the argumentative structure, and authors such as Stephen Toulmin, a contemporary American philosopher, have analyzed the argumentative structure into six elements. Such argumentation structure has been widely used in the field of PolicyAnalysis, among which the book Public PolicyAnalysis: An Introduction by William n. Dunn, An American scholar, gives a representative Introduction to policy argumentation.

Using Toulmin's concept, Dunn defined that the policy argument contains six elements: "I" (policy-relevant information), "C" (policy claim), "W" (warrant), "R" (rebuttal), and "backing" (backing). B) and qualifier (Q).[1] In short, the relationship between these six elements is as follows: policy information and argumentation grounds are the premises of the discussion, while refutation grounds are the opposite evidence. Both positive and negative grounds have their supporting bases. Researchers put forward policy propositions and judge the credibility of the propositions through the argumentation of the positive and negative sides.

In China, art appraisal, as a developing public issue, is mostly just policy information and policy propositions, and there is rarely a dialectical process of positive and negative discussion.[2] In the absence of an examination of options, it would be too presumptuous for researchers to assume that any one option is inevitable. From the perspective of policy argumentation, all possible schemes have their reasons and supporting bases but also have corresponding refutation reasons and produce different levels of credibility.

2 Policy Information on the Record of Artwork Authentication

2.1 Problems to Be Solved by the Policy

2.1.1 The Provenance of Artwork

Provenance is one of the important auxiliary pieces of information in judging the authenticity of works of art and can prevent the purchase of stolen goods such as theft and smuggling. Provenance records can prove the seller's innocence, protect the

[1] Dunn (1994).

[2] See Notice of the Ministry of Culture on Strengthening the Management of Art Market; Notice of the General Office of the Ministry of Culture on the Pilot Work of Art Appraisal Management; Approval of Beijing Municipal Bureau of Culture on Approval of Beijing tron Cultural Development Co., Ltd. as Pilot Units of Art.

interests of the buyer, and avoid both parties involved in illegality. The Association of Art Museum Directors (AAMD) and the American Association of Museums (AAM), The regulation seeks to require members to trace the provenance of works of art to 1970, but requires members to publish pictures and data on their websites for works that cannot be traced back to 1970 or for which a legal export certificate cannot be obtained. Portland Art Museum, for example, bought an 11th-century Bangladeshi Ganesha Stele. The provenance of the artwork can only be traced to auction records at Sotheby's in 2000 and Christie's in 2008, and the remedy is the publication of pictures and data on the artwork.[3]

The provenance of works of art is often difficult to investigate because unless it is an archaeological find with a clear record, a well-known piece that has been handed down in an orderly manner, an artwork with a record of being commissioned, or an actual record of being sold, the provenance usually changes hands over time and becomes increasingly unreliable.[4] Many counterfeiters, smugglers and art brokers take advantage of this blind spot to fabricate provenance, pretending that works of art are collected by famous artists, or creating provenance records of stolen or fake works under the pretext of public exhibitions to whitewash illegal works of art and scam buyers.

2.1.2 Guarantee of Artwork Defects

The defect type of art forgery is closer to the "lack of quality assurance" of the target.[5] The seller of works of art, in order to achieve the purpose of selling, will mark and classify the works for sale as famous and ancient works as far as possible; However, in order to avoid the liability of defect guarantee in civil law, such labeling and classification are usually positioned as "expression of opinion" rather than a "guarantee". If it is sold by an intermediary such as an auction company, there is an international auction practice of nonfidelity clauses in the standard contract, forming a disclaimer as a risk notification.[6] Although the law has strict requirements on the disclaimer statement of the seller or intermediary, for example, article 53 of The Auction Management Measures stipulates that the disclaimer statement is invalid when the auctioneer and trustee clearly know or should know that the auction object is defective, but the buyer is still at a relative disadvantage in the system. In addition to the buyer's own risk of forgery, if it is found to be a forgery, it is necessary to provide evidence, and then the judicial unit will decide whether the disclaimer statement of the seller or the intermediary is invalid, and the judicial results may not be all favorable to the buyer.

---

3 Gerstenblith (2010).

4 Buskirk (2003).

5 Zhang Ruiqin: Research on Legal Issues Related to Taiwan Oil Painting Fake, 2009 Master thesis of Taiwan Normal University, p. 25–27.

6 Guo Tianzhen: "Article 61 of the Auction Law: Who protects the interests," contains Modern Economic Information, No. 12, 2007, p. 101.

2.1.3 The Problem of Identity of the Target

There is no doubt that the object of sale shall be identical to the content of the contract between the parties. As stipulated in Article 135 of the Contract Law, "the seller shall perform the obligation of delivering to the buyer the subject matter or the documents for taking delivery of the subject matter and transferring the ownership of the subject matter." However, unscrupulous merchants may make use of modern reproduction techniques to produce identical copies, present them as originals, and then swap and replace them in the process of trading, and then deliver them as fakes.

For example, calligraphy and painting works have the so-called high-imitation printing technology of double-sided printing without dots. Because their copies have no traditional printing dot and can create an ink penetration effect on the back of the paper through double-sided printing, it is difficult to identify authenticity with the naked eye. If it is made with the same material as the original work and matched with exquisite mounting, it will be deceptive to a certain extent.[7] Other artifacts, along with the progress of reproduction technology, are bound to produce similar problems.

2.2 *Policy Objectives*

2.2.1 Distinguish Bona Fide Third Party

Bona Fide third parties (bona Fide Third Person) are third parties other than parties in legal relationships who are unaware. If the third party expresses his intention based on certain trust but finds that the actual situation of the right is inconsistent with the appearance of the expression, the law will give relevant protection to guarantee the proper and reasonable trust of the third party in good faith. For example, Article 87 of the Civil Law in Taiwan: "If the ideograph and the counterpart conspire to make a false expression of intention, the expression of intention shall be invalid. However, it should not be invalid against a bona fide third party." Article 92: "The intention of being defrauded means that its revocation shall not be used against a bona fide third party." Such provisions are protection for this purpose. In the art trade, however, this protection can easily be abused. Many counterfeiters, counterfeiters and smugglers will pretend to be good-faith third parties and pretend that fake or stolen goods come from others. They are not aware of criminal acts such as forgery and theft and try to escape crime. Therefore, one of the policy objectives of the record of art authentication is to make dealers of art have the basis to prove themselves as third parties in good faith. Those who cannot prove it should bear relatively more legal liability.

[7] Yin Yi: "A Historic Turning Point in the Identification of Chinese Calligraphy and Painting", including Ouyang Qiming and other chief editors: New Exploration of Art Identification, National Library of China Press, 2010 edition, p. 12.

2.2.2 Prevent Misrepresentation

The seller's misrepresentation of artwork commodities is prohibited by law. For example, Article 27 of The Auction Management Measures stipulates that the auctioneer shall not "falsely advertise the auction target and cause economic losses to the buyer;Article 8 of the Measures for The Administration of Business operation of Works of Art stipulates that business units of works of art shall not "forge or alter certificates of origin of works of art, documents of appraisal and evaluation of works of art and other transaction vouchers", etc. However, the seller will usually "opinion expression" and does not guarantee the true terms and other means to avoid liability, and it is sometimes difficult for the buyer to prove the specific loss caused by the misstatement. Art verification for the record of the second policy goals, are trying to through the format contract form, to regulate the seller to the art presentation of content, in order to provide the buyer can balance disclaimer of measures, such as fidelity terms the seller is not to let the seller for the art goods of all kinds of statements by more constraints, as well as, the lack of evidence from marketing content.

2.2.3 Prevent the Transfer of Trading Target

A palm off, "palm off," is a typical type of fraud in which a fraudster replaces an original with a fake to defraud someone of something. Although the General Principles of the Civil Law has rules to deal with this, such as Article 148, "If one party causes the other party to perform a civil juristic act against its true intention by fraudulent means, the defrauded party has the right to request the people's court or arbitration institution to cancel it." However, the cost of breaking the law is low compared with the huge profits that can be made by forgeries.

The third policy objective of the art authentication record is to prevent fraud in the trading of art objects. General methods to prevent the transfer of goods are not very suitable for works of art, such as trademarks, labels, bar codes, and even implanted chips, which are not easy to fix on works of art, and the cost of counterfeiting is compared with the value of the original works of art. There will still be forgers willing to take risks. Even if anti-counterfeiting measures can be imprinted on the artwork, the owner will have the suspicion that the artwork has been damaged. Therefore, photomicrography is another preventive measure. Just as the museum archived partial micrographs of Leonardo da Vinci's Lady with an Ermine in the Famous Polish film, comparison with preserved original microscopic image files can be used to judge the authenticity of artwork. This anti-counterfeiting measure is also actually used in the identification of authenticity of Chinese painting and calligraphy. For example, the scientific identification research Center of authenticity of Chinese painting and calligraphy of The Institute of Art and Science and Technology is used to record details such as the fiber structure of the paper by using multiple parts of the microphotography works as data for future comparison.[8] There are two preconditions for the application of this technique. One is that the original comparison data must be reliable. The second is that data must be stored in a fair, permanent and secure location. Artwork authentication records are an attempt to make artwork in the process of buying and selling and retain the initial microscopic photographic record for the buyer to compare the target objects.

3 Policies and Propositions on the Record of Artwork Authentication

The policy advocates that the government should establish or entrust a neutral unit to accept the application of the public for the record of art for sale. The archival content mainly includes the artwork information put forward by the applicant and the source guarantee signed by the applicant two data, the applicant has legal responsibility for the authenticity of the two data, that is, the applicant cannot put forward false and false artwork information but also good to verify whether the artwork is stolen goods obligation. After filing unit review, according to these document for the record content, and to apply for registration of art for more detail hd data sampling, data is kept in the record unit, in principle is not open to the public, public research institution, or police and inspection agencies may be due to the need of academic research or prosecuted cases, application read in case; Fees for hd data sampling and processing shall be borne by the original seller on a user-paid basis.

After completing the registration and HD data sampling procedures, the applicant will retrieve the artwork and obtain the "ID card" of the artwork. The applicant can resell this "ID card" together with the artwork in the future and become the original seller (i.e., the original seller) of this group of artwork "ID card", and the buyer who buys this artwork and obtains this group of artwork "ID card" will be the first buyer (i.e., the first buyer) of this group of artwork "ID card". The first buyer can, based on the "ID card" of the artwork held, apply to the filing unit for updating the "ID card" and comparing HD data sampling to confirm whether the seller has been filed with the unit and whether the artwork is consistent with the content of the filing. In the future, the artwork may be resold together with the "ID card" to a second buyer, who will update the "ID card" and compare HD data samples in accordance with the preceding steps.

The importance of updating the IDENTITY card and comparing HD data sampling in the art transaction process is that the former can confirm whether the work of art is legally acquired, while the latter can confirm whether the work of art is identical. Both measures need to be available to be effective. If there is no confirmation form of "id card", then a stolen artwork is likely to be sent to the record unit for HD

---

[8] Yin Yi: "A Historic Turning Point in the Identification of Chinese Calligraphy and Painting", including Ouyang Qiming and other chief editors: New Exploration of Art Identification, National Library of China Press, 2010 edition, p. 7–15.

data sampling after repeated resale, even if the comparison and match prove to be authentic, the buyer may not know it has bought stolen goods. If there is no HD data sampling, the buyer can only prove his legal ownership even if he obtains the "id card", which cannot avoid the risk of the artwork being transferred as a fake.

In nature, the artwork "id card" is similar to the quality guarantee issued by the original seller, which can be transferred with the artwork and has the nature of an "independent guarantee contract". An independent guaranty contract is a special contract established separately from the sale contract, rather than a "subordinate guaranty constraint".[9] Often seen in independent guarantee contract goods manufacturers to provide guarantees of the quality of the products, such as a home appliance being by retailers to sell to buyers, but when the home appliance malfunctions, buyers can guarantee the quality of the product, giving goods makers to maintenance service. Even if sales contracts only exist between buyers and retailers, the guarantee of quality is still.

The reason why it is difficult to implement independent guarantee contracts in art transactions is that it is difficult to confirm whether the goods and quality guarantee against which the buyer claims were issued by the original seller. For example, many auction companies and galleries will issue "certificate of authenticity", whose purpose is, of course, to win the trust of the buyer, but the purpose of the buyer, but not just to win the trust, more important is to resell, can win the trust of the next buyer; This written certificate of authenticity is not fixed, and it is easy to become a tool to escort forgeries. For example, the fake is sold with the certificate of authenticity. Therefore, auction companies and galleries are usually not responsible for the transfer of the certificate of authenticity.

To overcome this problem, the system of archiving works of art authentication replaces the guarantee attached to works of art by putting it on record in a neutral institution. Through the update of the "id card" and the comparison of high-definition sampling data, the validity of the ownership and identity of the artwork can be confirmed so that the independent guarantee contract of the work can be extended.

From the design of the system, the original seller bears the most legal responsibility, and the first buyer is the largest profit maker. Because the original seller must bear legal responsibility for the data and source of the artwork, the first buyer can be exempted from liability and become a third party in good faith as long as the original seller truthfully sells the artwork and authentication record to the second buyer. However, the legal liability of the original seller should not be extended indefinitely and must be limited by limitations. From the current relevant laws and regulations, damages caused by independent guarantee contracts, and "General Principles of civil Law" article 188: "the limitation of action for the protection of civil rights is three years… However, the people's court shall not protect such rights if it has been more than 20 years from the date of infringement. "It is reasonable to take 3 years as the legal liability of the original seller. In addition, the original seller has the right to know the object he must be responsible for, each "id card" transfer, the record unit

[9] Zhang Zhihao: Research on Liability for Guarantee and Quality Guarantee, Institute of Law, 2004, Chenggong University, p. 85.

should inform the original seller, only effective. Therefore, when the art "ID card" applied by the original seller has been expired for 2 years, no matter which hand of the buyer can no longer use the authentication record, the buyer needs to apply for a new "ID card" in the identity of the original seller.

Although the original seller has to bear more legal liability, the system is not completely without advantages for the original seller. Because the original seller can, through the transfer of an "ID card", know each buyer, just as many products guarantee services will require buyers to log on the company's website, the transfer of the authentication record is equivalent to the indirect development of potential customers for the original seller. In addition, if the original seller does not want to be burdened with excessive legal liability, then the content of the artwork can be described in conservative words or based on data and clearly explain the source of the artwork. For example, a signed "Zhang Daqian" cannot be sure whether the author is Zhang Daqian's painting and calligraphy works, the original seller can choose to record as "modern painting and calligraphy", and not record the author's name;And like a blue and white style of the Yuan Dynasty is unable to determine whether it is the imitation of later porcelain, the original seller can choose to put on record as "porcelain", and not put on record. Sellers of works of art may want to classify goods as masters or ancient for the purpose of getting a better price, but if they only want to make profits without any responsibility, it is against the principle of fairness.

In the same way, if the first buyer or any subsequent buyer wants to keep business information such as potential customers, that is, to avoid letting the original seller know the objects of subsequent transactions, he can choose to reapply for the authentication record and act as the original seller. If the first buyer, or any subsequent buyer, finds that the original seller's description of the artwork is too conservative, and his research reveals that the artwork may be an undervalued work by a famous artist, he may reapply for certification as the original seller and be legally liable for such opinion.

4 Reasons for the Record of Artwork Authentication

4.1 Arguments

The reasons for the record-of-art authentication are mainly based on the principle of "cost minimization and utility maximization". Since the art market's demand for art appraisal is mainly to solve the problem of liability attribution and damage compensation for fake and stolen goods, the design of the system can achieve the goal as long as it clarifies the responsibilities and obligations in the process of art trading.

Government departments, as neutral third parties, provide checks and balances between buyers and sellers so that high-risk sellers or buyers who have doubts and need to authenticate fakes can regulate each other's responsibilities and obligations through the guarantee of defects in the record of artwork authentication and bear the necessary expenses by themselves. Buyers who are confident in the authenticity of artworks, or those who can trust customers with their brands and goodwill, can conduct their transactions in accordance with their own business practices, without having to apply for a compulsory certification filing, and the government can avoid the suspicion of interfering with the market mechanism. The system itself tries to minimize the object of management and minimize the social cost needed to invest to maximize the social utility of limited government resources.

4.2 The Supporting Basis of the Argument

4.2.1 Views of Government Departments

(1) Saving government expenditure

The main work of the archival filing unit of government departments is to accept the archival filing of the public, keep the archival data and HD data sampling of artworks, and inform the original seller when renewing the ID card. The business content is mostly general administrative procedures with a relatively simple nature and low cost of personnel and equipment. In the early stage of policy implementation, if the number of cases accepted is not large, there is no need to set up a separate filing agency, but the relevant departments of the competent cultural authorities can support this business. This policy adopts the principle of user fee. The cost of maintaining the operation of the archival unit, keeping the data of archival works of art and renewing the "ID card" can be partially covered by the application fee, reducing the burden on the government. Its advantages are as mentioned by interviewee F: "It allows the institution itself to be viable and at the same time resolve future criminal or civil cases or financial problems such as mortgages with banks. I think that if there is no way to authenticate works of art in the future, this art authentication record system can go first." (Refer to interview transcript F12).

(2) Establish a database of circulating artworks

The classification of works of art, in the past due to the lack of incentives to actively declare, so the results are not clear. The policy of archival filing of artwork authentication allows buyers with warranty requirements for artwork defects to request sellers to apply for archival filing; The seller who has issued the certificate of authenticity is likely to take the initiative to apply for the authentication record in order to win the trust of the buyer, or to obtain more information of potential customers through the update of the "ID card". With the increase in the number of archival works, government departments can gradually establish a database of circulating works of art, which will become the basis for the classification of works of art in the future and can be provided to customs as comparative data for the export control of works of art to prevent the loss of precious cultural assets overseas.

(3) Detering the circulation of stolen goods and fake goods

From the perspective of the motives for filing, since the applicant is legally liable for the content and source of the application, those who want to make profits by selling works of art with false content or questionable sources are bound to be afraid and unwilling to apply. The buyer can indirectly judge the trustworthiness of the artwork by whether the seller can provide the authentication record and can confirm whether the artwork is stolen or fake through the update of the "ID card" and comparison of HD data samples. This policy can be in the scope of the open market to deter stolen goods and counterfeit the circulation effect.

4.2.2 Views of Art Appraisal Experts

(1) Avoid being involved in market disputes

Buyers in the art market demand art appraisals mainly to obtain warranties for defects. If the seller is unable to issue this guarantee, it will hope to obtain the endorsement of an art expert. This poses a dilemma for art appraisers: they may face complaints from sellers if fakes are found or claims from buyers if they are wrong. The policy of archiving art authentication allows art experts to avoid being involved in disputes between buyers and sellers and to return to the market. Primary responsibility for the transaction process is assumed by the main profiteer of the art trade.

(2) High-definition sampling data resources can be used as academic research materials

Microscopic surface texture, structure and other details of the data are an important basis for art identification, but the circulation of the market often does not easily obtain these data. For collections in public museums, limited by funds and manpower, only sample data can be established.

Among them, the collections of public museums are public property and almost never resold, so there will be no transfer of "ID card" and other problems. Many interviewees in this paper believe that HD sampling data from public collections can be carried out first. For example, respondent I thinks: "If it were an official public museum, it might be easier to do, and it might be useful when the country imports and exports artworks. I think it would be good if the people could apply for it when they need it. "(Refer to interview record I12) As interviewee M said," If this is to be done, it will be a big project, so the Imperial Palace must do it first; For private works of art, the premise is that the appraisal and valuation system mentioned above should be completed first before the latter can be put on record, which can be a long-term goal in the future. "(Refer to interview transcript M12).

Although private works of art are not easy to master, through the acceptance and filing of art authentication records, sample data of folk collections may be gradually established. Interviewee G also mentioned a similar idea: "The original idea of the art registration center is to put forward the registration application, we will put the relevant material analysis data of the art at the same time to build a file, to provide the need for identification in the future when the comparison data." (See interview record G12) The function of this kind of data is: "The personal information of buyer and seller need not be kept, but the transaction time and price should be recorded, so that the future can be used as the basis for price evaluation, and the scale of the industry can be grasped." (Refer to interview transcript G12).

Although the HD sampling database of artwork authentication records is mainly used as the basis for transaction comparison, it is equivalent to the establishment of an image database for private artwork, which can provide many samples for comparative analysis of public academic research institutions and has high academic value.

4.2.3 Views of Art Market Practitioners

(1) **Easy to obtain the trust of buyers**

Practitioners do not guarantee the authenticity of the terms will make buyers fear, and the authenticity of the warranty issued only by the artist is persuasive. Industry can almost rely on goodwill and word of mouth to accumulate the trust of buyers, which is relatively adverse to the establishment of a short time or small business scale of practitioners. The policy of archival filing of artwork authentication guarantees that practitioners have legal effects, and practitioners can choose the content of archival filing to determine the degree of guarantee and take 3 years as the time limit for claiming damages so that the liability to be borne will not expand indefinitely. Even individuals who do not have a large market share or a physical store can have the same sense of trust in the market as galleries and auction companies through art authentication records.

(2) **Benefit living artists**

Combining high-definition sampling technology to prevent forgeries in advance is the future trend of using technology to assist art appraisal. Respondent L said, "I think it is very good to record authentication, which can solve the problem of art for a long time. In ancient times, there was no technology. Now there is technology. It is time to break through these problems." (Refer to interview record L12) In particular, living artists can prove the authenticity of their works by themselves. Therefore, living artists or their galleries as the original sellers can almost be sure of the authenticity of the archival content. Art "id cards", which can be transferred to the next buyer along with the work, are more attractive to collectors than traditional paper certificates of authenticity. Interviewee H said, "It is easier and more credible to record the authentication of living artists." (Refer to interview record H12) When the artist is still alive, this measure is more urgent: "because now the method of high imitation is more and more sophisticated, anti-counterfeiting authentication record is very important, especially when the artist is still alive, like Wu Guanzhong, there is a catalog of all the works. (Refer to interview transcript H12).

(3) **Develop potential customers**

Collector lists are important business information for practitioners and are not easy to develop but difficult to maintain. The record of art authentication allows the original seller's guarantee responsibility to extend to the various buyers who take over, but at the same time, you can know the list of these buyers, and at the same time, you can bear the responsibility and get the relative reward; After the buyer knows the original seller, it is also possible to skip the middleman and contact the original seller directly in the future to save the cost of purchasing the artwork. Art certification filings will be particularly attractive to practitioners who need to develop a customer base and market awareness.

4.2.4 The collector's View

(1) **Obtain warranty for defects from the original seller**

Collectors often have nothing to do with the nonguarantee terms of practitioners, and the transferred certificate of authenticity may be falsified, so collectors can only admit that they have bad luck when they buy counterfeits. Through the art appraisal record can obtain the defect guarantee of the original seller, even if the art and "id card" through the change of hands, still valid, so that the collector can know the object of claim and obtain the basis of claim, safeguard their rights and interests.

(2) **Prevent the seller from transferring the artwork**

The record of art authentication can prevent works of art from being changed in the circulation process. Respondent B believes that "The record of art authentication feels more credible, because it can protect the owner of art works, so that the owner will not be stolen or sold without knowing it. In addition, this system is more secure to buyers, buyers can prove to buy, and the original record of the same." (see interview B12) art has the volume small, the high price of commodities, trademark, label, bar code identification marks such as difficult fixation on the art, the implants could make art injury, affect the value, by way of comparing photomicrography, can not affect art under the premise of appearance, to confirm the identity of the commodity, It is an effective way to prevent the seller from changing the artwork.

(3) **Prove oneself as the third party in good faith**

Collectors sometimes buy works of art in the hope that they can continue to resell them for a profit in the future. However, if new buyers find that the goods are fake or stolen after resale, not only the seller's reputation may be damaged but also may face lawsuits. Sometimes the collector's reluctance to take a loss, or his eagerness to dispose of a fake or stolen item, may turn from a well-meaning third party into a criminal. The record of art authentication allows each subsequent transfer of the original seller to leave a clear record so that the collector can prove his innocence or claim against the original seller and obtain legal protection due to the third party in good faith.

5 Reasons for Refuting the Record of Artwork Authentication

5.1 Reasons for Refutation

The main objection to the art authentication record is that the policy goes against the trading practices of the art market. The record of art authentication attempts to create a rational art transaction procedure. It assumes that security and a sense of security in the art transaction process are the primary goals pursued by both buyers and sellers while ignoring irrational factors in the art transaction process.

The consumption behavior of artworks not only aims at rational investment preservation but also includes perceptual aesthetic demand. Art is not the same as other goods with practical functions; the buyer to buy sometimes depends on the degree of love, as long as the price can be accepted, may be on the spot goods silver two, and do not require defects guarantee, authenticity guarantee certificate or other tedious procedures. In addition, art trading may also include social purposes such as arty, showing off wealth, social intercourse and even illegal purposes such as profiteering, speculation, money laundering and bribery, and become a "money game".

It is precisely because the art market contains various elements of rationality and sensibility, legality and illegality, beauty and ugliness, good and evil, full of gray areas, that it attracts all kinds of people to take what they want from it. For money game enthusiasts, counterfeit and stolen goods add to the excitement of the game; That is why there are so few legal cases of forgeries, out of proportion to the prevalence of forgeries, as many victims may choose not to report them to save face or seek redress by finding another victim. These irrational factors make the filing of art authentication seem like an "honest man's ideal", an attempt to circle a safe zone in the gray area of the art market.

5.2 The Supporting Basis of the Reasons for Refutation

5.2.1 Views of Government Departments

(1) Become a fake bleaching channel

As appraisal units only deal with general administrative affairs such as application procedures and high-definition data collection, they have limited ability to appraise artworks and will lack the ability to judge forgeries. Although the record unit will require the applicant to the legal responsibility for the authenticity of the contents for the record, if the applicant to the average person imperceptible fake (such as "qing imitation of longquan celadon" pretend "of the song dynasty longquan celadon") apply for verification for the record, purely in order to meet with verification record of vanity, but has no intention of selling the beneficiaries, Of course, no damages have been filed against him, and the forgery may continue to have the forensic record. Then, this measure is tantamount to indirectly recognizing the legal status of the fake by the government and becoming the absurd situation that the government endorses the fake.

(2) **Causes of "moral hazard"**

Moral hazard is the risk that one party may be harmed by the unethical behavior of the other because of a mismatch between use and effort. The original buyer in the absence of a seller's defect guarantee will bear the responsibility, carefully buy art, or take the initiative to consult experts. However, after having the art appraisal record, the buyer may abuse the appraisal record as the guarantee of marketing and claim, and buy the art with the appraisal record without fear, as a marketing gimmick;If they cannot resell before the expiration of 3 years, they may falsely accuse the original seller and threaten the seller with damages to achieve the purpose of returning the goods, so that they stand in an invincible position of commercial interests.

(3) **Unable to eliminate criminal behaviors**

There is a complex structure of accomplices in the criminal acts of art trading, and buyers are not necessarily innocent victims. Sometimes the sale of stolen goods is the result of mutual agreement between the buyer and the seller. For example, many stolen rarities are sponsored by the buyer. Sometimes forgeries are made when the buyer orders the counterfeiter in bulk at a very low price with the intention of reselling for a huge profit. These are the kinds of black-market transactions that cannot be guarded against, and the art certification filing simply keeps crimes out of the way. Enforcing the policy of recording art evidence does not mean that the government is eliminating crime.

(4) **Increase the trouble of filing units**

Although the filing unit is a neutral third party in good faith in the whole mechanism, it is easy to regard by the buyer as having the responsibility of supervising the seller because it accepts the seller's filing data. If the buyer fails to seek compensation from the original seller for damages, he may turn to the record-keeping unit, or even think that it is the authentication record that misleads him to cause his loss, and puts forward unreasonable demands such as damages and state compensation to the record-keeping unit, then the record-keeping unit will face endless judicial disputes and be exhausted.

5.2.2 Views of Art Appraisal Experts

(1) **Reduce the importance of art appraisal in the art market**

Even if there is no art authentication record system, do not want to be involved in market disputes art experts, they will be wise to stay out of the matter; The record of art authentication only reduces job opportunities for art authentication experts who originally served and taught in the art market. Because in order to avoid liability, the seller may simply be ambiguous or only describe the material of the artwork to the record, there is no need to issue an expert opinion or hire an expert as a consultant; On the other hand, the buyer may only care about whether the seller has the guarantee of defects, and no longer has the motivation to consult experts and improve their own appraisal ability. The filing of art authentication will reduce the importance of the professional ability of art authentication in the market.

5.2.3 Views of Art Market Practitioners

(1) **Increase operating costs**

Art market profits, that is, according to the features of information asymmetry, in the art of authenticity mixed pile ShaLi gold, QuWuCunJing, the amount of profit depends on the identification ability and the taste of high and low, the market is the weakest goes to the wall, selection of the field, to buy authentic is due payment, fake is need to bear the risk and cost, This is a problem both buyers and sellers face. The record of art authentication regards practitioners and sellers as parties with information advantages and requires them to bear more responsibilities and costs, thus reducing the space for profit while ignoring the fact that practitioners and sellers also need to bear the risks of fake and stolen goods.

(2) **Lack of incentives for high-priced and low-priced artworks.**

If it is a rare treasure, or most people are sure to be genuine "open goods", so even without the application of art authentication record, no guarantee to provide defects, still a pile of buyers rush to buy; If it is cheap stall goods, its price may be cheaper than the cost of applying for the record of art authentication, it is impossible to apply for the record of art authentication. Perhaps only those authenticities are difficult to distinguish, the price is not high or low art, and they will need to rely on art authentication records to win the trust of the buyer.

5.2.4 The collector's View

(1) **Do not want to be identified**

At the same time, as the transfer authentication is filed, the original seller will know the identity of the buyer, which will cause much confusion for collectors who do not want to be identified. Because of the secrecy of art collection and trading, in part because of security concerns, many collectors are reluctant to expose their work to the risk of theft. After practitioners know the identity of the collector, they may often come to sell and peddle, and the collector will be overwhelmed.

For some collectors, if the art is recorded but adverse to their export overseas, "because the art is logged, more than a hundred years of antiquities can not be exported. For collectors, art if the record is locked, if there are foreign buyers to buy at a high price, there is no way to sell, so collectors do not want to record, it is impossible for you to log on to his collection, to classification." (Refer to interview transcript C12).

In addition, in Taiwan, the registration of art authentication will also involve tax issues, which will reduce collectors' willingness to apply. For example, interviewee E said, "The reason why Taiwan's art trading process is not open is that government departments do not give special treatment to art trading like foreign countries. Therefore, today I finally bought a piece of art, and if it will be taxed heavily, I will not let my trading process be open. When I do not want to go public, the system does not work." (See interview notes E12) In some areas where there is no supporting measure for taxation, this system is likely to be unpopular.

As interviewee I said, "Private collectors do not necessarily want the government to know what their collections are because when collectors want to trade, import and export in the future, their freedom will be very low, and there will be tax problems. I do not think many people will be willing to use them." (Refer to interview record I12) or as interviewee K put it: "Unless it is state-owned art, there should be no collectors who want to be known by the government about their collections, so there will be no customers in this system." Most of these arguments are also based on the aforementioned perspective of freedom.

(2) **Damages still need to be arbitrated by art appraisal**

Although the record of art authentication is similar to the warranty of defects issued by the original seller, it does not guarantee that the original seller will accept all damages claimed by the buyer. When the original seller refuses to pay, insisting that the work being sold is genuine, then the problem is still back at square one: the buyer still has no choice but to use the judicial process, and the burden of proof remains on him, seeking a preponderance of the art of the evidence to prove that the object in question is a forgery.

(3) **Three years for the elimination of damages is too short**

Some collectors buy works of art for the purpose of preserving value and appreciation and may not sell them in a short period of time. Sometimes, they discover that the collection is a fake many years later, when it is likely to have already exceeded the three-year limitation of damages.

6 Credibility Analysis of Artwork Authentication Record

The policy design of artwork authentication records solves the problem of provenance and defect guarantees of artwork by requiring the original seller to take legal responsibility for the artwork data and source guarantees. High-definition data collection was performed to prevent the transfer of the target. The policy is motivated by the buyer's demand for defect guarantees and the seller's interest in gaining customer trust and developing customers. The implementation mode and inducement of policies echo each other with policy issues and policy objectives.

The rationale for the policy is that the clarification of responsibilities and obligations in the process of art trading has great social utility, while the scope of policy implementation focuses on both buyers and sellers, which can reduce the number of objects under management and social cost. Therefore, the rationale of "cost minimization and utility maximization" has high credibility.

However, the refutation of the policy points out that this policy violates the trading practices of the art market and ignores the irrational factors in the process of art trading. The greater the difference between a policy and social practice, the stronger the backlash. In addition, there is no permanent buyer in the art market. Buyers and sellers have overlapping identities and compete with each other. Buyers may become sellers one day and need to bear the liability of warranty for defects, which does not necessarily support this policy. The buyer also needs to be strong enough to force the seller to issue a defect guarantee.

Although refutation explains the realistic problems of the art market and reduces the credibility of this policy, it negates this policy by saying that it cannot solve "all" problems. It is a perfectionism that demands a policy, which is not very helpful for the improvement of the current situation. The policy goal of art authentication records is not to solve all irrational problems in the art market or to provide a final arbitration of art authentication. It is only through the artwork authentication record this independent guarantee contract to solve the source of the artwork, defect guarantee and the transfer of the target of three problems. The policy assumes that there are "rational" buyers and sellers in the art market, and that they share a common need for safety and security in the art trade even if their status is switched, and that these people need to be protected by the government; To abandon them simply because they are a minority is not the policy of an ideal government.

The criterion, therefore, is not how many problems a policy solves but how well it achieves its goals. From dismissed the reasons put forward various basis, many reasons can be through the supporting measures to guard against, for example from the government's position, if you worry about the policy become a fake bleaching of pipeline, the record unit can at the same time of acceptance for the record content, inform the applicant even if you do not sell the artwork, if the content is not solid, It may also face the legal liability of prosecution by the filing unit, because its behavior may involve the suspicion of forging documents and obstructing official duties. For example, from the standpoint of the collector, if he does not want his identity to be exposed, he can ask the seller to reapply for the art authentication record or simply give up the right to update the authentication record and compare the high-definition data, and the privacy of his identity can still be maintained. For other problems, countermeasures can be found, or policy stakeholders can shift costs and adjust their positions to solve them.

7 Conclusion

Based on the arguments and reasons for refutation, this policy is highly credible in terms of cost and efficiency. However, due to the lack of such trading practices in the art market, part of the credibility is reduced, so the comprehensive credibility is "moderate".

Predictably, a good place to start for this policy is to work with galleries, auction houses or living artists who already have certificates of authenticity. Such operators may have a high willingness to guarantee defects, while living artists can guarantee the validity of defects and avoid the risk of damage claimed by the buyer. Art authentication records are based on such a concept, combined with high-definition data, so that the effectiveness of warranty defects can be extended to the next buyer.

The first and fourth years of implementation will be critical to see how well the policy works. Because the number of applications in the first year represents the effect of policy advocacy and will reflect the acceptance of policy stakeholders such as practitioners and collectors, the fourth year is due to the limitation of expiration of the first application for the record of art authentication, and the time point of reapplication will reflect the willingness of the buyers to assume the guarantee of defects and act as the new original seller. The implementation of any policy requires full communication with policy stakeholders to highlight the advantages of the policy and reduce the backlash of the policy.

References

Dunn WN (1994) Publicpolicy analysis: an introduction, 2nd edn. Englewood Cliff, NJ: Prentice Hall, pp 66-68

Gerstenblith P (2010) International cultural property. In: Hutt, S. (ed.) Year book of cultural property law 2010. California: Left Coast Press, p. 142

Buskirk M. The Contingent Object of Contemporary Art. The contingent object of contemporary art. MIT Press, (2003), p. 167

Bibliography

Monograph in Chinese

Huang Maorong. General Introduction to Debt Law [M]. Beijing: China University of Political Science and Law Press. 2003: 394

Huang Xifeng. Cultural Industry Policies and Laws and Regulations [M]. Beijing: Peking University.2013: 8

Lin Rikui. Art Pawn and Auction [M]. Zhejiang: Zhejiang Gongshang University Press. 2009: 8

Liu Cheng-weiyi. Study on The Principle of Consideration in Anglo-American Law [M]. Beijing: Law Publishing House, 2006: 18–35

Liu Ningyuan. Principle and Practice of Auction Law [M]. Shanghai: Shanghai People's Publishing House, 1998: 8–32

Liu Ningyuan. Research on China's Auction Legal System [M]. Beijing: Peking University Press. 2008: 19–48

Liu Shulin, Wang Mingxi. Basic Theory and Extension of Auction [M]. Shanghai: Economic Science Press, 2011: 1

Liu Shuangzhou. Principles of Auction Law [M]. Beijing: China University of Political Science and Law Press. 2010: 59–107

Luo Bing. International Art Trade [M]. Beijing: Communication University of China Press, 2009: 184

Qin Chunrong. Art Auction [M]. Shanghai: Shanghai University Press, 2004: 49–72

Editor, National People's Congress Legal Working Committee. Interpretation of Tort Liability Law of the People's Republic of China.] Beijing: Legal Press.2010: 19–45

Tao Yu. Introduction to Art Market [M]. Beijing: China Architecture and Architecture Press, 2011:257

Tian Shaohua, Yang Qing. Research on Expert Civil Liability System [M]. Beijing: China Procuratorial Press, 2005: 77–389

Tian Tao, Wang Fenghai. Case Guide of Auction Law [M]. Beijing: Law Press, 2004: 234

Tian Tao, Wang Fenghai. The Case Guide of Auction Law [M]. Beijing: Law Press, 2007: 256

Tian Tao. Case Guide to Auction Law, Part III [M]. Beijing: Law Press, 2010: 3–5

Wang Zejian. Civil Law Theory and Case Study (II) [M]. Beijing: Peking University Press, 2009a

Wang Zejian. General Principles of Civil Law [M]. Beijing: Peking University Press. 2009b: 498

Wang Zejian. Tort [M]. Beijing: Peking University Press, 2016: 177–240

Wang Zejian. Principle of Debt Law [M]. Peking University Press, 2013: 39–44

Z. Zheng, *The Legal System of Art Auction in China*,
https://doi.org/10.1007/978-981-19-0128-7

Wang Zheng. Art Investment and Market Laws and Regulations [M]. Chengdu: Sichuan University Press, 2011: 54
Xi Mu. Introduction to Chinese Art Market (Volume 1) [M]. China Bookstore. 2010a: 17
Xi Mu. Introduction to Chinese Art Market (Volume 2) [M]. China Bookstore. 2010b: 23
Xu Hui. Foundation of Art Law [M]. Beijing: Science Press. 2010: 20–23
Yao Zhiming. Research on The Principle of Good Faith and Collateral Obligation [M]. Taipei: Yuanzhao Press, 2013: 51–72
Zhang Peitian, Ed. Guide to Auction Law [M]. Beijing: China University of Political Science and Law Press, 1991: 13
Zhang X B. Tort Law in China. Beijing: China Social Sciences Press, 1995: 254–255
Zhao Songling. Gem Appraisal [M]. Taipei: Taipei Art Book Company, 1993: 52
China Auction Industry Association. Auction Case Analysis [M]. Beijing: China Financial and Economic Press. 2003a
China Auction Industry Association. Case Analysis Tutorial of Auction Law [M]. Beijing: China Financial and Economic Press. 2007
China Auction Industry Association. Exploration of Auction Theory and Practice [M]. Beijing: China Financial and Economic Press. 2003b
Chinese Auction Industry Association. New Auction Related Laws and Rules [M]. Beijing: China Financial and Economic Press. 2010
Zhou Lin. Practical Manual of Art Law [M]. Beijing: International Culture Publishing Company, 1998: 12–25
Zhou Xuefeng. Corporate Audit and Expert Responsibility [M]. Beijing: People's Court Press, 2007: 101–102
Zhu Fumei. Scientific Identification and Criminal Investigation [M]. Author issue.2004: 499

Chinese Translation

Basell Maxine. Good and Evil in Art and Law [M]. Translated by Gan Qiao. Beijing: Law Press. 2011: 145
Grose. The Origin of Art [M]. Translated by CAI Muqiao. The Commercial Press. 1984: 54
Gombrich. History of Art [M]. Translated by Fan Jingzhong. Lin Xixiao. Tianjin: Tianjin People's Fine Arts Publishing House. 1998: 36
Paul Klemperer. Auction: Theory and Practice [M]. Translated by Zhong Hongjun. Beijing: China Renmin University Press. 2006: 23–90
Leonard D. Duboff, Christy KING. Summary of Art Law [M]. Translated by Zhou Lin. Beijing: Intellectual Property Publishing House. 2011: 45–124
Schwab. Introduction to Civil Law [M]. Translated by Zheng Hong. Beijing: Law Press. 2006: 234
Walter Beemer. Philosophical Analysis of Contemporary Art [M]. Translated by Sun Zhexing and Li Yuan. Beijing: Commercial Press. 2012: 78
Vija Krishna. Auction Theory [M]. Translated by Hu Jun and Zhang Cong. Shanghai: Shanghai People's Publishing House. 2012: 45–80
James GOODwin. The International Art Market, Part 1 (Part 2) [M]. Jing Yizhong, Lai Jingbo, pei Zhijie. Beijing: China Railway Publishing House. 2010: 23–67

Chinese Paper

Bai Yu. Information asymmetry and managers' obligation to explain [J]. Shandong Social Sciences, 2009(03): 119–121+157

CAI Zhaoqi. Collection of flavor [J]. Guanghua Journal. 1995(81): 32–50

Geng Lin, Cui Jianyuan. Journal of social sciences of Jilin university, 2016, 56(03): 21–29

Gou Chuanzeng, GUAN Zhen, Wang Xiaodong. A Preliminary study on several Issues concerning the Enactment of auction Law [J]. Politics and Law, 1994(04): 48–50

Guo Fuqing. Preliminary study on the Establishment of China's Auction Legal System [J]. Legal and Commercial Studies (Journal of Central South University of Political Science and Law), 1995(01): 50–54

He JIAN. Commentary on Article 54, Clause 1, Clause 2 (Obvious unfair System) of Contract Law [J]. Jurists, 2017 (01): 155–174 + 180.

Jiang Shibo. An Analysis of the Effect of the Disclaimer clause of the Auctioneer's Defect Guarantee from an Auction Case [J]. Law Science, 2008(06): 150–154

Jiang Shuming, LIANG Chengliang. Thinking on the construction of liability for damages of trust interests [J]. Times law, 2012, 10(06): 65–74

Li Zhanghui. Analysis on the legal relationship of auction [J]. Application of Law, 1994(09): 11–14

Li Hailong. Journal of Zhejiang university of technology (social science edition), 2012, 11(02): 230–234

Li Wei. Discussion on the Legal Characteristics of Auction and The Rights and Responsibilities of parties [J]. Modern Law, 1998(02): 90–92

Liu Y, Liu Y, Liu Y, et al. The role of the auction contract in the development of the Auction System [J]. Shandong adjudication, 2009, 25(02): 43–44

Lin Ailian. Journal of Shanghai University of Political Science and Law, 2006(06): 31–36

Lin Chenger. On the Principle of good faith and the Function of Prohibition of abuse of rights [J]. Taiwan Native Law Journal, 2001 (22): 1–176

Liu C W. The Formation and Evolution of consideration Theory in Anglo-American Contract Law [J]. Peking University Law Review, 2007(01): 106–134

Liu Ningyuan. Journal of East China University of Political Science and Law, 2008(05): 44–51

Liu Ningyuan. Question on exemption of Warranty Liability for Defects in Auction Law [J]. Law Science, 2000(01): 38–41

Liu Liu Ningyuan. Question on exemption of Warranty Liability for Defects in Auction Law [J]. Law Science, 2000(01): 38–41

Lou Jianbo, Jiang Xuelian. A Study on the jurisprudence of Fiduciary Duty—On the Interaction between trust Law and fiduciary Duty rules in Civil Law Countries [J]. Social Science, 2017(01): 92–102

Luo Bangtai. Study on Authenticity identification and Intrinsic Information of Calligraphy and Painting [A]. Ye Sanbao, Ed. Unique vision: Investment and Collection of Chinese painting and Calligraphy [C]. Shanghai: Shanghai People's Fine Arts Publishing House. 2003: 205

Ma Changjun, XU Ziliang, Di Qing. People's Justice, 2008(22): 96–99

Mou Jianping. China Mining News, 2016-01-30 (009)

Mou Xiankui. An empirical study of the relationship between the information of the Weak and the information of the Weak [J]. Law Science (Journal of Northwest University of Politics and Law), 2007(04): 78–85

Good will last. On civil Liability of Experts—The Significance of its Theoretical Framework [A]. Liang Huixing, Ed. Jurisprudence of Civil Law and Legislation research (II) [C]. Beijing: National School of Governance Press. 1999: 297

Michitaro Urawa. Expert Responsibility in Germany [A]. Edited by Liang Huixing. Essays on Civil and Commercial Law (Vol. 5) [C]. Beijing: Law Publishing House, 1996: 540

Shi Haomin. On the Relevant legal issues of auction [J]. Journal of Political Science and Law, 1989(04): 39–43

Su Yongqin. Economic Analysis of liability for negligence in Contracting [J]. National Taiwan University Law Review. 2004 (33) 01: 183–218
Sun Xin. Extensive Knowledge and Fine Appreciation—On Qigong's Painting and Calligraphy Appraisal and Scholarship Methods. Fine Arts Observation, 2000 (04): 110
Tang Haiqing. Legal Protection of counterfeit art consumers [J]. Economic Research Guide, 2009(31): 116–117
Wang Yumiao. A preliminary study on the legal relationship of auction [J]. Modern Economic Information, 2013(16): 400–404
Wang Xu. Analysis of legal Attributes of Auction Rules [J]. Frontiers, 2008(08): 109–112
Wang Yan. Some Problems in Auction Legislation [J]. Journal of Law, 1996(04): 21–22
An interview with Fu Shen, Director of The Chinese Art Department of the National Oriental Museum of Art [N]. The Associated Press. 1989–27
Wu Bingheng. Journal of Shanghai university of political science and law (collection of rule of law), 2012, 27(04): 41–46
Wu Xuli. Whether there is legal Liability for auction of fake goods [J]. Application of Law, 1999(01): 30–31
mutoh. Information Obligation and Guarantee Responsibility of auctioneers—From the perspective of the Legal Status of Intermediaries [J]. Law science (journal of northwest university of politics and law), 2017, 35(06): 156–167
Mutoh. Contract relationship and agency effect in auction [J]. Jurist, 2015(03): 95–110+178
Xu Jianrong. A point of view on the national expert for the fidelity of calligraphy and painting [A]. Ye Sanbao, editor. Investment and Collection of Chinese painting and Calligraphy [C]. Shanghai: Shanghai People's Fine Arts Publishing House. 2003: 68
Zhang Y, Zhang Y, Zhang Y, et al. Perspectives on Illegal Behaviors in Auction Activities [J]. Law Science, 1993(08): 24–25
Yin Qiushi. On the principle of explicit Name in Agency and its Exceptions [J]. Politics and Law, 2016(01): 76–89
Zhang Peng. Thoughts on perfecting China's auction legal system [J]. Journal of law, 2009, 30(05): 112–114
Zhang Qiu-hang, Liu Hui. My opinion on the Meaning of basic Principles of Auction Law [J]. Journal of Law, 1996(02): 22–23
Zhang Yongbin, Zhao Zuwu. On the Application of special Exemption Clause in Auction Law and Its Legal Interpretation [J]. Journal of East China University of Political Science and Law, 2002(02): 30–34+41
Zhou Zhongyong, He Yongdong. On several Legal Issues of Auction [J]. Law Review, 1988(01): 80–81

Dissertation

The guitar. On the Civil Liability of auctioneers for "fake" Works of art [D]. Capital University of Economics and Business, 2016
Liu Junhong. Research on Legal Issues of Chinese Art Auction [D]. Renmin University of China, 2012

Foreign Literature

Adler, Brenna. "The International Art Auction Industry: Has Competition Tarnished Its Finish?" [J] Northwestern Journal of International Law & Business 23 (2003)

Annesley, Noel. "Attributing Old Master Drawings." [J] In The Expert versus The Object-Judging Fakes and False Attributions In Edited by Ronald D. Spencer, 79–88. New York: Oxford University Press (2004)

Bachman, Robert. "the Agency: Auctioneer's Duty to Disclose Material Facts of Agency to Seller." [J] Marquette Law Review 33 (1949)

Bagwell, Laurie Simon and B. Douglas Bernheim. "Veblen Effects and the Theory of Conspicuous Consumption." [J] American Economic Journal Review 86, no. 3 (1996)

Bandle, Anne Laure. "Fakes, Fears and Findings—Disputes over the Authenticity of Artworks." [J] Transnational Dispute Management 2 (2014)

Bandle, Anne Laure. "Legal Questions of Art Auctions (Rechtsfragen der Kunstauktion)." [J] International Journal of Cultural Property 18, no. 4 (2011)

Bowen, Don. "Condition Reports for Artworks." [J] Picture Framing Magazine (1996)

Brandly, Mike. "Auctions: Does the Offering Cause a Desire to Own?" [J] Mike Brandly: Auctioneer Blog. Accessed February 7, 2016

Bridge, Michael G. The Sale of Goods. Oxford: Oxford University Press, 1997

Samuel Butt. "Authenticity Disputes in the Art World: Why Courts Should Plead Incompetence." [J] Columbia Journal of Law & the Arts 28 (2005)

Cahill, John. "'Keeping it Real': A Brief Primer on the Law of Art Authenticity." [J] Columbia Journal of Law & the Arts 35 (2012)

Carducci, Guido. "The Growing Complexity of International Art Law: Conflict of Laws, Uniform Law, Mandatory Rules, UNSC Resolutions and EU Regulations." [J] In Art and Cultural Heritage—Law, Policy and Practice, Edited by Barbara T. Hoffman, 68–86. New York: Cambridge University Press, 2006

Cartwright, John. "The Rise and Fall of Mistake in The English Law of Contract." [J]. Fraud and Duties to Inform in European Contract Law, edited by Ruth Sefton-Green, 65–86. Cambridge University Press, 2005

Cassady, Ralph Jr. Auctions and Auctioneering. Berkeley: University of California Press, 1967

Clark, Michael J. "The Perfect Fake: Creativity, Forgery, Art and the Law." [J] DePaul University Journal of Art and Entertainment Law 15 (2004)

De Marchi, Neil. "Introduction." In Auctions, Agents and Dealers—The Mechanisms of The Art Market 1660–1830, Edited by Jeremy Warren and Adriana Turpin, 1–10. London: The Wallace Collection, 2008

De Marchi, Neil and Hans J. Van Miegroet. "Art, Value and Market Practices in the Netherlands in the Seventeenth Century." [J] Art Bulletin 76, No. 3 (1994)

Dutton, Denis. "Authenticity in Art." [J] in The Oxford Handbook of Aesthetics, edited by Jerrold Levinson, New York: Oxford University Press, 2003

European Fine Art Foundation. TEFAF Art Market Report 2017, prepared by Clare McAndrew. Helvoirt: European Fine Art Foundation (TEFAF), 2017

European Fine Art Foundation. TEFAF Art Market Report 2016, prepared by Clare McAndrew. Helvoirt: European Fine Art Foundation (TEFAF), 2016

Fawcett, James J., Jonathan M. Harris and Michael Bridge. International Sale of Goods in the Conflict of Laws. Oxford Private International Law Series. Oxford: Oxford University Press, 2005

Fentiman, Richard. International Commercial Litigation. New York: Oxford University Press, 2010

Fleming, James Jr. "The Similarity of The Reasonable Man in The Tender Cases" [J] Missouri Law Review 16, no. 1 (1951)

Friedlander, Max J. "On Forgeries." In The Expert versus The Object-Judging Fakes and False Attributions In The Visual Arts, Edited by Ronald D. Spencer, 39–43. New York: Oxford University Press, 2004

Gerstenblith, Patty. "Getting Real: Cultural, Aesthetic and Legal Perspectives on the Meaning of Authenticity of Art Works." [J] Columbia Journal of Law & the Arts 35 (2012)

Goldstein, Malcolm. Landscape with Figures: A History of Art Dealing in the United States. New York: Oxford University Press, 2000

Harris, Luke. "The Liability of Experts for The Misattribution of Works of Art." [J] Europa Institut, University of Zurich on Kunst und Recht Haftung von Gutachtern im Kunstrecht, Zurich, November 27, 2012

Harter-Bachmann, Sebastian. "Truth in Art and Law: Allocating the Risks Associated with Attribution in the Art Auction House." [J] Master of Jurisprudence Thesis: Jurisprudence. University of Durham, 2007

Hill, Jonathan and Adeline Chong. International Commercial Disputes, Commercial Conflicts of Lawsin English Courts. Oxford: Hart Publishing, 2010

Hodgkinson, Tristram. Expert Evidence: Law and Practice. London: Sweet and Maxwell, 1990

Huda, Shireen. Pedigree and Panache: A History of the Art Auction in Australia. Canberra: ANU E-Press, 2008

Hudson, A.H. "A Tale of Two Urns—Dating and Attribution of Art and Antiques." [J] Art Antiquity and Law 10, no. 3 (2005)

Hudson, A.H. "Attribution of Paintings and Sale by Description." [J] Art Antiquity and Law 8, No. 2 (2003)

Keating, J. Michael Jr. "Getting Reluctant Parties to Mediate: A Guide for Advocates." [J] Alternatives to the High Cost of Litigation 13, No. 1 (January 1995)

Lord, Richard A., ed. Williston on Contracts. A Treatise on the Law of Contracts, 4th ed. Westlaw. Thomson Reuters, 2003

Meisel, Frank. "Auctioneers and Misdescriptions: Between Scylla and Charybdis." [J] Modern Law Review 73 (2010)

Meisel, Frank. "Auctioneers and Buyers: A Special Relationship?" [J] Journal of Professional Negligence 21, no. 4 (2005)

O 'connor, Authenticating the Attribution of Art—Connoisseurship and the Law in the Judging of Forgeries, Copies, And False Attribution. [J] In The Expert versus The Object-Judging Fakes and False Attributions In The Visual Arts, Edited by Ronald D. Spencer, 3–27. New York: Oxford University Press, 2004

Osburgh, Carolyn. Authenticity in the Art Market—A Comparative Study of Swiss, French and English Contract Law. Leicester: Institute of Art and Law, 2005

Pardo-Guerra, Juan Pablo. "Priceless Calculations: Sociotechnical Appendages of Art." [J] European Societies 15, No. 2 (2013)

Reeves, Van Kirk. "The Rights and Risks of Experts in French and American Courts" [J] IFAR Journal 12, No. 4 (2011)

Reeves, Van Kirk. "The Risks of Experts in French and American Courts" [J] IFAR Journal 12, No. 4 (2011)

Simmons, Lucian J. "Provenance and Auction Houses In The East China Sea" [J]. Papers Emanating from the Seventh PCA International Law Seminar, May 23, 2003, Edited by the International Bureau of the Permanent Court of Arbitration, 85–98. The Hague: Kluwer Law International, 2004

Singer, Kai B. "'Sotheby's Sold Me a Fake!'—Holding Auction house Accountable for Authenticating and Attributing Works of Fine Art." [J] Columbia Journal of Law & the Arts 23 (2000)

Spencer, Ronald D. "Buyer's Rescission for High Value Art robbery—Spreading the Risk." [J] Spencer's Art Law Journal 1, no. 3 (2011)

Spencer, Ronald D. "Opinions about the Authenticity of Art." Spencer's Art Law Journal 2, No. 2 (2011)

Spencer, Ronald D. "When Experts and Art Scholars Change Their Minds." Spencer's Art Law Journal 1, No. 1 (2010)

Spencer, Ronald D. "Introduction." In The Expert versus The Object-Judging Fakes and False Attributions In The Visual Arts, Edited by Ronald D. Spencer, XI–XVIII. New York: Oxford University Press, 2004
Spencer, Ronald D. "The Risk of Legal Liability for Attributions of Visual Art." [J] In The Expert versus The Object-Judging Fakes and False Attributions in the Visual Arts, Edited by Ronald D. Spencer, 143–187. New York: Oxford University Press, 2004
Stebbins, Theodore E. Jr. "The Art Expert," [J] In the Expert versus the Object-Judging Fakes and False Attributions In the Visual Arts, Edited by Ronald D. Spencer, 135–142. New York: Oxford University Press, 2004
Varner, Elizabeth. "Arbitrating Cultural Property Disputes." [J] Cardozo Journal of Conflict Resolution 13 (2012)
Vyas, Stephanie G. "Is There an Expert in the House? Thomson V. Christie's: The Case of The Houghton Urns." [J] International Journal of Cultural Property 12 (2005)
Weber, "Liability for the Acquisition of Faked or opposed Works of Art in US Law." [J] in Kulturguterschutz -- Kunstrecht - Kulturrecht, Festschrift fur Kurt Siehr Zum 75. Geburtstag aus dem Kreise des Doktoranden- und Habilitandenuva "Kunst und Recht," Edited by Kerstin Odendahl and Peter Johannes Weber, 409–431. Baden-baden: Nomos, 2010